USA TO Z

A Celebration of American Popular Culture

RAY JONES

CUMBERLAND HOUSE
NASHVILLE, TENNESSEE

USA to Z
PUBLISHED BY CUMBERLAND HOUSE PUBLISHING
431 Harding Industrial Drive
Nashville, Tennessee 37211

Cover design by Gore Studio, Nashville, Tennessee

Library of Congress Cataloging-in-Publication Data

Jones, Ray, 1948–
    USA to Z : a celebration of American popular culture / Ray Jones.
        p.   cm.
    ISBN 1-58182-397-5 (pbk. : alk. paper)
    1. Popular culture—United States—Dictionaries. 2. Americana—Dictionaries.
I. Title.
E169.04J73 2004
306'.0973'03—dc22

                                                                    2004008666

Printed in the United States of America

1 2 3 4 5 6 7 8 9 10—08 07 06 05 04

CONTENTS

M

N

O

S

T

U

Z

INTRODUCTION

To Catch Lightning in a Bottle

W HAT DO Raggedy Ann dolls, grizzly bears, Wurlitzer jukeboxes, Carlsbad Caverns, Model T Fords, Stetson hats, Georgia peaches, Humphrey Bogart, and Patsy Cline have in common? They are all wondrously American phenomena, as much a part of our national heritage as the flag or the Constitution. What about sizzling hot Louisiana pepper sauce, Airstream trailers, drive-in movies, Radio Flyer wagons, Navajo rugs, the Golden Gate Bridge, John Steinbeck, Jack Benny, and the legend of the *Edmund Fitzgerald*? You guessed it—the connection is the same. All these people, places, products, and ideas are part of what makes America great—and makes us very happy to be Americans. They have something else in common, too— you'll read about all of them right here in this book.

USA to Z is a celebration of American culture. It's not about laws, politics, or taxes, not about dusty old documents, corroding bronze statues, or worn-out arguments in the halls of Congress. Instead it's about M&M's and Ivory Soap, the movies of Old Hollywood and mystery novels set in old New York, bluegrass music and Benny Goodman jazz, the legend of John Henry and Charlie Brown's *Peanuts* gang, wild Maine blueberries and Idaho potatoes—the real America that people have lived in for generations and that we still enjoy today.

The pages of *USA to Z* are filled, not just with legendary products such as the Victor Talking Machine or amazing places like Yellowstone National Park, but also with exemplary people who had, as they say, *the right stuff*. One such American was Benjamin Franklin. Every schoolchild knows the contributions Franklin made to American independence. Most know that he published *Poor Richard's Almanac*, invented bifocal eyeglasses and the Franklin stove, and gave Philadelphia its first street lighting, night watchmen, insurance company, fire department, and college. Franklin was the quintessential American because he was interested in everything. High on the endless list of things that fired his imagination were lightning and electricity—a twin fascination that caused him to go out and fly a kite during a thunderstorm. This was a remarkably dangerous thing to do (don't you try it!), and old Ben might very well have gotten himself fried. Instead, he watched in amazement as a bolt struck the kite and zipped down the wire he had attached to it, causing a key he had suspended in a glass jar to jump and jiggle. Having thus accomplished his purpose of demonstrating that lightning is electricity, Franklin became the first man in history to catch lightning in a bottle. In one way or another, Americans have been doing that ever since.

The American spirit is like electricity—hard to define, but you can sense the current. Sometimes it's warm and sometimes shocking, but it's always present. You can feel its vibrations in an Aaron Copland symphony or the rumble of a Harley-Davidson motorcycle. You can see it in a Frank Lloyd Wright house, a Martha Graham ballet, or an art deco lampshade. You can taste it in a handful of wild Maine blueberries, a Toll House cookie, a bowl of Texas chili, or a sip of Jack Daniel's Tennessee Whiskey. You can hear it in a passage from John Steinbeck's *Of Mice and Men,* a Dorothy Parker wisecrack, or the call of a wilderness loon.

To catch the spirit, all you have to do is open your eyes, your ears, and your heart and immerse yourself in that great American pastime, the enjoyment of life. The fact is, the pursuit of happiness is the main point of being an American. It says so right there in the Declaration of Independence. Having fun is patriotic.

USA to Z was written because it was a lot of fun to write and in hopes that you'll have fun reading it. What is more, it was written to show that we have powerful connections: between each of us as Americans, between all the products, places, and people mentioned in *USA to Z,* and thousands of other wonders not mentioned. The bonds, like magnetic charges of electrical energy, are there. You just have to know how to make the connections, and making them is a big part of the enjoyment of reading this book.

To help you explore these connections, *USA to Z* has been organized in an unusual manner. As the title suggests, individual sections are arranged alphabetically, but at the end of each one you'll find a list of links calling your attention to related topics. These links are much like the ones you often encounter at an Internet website, only in this case, no mouse or clicking is required. All you have to do is turn to the page indicated. As a result, there are hundreds, even thousands of ways to read this book, and no way to predict what sort of adventure you will have when you turn its pages. For instance, when you've finished reading about Carlsbad Caverns, you may decide to jump over to the sections on Mammoth Cave, Batman, or the Empire State Building. Why Batman or the Empire State Building? Read on and find out.

Even more fun can be had by going out and sampling America's wonders—flying a kite in a thunderstorm—not literally, please—so to speak. Those who want to experience firsthand any or all of the marvels mentioned on the following pages will find assistance near the conclusion of each section. Want to taste the very best New York City bagels? Visit the Kentucky Horse Park? Own a Maine coon cat? Paddle an Old Town canoe? See a gray wolf or a grizzly—hopefully from a respectful distance? Sizzle up the world's best buffalo burger? Wrap yourself in a Pendleton blanket? Buy the Brooklyn Bridge? Dance the lindy hop? *USA to Z* offers names, addresses, and telephone numbers that may help.

So go to it. And see if you can catch a little lightning in a bottle.

USA TO Z

A

HENRY AARON

Gentle Giant of Baseball

AND THEN there was Hank.

Unlike the many bad boys of baseball and other sports whose antics grab headlines, Henry Louis Aaron has always been a soft-spoken and unassuming man. Unlike so many less-talented players whose flamboyance helped make their names household words, Aaron pursued excellence in his own quiet way. The loudest noise he ever made was the sharp crack heard when his bat met the ball, which it did with stunning regularity during his twenty-two-year major-league career.

"I let my statistics do my talking for me," says Aaron.

Hank Aaron's statistics: at bat, 12,364; hits, 3,771; runs batted in, 2,297 (an all-time major-league record); home runs, 755 (an all-time major-league record); lifetime batting average, .305.

The statistic everyone now associates with Hank Aaron is the number 715. The legendary Babe Ruth hit 714 major-league home runs, a record most said would never be broken. When Aaron stepped to the plate for his first at bat of the 1974 season, he had already equaled Ruth's record. Los Angeles Dodgers starting pitcher Al Downing fired a fastball into the strike zone, and just as he had done so many hundreds of times before, Aaron sent it rocketing over the outfield fence. The event stopped the game for an hour, caused the networks to break in on their regular programs with the news, and brought the country to a near standstill for a couple of days. If real history can be made by a sporting event, Aaron did it on that day.

Born in 1936, Aaron spent his childhood in Mobile, Alabama, where he practiced his hitting skills in the backyard whacking bottle caps with a broomstick. By age sixteen he was already playing semi-professional baseball, and in 1951, he signed as a shortstop with the Indianapolis Clowns of the Negro Leagues. One year later the Milwaukee Braves bought his contract and sent him to the minor leagues to gain experience. Mostly it was minor-league outfielders who got the experience, along with plenty of exercise, chasing after Aaron's hits. Usually, their running was in vain since more often than not Aaron sent the ball sailing over the outfield wall and out of reach.

It was a scene repeated often in the major leagues after Aaron became a regular fixture in the Braves lineup in 1954. An opposing pitcher would get behind in the count, try to slip a fastball over the plate, and crack! There it would go. To this day there are retired pitchers with cricks in their necks from jerking their heads around to watch an Aaron blast leave the park.

In 1956, Aaron won the National League batting crown with an average of .326. The following year he was named the league's most valuable player when he hit forty-four home runs and led the Braves to a World Series victory over a strong New York Yankees team. Despite this and the fact that year after year he pounded out thirty, even forty or more, home runs, his accomplishments were not widely celebrated. A late 1950s baseball card even mistakenly pictured him batting left-handed. Sportswriters and the public were fascinated by Mantle, Mays, and Maris—not Hank Aaron. It was only after Aaron began to close in on Babe Ruth's record that many realized this quiet but powerful man had been hammering baseballs out of parks for nearly two decades.

To their discredit, there were many who did not want see Aaron break Babe Ruth's record. Almost certainly, had he lived to see his record broken, Ruth himself would not have been one of them. When news of Aaron's record-breaking homer came in 1974, Ruth's widow said, "The Babe would have been proud."

"I didn't want them to forget Ruth," Aaron said. "I just want them to remember me."

People will certainly remember him, and not just because he could play baseball. Today, Aaron serves as a senior vice president in the Braves organization and helps the club develop new talent. He also promotes a host of civic causes and charitable organizations.

In 1974, Aaron became one of only a few sports figures ever to address the U.S. Congress. Referring to his own sense of patriotism he said, "I have great respect for the flag and what it symbolizes. To me the flag has been more than merely an inspiration. Ever since my first game . . . I have been aiming for the flag in more ways than one."

TBS television has produced an award-winning documentary of Aaron called *Chasing the Dream.* You may be able to catch it sometime on a rerun.

Hank Aaron was elected to the Baseball Hall of Fame in 1982. A visit to the Hall is well worth it, but the best way to get into the swing of this great sports tradition is to go to a game. Although watching baseball on television is better than no baseball at all, it has been compared by some to "watching paint dry." It is far more thrilling to experience a game in person. If you can't get to a major-league park, there is almost certainly a minor-league team in your area. Go see a game, have a hot dog, and for heaven's sake, root for the home team.

GO TO:

PAGE 313 FOR YOGI [BERRA]
PAGE 93 FOR TY COBB
PAGE 151 FOR JOHN HENRY: STEEL-DRIVING MAN

ACOMA, NEW MEXICO

City in the Sky

ON A mesa top hundreds of feet above the desert in western New Mexico stands another, more ancient Santa Fe. Like the state's capital city, it has earth-tone stone and adobe buildings, a grand old church, and beautiful pottery for sale. But this place is very much older than Santa Fe or any other city in America. Some believe the Acoma Pueblo, or "Sky City" as it is sometimes called, is the oldest continuously inhabited place on the continent. Archaeologists believe people may have lived on the mesa for as long as two thousand years.

Acoma looks old, too—very old. Its multistoried homes and kivas give the impression they were built by the same elemental forces that shaped the surrounding desert. Driving toward the pueblo along the narrow access road from the north, it is nearly impossible to distinguish its buildings from the barren rocks on which they stand. Even at the pueblo visitor center, only about a quarter of a mile from the village, it is hard to tell the houses from the boulders. Some visitors may not see the village at all until their tour guide points it out to them. The pueblo appears to be—and is—part of the land itself.

The word *Acoma* means "People of the White Rock." The Acoma Pueblo people have been clinging to their white rock (actually its color is a light reddish brown) for longer than even they can remember, although there is a tribal myth describing a migration ages ago from the North. The Acomas had already been here for eons by the time the explorer Coronado visited them in 1540 during his vain search for Cibola, the mythical city of gold. The only golden things Coronado found were the tall sunflowers that swayed over the trackless great plains to the east, but his coming presaged major changes for the Acomas and other southwestern peoples. The next time Europeans came to Acoma, they would bring disaster.

During the 1590s the Spanish founded the province of New Mexico and began to settle the Rio Grande Valley. In 1598, a small party of soldiers led by Don Juan Zaldivar arrived at Acoma to trade and look for gold (the ever hopeful Spaniards never stopped looking). Urged on by the fiery oratory of their Chief Zutucapan, the Acomas ambushed the Spanish. Most of the soldiers were killed, and Zutucapan himself struck down Zaldivar with a huge club. Four of the soldiers escaped, however, and carried word of the killings to Spanish authorities. Soon a small army under the command of Zaldivar's brother was dispatched to punish the Acomas.

Confronted by steel swords, muskets, and cannon, the Acomas fought back with stone-tipped spears and arrows. Throwing rocks and rolling boulders down on their attackers, they managed to hold out in their fortresslike town atop the mesa for several days. Finally, the Spanish managed to work their way up and in a pitched battle at the top slaughtered more than eight hundred Acoma warriors. Only two of the armored Spaniards were killed. Zaldivar rounded up as many captives as he could and herded them to Spanish headquarters on the Rio Grande. As punishment, each male prisoner had a foot chopped off and the entire tribe was sentenced to slavery for the next twenty years. Eventually all who survived this ordeal returned to the Acoma mesa and rebuilt their city in the sky.

Perhaps the most remarkable structure they built was a church. Supported by seven-foot-thick stone and adobe walls, the San Estevan Franciscan mission was completed in 1629. The huge beams that held up the ceiling were brought from forests on distant Mount Taylor. Because they were to be used in a consecrated structure, the heavy beams were never allowed to touch the ground during the entire forty-mile journey to the mesa. Today, the old church still stands, as does much of the ancient pueblo.

A few Acomas, mostly potters and other artists, still live on the mesa, but the majority of the tribe inhabits small towns and villages such as Acomita and McCartys elsewhere on their 248,000-acre reservation. The old pueblo is considered a holy site and is off-limits to electricity and running water, one of the reasons it is difficult to live there year-round. Even so, every Acoma family maintains a second home on the mesa, which they occupy during religious festivals such as San Pedro's Day, Santa Ana's Day, and the Feast of San Estevan.

Except when the village of Old Acoma is closed to outsiders during special religious observances, the pueblo is open to the public. Visitors register at the Acoma Pueblo Visitor Center, take a bus to the top of the mesa, and follow a tour guide through the pueblo. Acoma pottery, thought by many to be among the best in the Southwest, is offered for sale at many locations in the village.

If you could visit only one place in New Mexico—and that would be a shame, since the state has a lifetime of magical experiences to offer—this is the place you should choose. The view from the mesa is beautiful, and San Estevan is unlike any other religious edifice on this continent. What is more, you'll find that purchasing pottery from the artist who made it is much more soul-satisfying than buying it from a shop in the city.

Old Acoma Pueblo is located to the south of Interstate 40, about fifty-five miles west of Albuquerque. For information or to confirm the date of a visit, call (800) 747-0181, or write to Old Acoma Pueblo, P.O. Box 307, Acoma, NM 87034.

GO TO:
PAGE 169 FOR CHIEF JOSEPH'S LAST STAND
PAGE 205 FOR NAVAJO RUGS
PAGE 223 FOR PENDLETON BLANKETS
PAGE 228 FOR PUEBLO POTTERY
PAGE 249 FOR CHIEF SEATTLE'S PLEA

SAMUEL ADAMS

Brewing Up a Revolution

EVERY ELEMENTARY school kid who has cracked an American history book knows that Samuel Adams was a freethinker. It was Adams who urged on the raiding party of outraged Massachusetts tax resisters who dressed up like Indians and dumped a load of British tea into Boston Harbor. Without the Boston Tea Party, there might have been no American Revolution. What most of the schoolbooks don't reveal is that Adams was much less interested in tea than in beer.

A 1743 Harvard graduate, Adams went into business as a brewer. Some of those who drank Adams's beer and took the time to write about it said the stuff was tasty. Unfortunately Adams was a lousy businessman, and his company went belly-up in 1764. Thereafter Adams devoted himself to a far more intoxicating pursuit: politics. The British probably wished he had gone on brewing beer, since he soon became one of the most vociferous advocates of American independence. If the British could have gotten their hands on Adams, they most certainly would have hanged the man. They did not, and Adams went on to win a seat in the Continental Congress, to sign the Declaration of Independence, and after the revolution to serve as governor of Massachusetts.

Following the revolution nothing was heard of Samuel Adams Beer for more than two centuries. Then in 1985 Adams's great-great-grandson Jim Koch revived his family's eighteenth-century beer recipe and launched the Boston Beer Company. Most who have tried it say Samuel Adams Beer is delicious and fairly bubbling with the spirit of its originator and namesake.

Samuel Adams is a premium beer available throughout the U.S., but it is seen and served most often in New England. For information, write to Boston Beer Company, 30 Germania Street, Boston, MA 02130, or call (617) 522-9080. Tours of the Boston brewing facility are available.

GO TO:

PAGE 60 FOR BOSTON TEA PARTY
PAGE 86 FOR CELESTIAL SEASONINGS TEAS
PAGE 168 FOR JACK DANIEL'S
PAGE 274 FOR U.S. CONSTITUTION (BILL OF RIGHTS)

AIRSTREAM TRAILERS

Heaven on a Trailer Hitch

OWNERS SAY they glide along as if on a stream of air. They also say owning one is like being able to hitch "a little piece of heaven" to the back of your car.

Among the most commonly seen and delightful leftovers from the art deco era is the ever popular Airstream trailer. Looking like silver-plated turtles or armadillos, Airstreams have glided along America's highways for generations, their polished aluminum skin mirroring the gorgeous country they pass through. Inside and out, these grandparents of the modern travel trailer have changed little over the years, and their owners would not have it any other way.

Airstreams were extra-modern and of the very highest quality from the beginning, and they remain so today. Owners of Airstreams

are so proud to have them, they often roll down the road in huge caravans made up exclusively of other Airstreams. Lesser models are
not allowed to keep company with them.

The sparkling Airstream trailer was the brainchild of California
publisher Wally Byam. During the 1920s his magazine printed a
freelance article containing instructions for building a travel trailer.
Apparently the directions were faulty since Byam was hit with an
avalanche of complaints. Byam responded by designing his own
"dream" trailer. Readers liked Byam's streamlined concept so much
that he was soon selling plans and building trailers instead of publishing a magazine.

Byam opened his first Airstream plant in 1931, right in the
middle of the Great Depression. Despite the hard times, he was able
to sell his sparkling trailers for up to $1,200 a unit—they go for much
more than that today—and his factory could hardly keep up with
the demand. Apparently people still yearned for quality even when
money was tight. Quality was, and remains today, what Airstreams
are all about. Employing designs and construction techniques
drawn from the aircraft industry and using only the best materials,
Byam gave his customers true value for their dollars. As a result,
Airstream was the only one of more than three hundred trailer manufacturers to survive the depression years.

Airstream owners have always considered themselves a breed
apart. During the 1930s and 1940s they took to traveling together,
sometimes in large caravans. Byam himself led a caravan of fifty
Airstreams to Central America in 1951. Afterward, Airstream caravans became an institution, and the Wally Byam Caravan Club
International was formed to organize trips and keep members
informed. Actually, the Airstream trailers, not the owners, are registered as members of the WBCCI. Today, there are almost twenty
thousand trailers in the organization. Nonmember trailers are sometimes sniffingly referred to as "baldies" because they lack the prominent registration number. Each year more than fifteen hundred
events are held for member trailers and their owners, who may
come along for the ride.

It is said that the typical Airstream owner is over fifty-five,
retired, married, group oriented, and not badly fixed financially.

Airstreams can cost $40,000 or more, and the price tag for vintage models may go even higher. Even so, owners invariably say the gleaming, rounded-off trailers are well worth the money. After all, NASA used a big Airstream as a quarantine unit for returning astronauts. If they are good enough for the space jockeys, then why not the rest of us? Some owners love their Airstreams so much they have sold their homes and taken to living full-time in their trailers.

The Airstream Company continues to thrive. Airstream now makes fiberglass trailers and motor homes in addition to the original aluminum-bubble model. The vintage caravan models are referred to as "Airstream Classics."

Want to buy your own Airstream? You can find them at Airstream dealerships located throughout the country, but be prepared to part with a few of those nickels you've been dropping into that old coffee can. For more information about the company and its product line, write to Airstream Inc., 419 West Pike Street, P.O. Box 629, Jackson Center, OH 45334, or call (937) 596-6111. Owners of "baldies" who would like their trailers to join the Wally Byam Caravan Club International should write to WBCCI, 803 East Pike Street, Jackson Center, OH 45334, or call (937) 596-5211.

GO TO:

PAGE 149 FOR HARLEY-DAVIDSON MOTORCYCLES
PAGE 193 FOR MODEL T FORD
PAGE 202 FOR ALL-AMERICAN MULES

ALADDIN LAMPS

Soft Light for Magical Evenings

AROUND THE turn of the twentieth century, everyone in America was excited about electric lights. Thanks to the wires beginning to line the nation's streets and byways, Edison's bottled lightning was brightening homes and cities coast to coast. Electricity was the future, right? Well, not according to folks at the Mantle Lamp Company of America, which started doing business in 1908.

The company's founders had invented a new type of lamp that used a heat-sensitive mantle to produce a soft, white light. Powered by burning kerosene, the lamp was easy on the eyes but plenty bright enough for reading, sewing, and guitar picking. The Mantle Lamp Company's investors figured there would be lots of rural people who could not get electricity or who were just too darned old-fashioned to use it. And they were right. While city dwellers were rushing to have their homes wired for electricity, their country brethren moseyed down to the general store to buy the almost magical Aladdin lamps.

For generations Aladdin lamps have been a fixture in rural homes and in quite a few city houses as well. They have played a key role in the country's development, bringing quality lighting to families that previously had none. Today, Aladdins are treated by many families as heirlooms, and no wonder. Many classic models are highly valuable antiques.

Now here is the surprise. The company that created those first quality kerosene lamps still makes them. Located in Nashville, Tennessee, it is known today as Aladdin Industries, and in addition to its lamps, Aladdin manufactures Stanley Steel Vacuum Bottles along with a host of other fine products.

Even in this all-electric age, Aladdin still sells plenty of its kerosene lamps. They come in awfully handy when a hurricane or ice storm knocks down the power lines. They are also great for woodsy cabins and fish camps. And for a romantic evening they provide exactly the warm glow you want. Who says brighter is better?

For information on Aladdin lamps and other products, call (800) 457-5267, or write to Aladdin Mantle Lamp Company, 681 International Boulevard, Clarksville, TN 37040.

GO TO:

PAGE 115 FOR THOMAS EDISON
PAGE 226 FOR POTBELLY STOVES

ALL-DAY PREACHING AND DINNER ON THE GROUNDS

Best Food and Friends This Side of Heaven

THE BEST pecan pies on earth—not counting the ones baked by your grandmother—are to be found at church. Especially delicious are the ones brought in potluck style to an "all-day preaching and dinner on the grounds." To most Americans, it may seem unthinkable to spend all day at church, even on Sunday. For old-fashioned religious communities, however, especially those in the Deep South and parts of the Midwest, the "all-day preaching" is a long and cherished tradition.

In the past, most of these extended religious services began around ten or eleven o'clock in the morning, the usual churchgoing time, and ran on far into the afternoon. Sometimes they continued until well after dark. The hours were taken up with a variety of activities such as hymn sings, prayer meetings, and Bible studies. Those in attendance usually were treated to at least two and maybe three or more sermons delivered by the local minister and/or a visiting evangelist.

Of course the highlight of the day was the dinner, normally served picnic style on the ground or on folding tables outside the church. The potluck offerings often included the likes of fried chicken or baked ham, potato salad, boiled corn, string beans, rolls, biscuits, coconut cake, lemon or pecan pie, and plenty of iced tea or hot coffee served from large pitchers. Needless to say, no alcoholic beverages were served or countenanced.

All-day preachings and dinners on the grounds are rare nowadays. The availability of Sunday shopping as well as televised football and other sports on Sunday afternoons have made community religious activities of this sort very hard to organize. Even so, the congregations of some smaller rural churches continue the tradition, to the considerable betterment of their spirits and stomachs.

To find an all-day preaching and dinner on the grounds, you'll have to look far and wide and ask around. Little towns in Georgia, Alabama, Mississippi, Tennessee, and the Carolinas are likely places to look. If you do come across one, stop by. You'll almost certainly be welcome.

GO TO:
PAGE 48 FOR BEAN SUPPERS
PAGE 86 FOR CELESTIAL SEASONINGS TEAS
PAGE 218 FOR PAPER-SHELL PECANS

ALLIGATORS

Dragons of the Deep South

A CAJUN version of the Santa Claus myth replaces the reindeer with alligators. This conjures a charming image but raises troubling doubts about what is likely to happen when Santa Claus lands on the roof with all his gifts. Might not the alligators scuttle down into the house and eat the children, if not the parents, the packages, and Santa himself? Real alligators are rather single-mindedly intent on supper, and they will eat almost anything.

Alligators have been around a lot longer than people. They are contemporaries of the dinosaurs—and they look like it, too. With their armor-plated bodies, powerful, thrashing tails, and burning, reptilian eyes, they would have fit perfectly into the world of seventy million years ago. Somehow alligators escaped the great extinction that wiped out their dinosaur relatives and have survived right down to the present day.

Naturalist William Bartram, who visited Florida during the late 1770s, noted alligators "in such incredible numbers and so close together from shore to shore that it would have been easy to have walked across on their heads had the animals been harmless." Lucky for him he did not try it.

Over the years, the great numbers of alligators that once inhabited southern swamps and rivers steadily dwindled. Hunted for their valuable hides, they became quite rare by the 1960s. It seemed that the demand for alligator shoes, belts, and purses might finally send the alligator the way of the tyrannosaur and the carrier pigeon. However, the alligator's plight was not so serious as naturalists once feared. The federal protection of the 1970 Lacey Act, which outlawed interstate trafficking in poached alligator hides, proved so effective that the big reptiles made a stunning comeback. Today, they prosper in nearly every southern state.

Alligator leather and meat remain popular, but the demand is now met through controlled hunts and alligator ranches. Approximately three hundred thousand pounds of meat and fifteen thousand hides are sold each year, fueling a multimillion-dollar industry.

Apparently alligators are less disturbed by suburban sprawl and other human activities than many wild creatures. It is not uncommon for Floridians to lose a pet to an alligator or to find one in their swimming pool. More than one casual fisherman has hooked an alligator (and no doubt cut his line). Alligators have jaws like steel traps and have been known to bite the side out of a wooden boat.

More lucky and far more numerous than buffalo, the alligator is an all-American critter but found mostly in the South. They can be seen in considerable numbers in the Everglades National Park and in many other southern parks and preserves. Gators are not very active, and in the water they look much like partially submerged logs (just keep in mind that logs don't bite, but alligators do). Enjoy and appreciate them from a distance. An excellent opportunity to observe alligators and other wildlife is offered by Everglades Day Safaris. For more information, write to Safaris, P.O. Box 1193, Sanibel, FL 33957, or call (239) 472-1559 or (800) 472-3069. You can also e-mail your request for information to gator@ecosafari.com. Most safaris include a lunch featuring alligator meat. Some say it goes down best with a little Tabasco.

GO TO:
PAGE 64 FOR AMERICAN BUFFALO
PAGE 38 FOR ARMADILLO

PAGE 294 FOR GRAY WOLF
PAGE 143 FOR GRIZZLY BEAR
PAGE 264 FOR TABASCO

APPALACHIAN COUNTRY STORES

Penny Candy and Mountain Music

T HE WORLD'S liveliest music cannot be heard in concert halls or at pop festivals, and most of it is not recorded on CD or DVD either. To hear this music, you must climb into the Southern Appalachians where the old masters still hold sway. For the hill folk of Georgia, North Carolina, Tennessee, Kentucky, Virginia, and West Virginia, music is not so much a high calling as it is an everyday part of life, and that doesn't mean the radio or MTV. All they need is a beat-up old banjo, a cane-backed chair, and maybe a wall to lean against, and they are ready for a performance. A small, attentive audience helps but is not required. In winter, a hot fire in a potbelly stove is also considered helpful, since it may put a little extra nimbleness in the fingers.

Almost any day of the week, but especially on Saturday, mountain musicians gather around the big coal stove at the Todd General Store in tiny Todd, North Carolina. "Tiny" may be a generous description of Todd, since the general store is about all that's left of the place. Back before the Great Depression of the 1930s, Todd was a busy little town with its own railroad terminal, a roundhouse, and a prosperous logging business to keep folding money in the pockets of hard-working local folk. People from the area were proud to say their town had "nine stores, four doctors, and a dentist." But the trees were cut down, the depression destroyed the railroad, and a flood in 1940 took away most of the buildings. The doctors, the dentist, and most of their patients moved away. Those who remain buy their milk, beans, candy, and snuff at the Todd General Store. And if they happen by at the right time, they may hear some wonderful mountain music. The Todd store features what its owners describe as a bull pen, a small sitting area set aside for fiddlers and their fiddles, pickers and their banjos, or high-country storytellers and their yarns.

In Valle Crucis, several dozen winding mountain miles to the west of Todd, the old-time Mast General Store is also a magnet for musicians. On almost any day, you might see them bowing their fiddles or picking away at guitars and dulcimers on the wooden bench out front, or on stools near the huge stove at the heart of the store. While listening to them, you may dig through the darnedest assortment of merchandise you're likely to see anywhere: buttons, screws, cheese, thread, kitchenware, books, nails, machinery, canoes, picks, axes, shovels, pans, bobbins, bottles, cans, shoes, aprons, clothing, groceries—both ordinary and gourmet--and just about anything else you might want or imagine you want. To put it another way, the Mast is an old-fashioned country store and as such has a bit of everything.

The store's clapboard façade sags a little, which is no surprise since it was built in 1892. Like many country stores, this one got its name from the family that owned and ran it the longest. W. W. Mast and his son Howard operated the business for more than eighty years, and the characters of these two men permeate the store to this day. It is said by locals that the Masts "hated like the devil" to turn away a customer. So they had something for everyone—crowded on shelves, piled on counters, or sitting around in barrels. For farmers, they had seed, plows, and straw hats. For carpenters, they had nails, overalls, and good, stout work boots. For churchgoers, they had Sunday suits and ladies' gloves and hats. For mothers, they had candles, mixers, and elixirs; and for the bereaved, caskets on discreet display in an upstairs room. And, of course, for a child with a penny, they always had a twist of licorice and a bright smile.

It used to be that people with an ailment didn't go to a doctor or a pharmacy. Instead, they dropped in at the country store where the keeper had sage advice for them and almost certainly something on the shelf to clear up the problem. For aches and pains, the Masts could offer a variety of liniments that were as effective on horses as people. For those fabled female complaints, they had the Lydia E. Pinkham Vegetable Compound. For a case of the blues, they were always handy with a tonic or a bottle of Moxie Water.

Under assault by a modern world of interstate highways, clinics, druggists, department stores, and supermarkets, the Mast Store eventually fell into decline. Howard Mast finally gave up the business in 1977, but luckily that was not the end of it. The store's current owners run the place in the best old-fashioned tradition. Rumor has it there is still a casket on display somewhere upstairs, and downstairs you will still find plenty of penny candy.

The Todd General Store is located in Todd off Route 194, about twelve miles north of Boone, North Carolina. Write to Todd General Store, Todd, NC 28684, or call (336) 877-1067. The Mast General Store is located in Valle Crucis on Route 194, about eight miles south of Boone. Write to Mast General Store, Valle Crucis, NC 28691, or call (963) 963-6511. For mail order, call (866) FOR-MAST ([866] 367-6278).

GO TO:

PAGE 53 FOR BLUEGRASS
PAGE 95 FOR COCA-COLA
PAGE 110 FOR DR PEPPER
PAGE 166 FOR IVORY SOAP
PAGE 225 FOR LYDIA E. PINKHAM VEGETABLE COMPOUND
PAGE 282 FOR VERMONT

APPALACHIAN SPRING

Music for Martha and the Mountains

AMERICA'S MOST popular piece of classical music was written—no surprise here—by an American. Aaron Copland's *Appalachian Spring* is on nearly everyone's list of musical favorites. Country, rock, and bluegrass fans love it as much or even more than do classical music buffs. That is probably because it is so rich in folksy American feeling. The central theme that runs through it is an old Shaker hymn, and thanks to Copland, you can probably hum it.

Of all the world's best-known and loved musical scores, this one has the happiest title. The name and the music go together like apple pie and Cheddar cheese. It is impossible to hear the music and not actually think of spring in the Appalachians—of mountain streams bubbling with melted snow or of the year's first blossoms bursting open in a hollow somewhere high in the Smoky Mountains. But here is the fun part. Those were not the things Aaron Copland was thinking of when he wrote the music back during the early 1940s.

"It's an odd thing about that title," Copland said in an interview many years after *Appalachian Spring* premiered as a ballet in 1944. "Today, when I hear the piece or conduct it, I think of the mountains and the springtime just the way everyone else does, but that was not what was on my mind when I wrote the music. Actually, I was thinking of Martha Graham and of how beautiful she was when she danced."

Originally, Copland titled the piece *Ballet for Martha*, and he coaxed Graham to dance at its first performance in Washington, D.C. In Graham's opinion, the title was "as simple and direct as the Shaker theme that runs through the music," but she did not think it appropriate for a ballet. "I took some words from the poetry of Hart Crane and retitled it," she said. The new title she chose was *Appalachian Spring*.

When Copland found out what had happened, he confronted Graham. "Martha, what have you done with the title?"

"Changed it," she said. "I like this one better."

"Does it have anything to do with the ballet?"

"No," said Graham, "I just liked it better."

The composer did not argue—he never, ever argued with Martha Graham—so, the new title stuck. Like all great classical pieces are destined to do, *Appalachian Spring* has outlived its creators. Copland and Graham died within a few months of each other during the early 1990s.

You can find a copy of *Appalachian Spring* at any record shop. Keep in mind, the music comes in two versions, a concert suite and a longer ballet performance suite. You may find that you enjoy both.

Symphony orchestras often include the concert version of the piece in their spring offerings. If there is a symphony orchestra in your community, support it with your donations; ticket prices almost never cover the cost of operating a fine orchestra. Better still, take the family out to a concert. You'll be doing them and yourself a favor.

GO TO:
PAGE 34 FOR APPALACHIAN COUNTRY STORES
PAGE 100 FOR AARON COPLAND
PAGE 141 FOR MARTHA GRAHAM
PAGE 232 FOR AMERICAN QUILTS

ARMADILLO

Creature Designed by Rube Goldberg

LIKE MOST other American critters—including people—the armadillos seen today in Texas and throughout much of the South are the descendants of immigrants. These armored creatures did not arrive on U.S. soil until well into the nineteenth century. Having migrated from South America, they first came to the attention of Texans in 1879 when a woodcutter came across one just outside San Antonio. The amazed woodsman hauled the armadillo along with his load into the city, where the creature attracted throngs of curious residents and eventually fetched a price of $30.

It is hard to imagine anyone would think an armadillo was worth that much nowadays. You can't eat them, they are certainly not cuddly, and there are so many of them around that they could hardly be considered curiosities. Even so, people seem to love them. The armadillo has been more or less adopted as the emblem of the American Southwest.

A sort of anteater with armor, the armadillo uses its powerful claws to rip open rotten logs and tear into ant and termite nests, where it licks up from fifty to one hundred insects at a time with its long, sticky tongue. The variety most commonly seen in this country, the nine-banded armadillo, grows up to thirty-two inches long and may weigh up to fifteen pounds. Covered from head to tail with thick layers of armor, the armadillo is impervious to most predators. Dogs, however, are sometimes able to turn them over and get at their soft underbellies, with fatal results for the armadillos.

Not widely admired for their intelligence, armadillos are considered by some Southwesterners to be the "stupidest creature on four legs." Like most prejudiced beliefs, this one is wide of the truth. The fact is, armadillos are much stupider than that. Compared to an armadillo, a chicken is a genius.

Here are examples of armadillo jokes frequently heard in Texas:

Question: Why did the armadillo cross the road?
Answer: He didn't. He just sat there waiting for the next eighteen-wheeler.

Question: What's the difference between an armadillo and a concrete block?
Answer: When a car is approaching at night, a concrete block won't run around in circles in the middle of the road.

Question: What's the difference between an armadillo and a piece of driftwood?
Answer: The driftwood may float across the river, but the armadillo will try to walk across on the bottom.

All the curious behaviors alluded to by these jokes can be observed in armadillos. Countless automobile tires have been ruined by armadillos who could not figure out how to get out of the way of an oncoming vehicle. One less-than-serious nature writer has suggested that the animal's successful migration into the eastern states was made possible by pioneer armadillos who scuttled across the bottom of the Mississippi. Probably the armadillos crossed the Mississippi the same way most of us do, on highway bridges. Today, armadillos have advanced all the way to Florida, where they have no doubt provided more than one alligator with a tasty, if somewhat crunchy, morsel.

Early Spanish explorers must have been astonished when they first encountered armadillos and gave them their name, which means "little armored things." The Spanish saw the armadillo as somehow symbolic of the New World. Nice compliment, that. No doubt, the best place to see armadillos is Texas. For a copy of the Texas State Travel Guide, write to P.O. Box 141009, Austin, TX 78714, or check out the state's official visitors website at www.traveltex.com.

GO TO:

PAGE 32 FOR ALLIGATORS
PAGE 64 FOR AMERICAN BUFFALO
PAGE 294 FOR GRAY WOLF
PAGE 143 FOR GRIZZLY BEAR
PAGE 134 FOR RUBE GOLDBERG

ART DECO

Tomorrow, Tomorrow, and Tomorrow

THEY WERE no old fogies, our grandparents and great-grandparents. No indeed. Rather, they were thoroughly modern people who approached their future with a boldness and confidence that we who have stepped so timidly into the twenty-first century could never hope to match. They embraced the twentieth century with such eagerness that it seemed they could hardly wait to reach tomorrow. For evidence of this, one need only look at the buildings they built, the cars they drove, and the jewelry they wore when they were young.

Today, we call it "art deco," but the term is ours, not theirs—it was coined by an art historian during the 1960s. For the people who lived during the so-called art deco era, the 1920s and 1930s, it was merely the look of the future.

What is art deco? Essentially, it is a form of futuristic decor used in interior, industrial, graphic, and architectural design. When art deco first appeared early in the twentieth century, it reveled in light, color, and the myriad of wonders made possible by the machine age.

Like most artistic trends, art deco is difficult to describe. It is the sort of thing for which you must develop an eye, but once you have, you will recognize it whenever and wherever you see it. There are any number of themes and characteristics that frequently show up in art deco: sunbursts and fountains symbolic of a dawning age; an emphasis on speed, power, and flight, celebrating all the new transportation and communication options that appeared early in the twentieth century; geometric shapes paying homage to the machine, once thought to be the solution to all our problems; ancient cultures representing a fascination with Mayan and Egyptian civilizations; and the stacked, almost cubist shape of the skyscraper, suggesting power and activity on a monumental scale.

When art deco is mentioned, people are likely to think of the old oceanfront hotel district of Miami Beach. Many of the buildings in this historic quarter resemble enormous, colorfully decorated wedding cakes. They are a delight to behold and taken together represent an American architectural treasure, but they show only one side of art deco design. Keep in mind that the Chrysler and Empire State Buildings are also art deco, and these all-business structures are in no way suggestive of wedding cakes.

Wherever you go in America, elements of art deco architecture and design remain. Old public buildings, department stores, service stations, and homes built during the 1920s and 1930s may be just as authentically deco as anything you are likely to see in Miami Beach. Train stations and airports are often deco. So are movie theaters, ballrooms, and many older hotels. Even old factories and warehouses often show the telltale marks of art deco design.

Art deco elements were often used to jazz up consumer products such as clocks, watches, lamps, and appliances. Bakelite table radio chassis were molded into sleek, streamlined shapes. Some deco lamps looked as if they might have once lit a pharaoh's chamber. Many such deco items are now hot properties in the antique industry.

Art deco architecture is not always art and not always beautiful. But sometimes it is both. Frank Lloyd Wright experienced an extended art deco period, and evidences of its influence can be seen in many of his most memorable homes and buildings.

The style is once again growing in popularity. One can also see art deco concepts reflected in the interior designs of homes and buildings, some of which were completed only recently. The overall design aims at producing a clean, cohesive environment that suggests machinelike efficiency, with furnishings that have industrial materials such as glass and metal incorporated into their design.

In a technical, art history sense, the term "art deco" refers to the eclectic style exemplified by a famous design exposition called *Arts Decoratifs Industriels et Modernes.* In Europe the style was frequently referred to as *moderne.* First widely applied in Europe, the style migrated to the United States, where it reached a peak of popularity during the early to mid-1930s. On this side of the Atlantic, however, art deco developed such a daring flare that it became largely an American phenomenon.

Europeans don't see much of their own design history in the hotels of Miami Beach, let alone the Empire State Building. We Americans, on the other hand, tend to think of the old skyscraper as entirely our own. It is only natural that a skyscraper be beautiful. Why, after all, would King Kong want to climb an ugly building?

To see and enjoy art deco architecture, you may only need to drive or walk around your own town. Older business areas and residential neighborhoods should have plenty of splendid examples. For samples of art deco consumer goods, look first to your own closet or kitchen cabinets. Maybe your mixer has that 1930s look. If not, antique shops in your area will likely have art deco items aplenty to delight you.

Many large cities have art deco societies and groups dedicated to the preservation of historic architecture. Among the most active of these is the Art Deo Society of Los Angeles, P.O. Box 972, Hollywood CA 90078, (310) 659-3326. Also quite active is the Art Deco Society of New York, P.O. Box 160, Planetarium St., New York, NY 10024, (212) 679-DECO (3326).

However, Miami Beach is likely the epicenter of the world art deco movement, and everyone should experience its colorful historic district at least once. For advice on seeing the district and information on walking tours, contact the Miami Design Preservation League at P.O. Box 190180, Miami Beach, FL 33119, call (305) 672-2014, or visit the website at www.mdpl.org. Inquire about the annual Art Deco Weekend in Miami.

GO TO:

Page 120 for Empire State Building
Page 299 for Frank Lloyd Wright
Page 136 for Golden Gate Bridge
Page 211 for Old Hollywood
Page 159 for Hoover Dam

B

BAKED BEANS

Surest Test of a New England Christian

WANT TO do it right? In the morning, dig a hole in the ground and build a roaring wood fire over a pile of large stones. When the stones are white hot and smoking, place them—very carefully—in the bottom of the hole. Then take a heavy clay pot, fill it with beans, add a cup or so of maple syrup, and throw in a hunk of pork fat (that is, if bear fat is unavailable). Put the pot in the hole on top of the hot rocks, cover it with soil or sand, and then forget about it for the rest of the day. When suppertime rolls around, dig up the pot, and you'll have what you need. Add a loaf of steamed brown bread and a scoop of fresh, creamy butter, and you'll have heaven itself.

Recipes for baked beans are as numerous as kitchens, especially in New England, where the sweet and spicy legumes serve as a sort of national cuisine. Every Yankee has his or her own favorite "world's best" recipe for this delicacy, but none are fancy. The basic ingredients are yellow-eye, Jacob's cattle, or soldier beans—New Englanders consider pinto beans an insult to the palate—a slab or two of salt pork; a little maple syrup, brown sugar, or molasses; a handful of chopped onion; and a dash or so of dried mustard, salt, and pepper.

Many bean chefs believe that when the dish cannot be prepared in a hole as described above, beans are best when baked in a brick oven. Bean-loving author Robert Coffin, an expert on the ways and eccentricities of New Englanders, did not hold with the brick-oven theory, however. In his classic study *Mainstays of Maine*, Coffin reminded fellow purists that baked beans were the stuff of deep-woods lumber camps, where all the cooking was wood-fired. Coffin would have been horrified at the thought of his favorite food turn-

44

ing hot and bubbly in a gas or electric oven or—perish the thought—
a microwave. He was convinced the beans would come out "wicked
good" only if they were "done up proper" in a woodstove.

True-blue baked bean aficionados may well agree with Coffin.
The trouble is that even in New England most folks don't have cook-
stoves that use wood for heat nowadays. But Coffin had a fix for
that. Simply ask around until you find someone who does own a
woodstove, and let them do the bean baking. New Englanders are
duty bound to pitch in when a neighbor lacks proper facilities. "It
is," said Coffin, "the surest test of a New England Christian."

For those less strict than Coffin, excellent brick-oven beans can
be had just about anywhere if you don't mind buying your beans off
a shelf. The B&M Company of Portland, Maine, bakes excellent
beans in their huge brick ovens and cans them in a variety of sizes—
for your convenience and their profit. You may find B&M products
at your grocers. If not, write to Burnham & Morrill Company, Portland, ME 04104, or call My Brands at (888) 281-6400.

GO TO:

PAGE 48 FOR BEAN SUPPERS
PAGE 157 FOR HOMINY GRITS
PAGE 226 FOR POTBELLY STOVES
PAGE 52 FOR BLUEBERRIES

BATMAN AND ROBIN

Like a Bat out of Gotham City

FORGET THE movies. The real Batman is and always will be the cartoon character Bob Kane created for Detective Comics more than a
half century ago. A guy like Batman, with his batcape, batcave,
batsignal, batmobile, and boyish sidekick, Robin, doesn't make much
sense outside the garish, color-paneled universe of the comic book—
that peculiar American contribution to world literature. Neither does

Gotham City, the surrealistic megalopolis where Batman outwits and outmuscles exotic villains such as the Joker and the Penguin.

"Sock! Take that! Pow! You're going back on ice, Penguin." Lines like that are best suited to the blocky still scenes and swollen dialogue balloons of a comic book. When they attempt this sort of banter on the big screen—and they do—it's unconvincing and distracting. But not so in the comics. Yes, it is a little hard to believe Batman and Robin could deliver clever little quips and carry on witty conversations while smashing furniture, crashing through windows, and collaring troops of murderous bad guys. But you can imagine it. That's the magic of the comics. You can imagine almost anything.

You bet, the blockbuster movie *Batman* and its various sequels are a lot of fun. With their rapid-fire razzmatazz, eye-popping visual effects, and violence, violence, and more violence, they are pure Hollywood gold. Their one unfortunate drawback is that they do all the imagining for us. With comics it's different. With comics, the imagining takes place up there in the private screening room of your mind. With comics, you don't care if the dialogue is believable. The art and action are right there on the page, and you can hold them in your hands. Batman and his pal Robin can cut loose with an insulting quip or disgusting pun with every sock, pow, and whack, and you love it.

The comics were the perfect medium for an artist the likes of Bob Kane. As a child, he doodled not just in his school notebook, as most children do, but on walls, sidewalks, advertising posters—everywhere. By age ten, Kane already knew he wanted to be a cartoonist and started copying the Sunday comics freehand for practice. Kane got his big break at the very early age of eighteen with Detective (DC) Comics, which had just released the enormously successful Superman series. Kane begged his editor for a chance to create his own superhero and was given a single weekend to come up with an idea. On Monday, Kane stepped into the editor's office and presented him with . . . Batman, complete with mask, cape, signal, and batmobile.

The inspiration for Batman came from the Douglas Fairbanks Jr. movie hero Zorro, who wore a mask and kept his black horse in a cave. The idea for Batman's winglike cape was lifted from drawings of a flying machine conceived by another incurable doodler, Leonardo da Vinci. On one of the drawings da Vinci had scribbled the words "Your bird will have no model but that of a bat." And who was the model for Bruce Wayne, Batman's boring daylight persona? Just say the names aloud and you'll get the answer: Bruce Wayne—Bob Kane.

The "caped crusader" first appeared in DC Comics in 1939, the same year the twentieth century's most interesting and revolutionary world's fair opened in New York. The fair envisioned a utopian "World of Tomorrow" that would never really come into existence except in science-fiction movies and comic strips. The Batman comics owed much to the fair's modernist spirit: the streamlined shapes, the bizarre gadgetry, and the fanciful deco-style architecture.

Gotham City itself, however, represents a far less optimistic view of the future than the one offered us by the 1939 New York fair of fairs. In creating Gotham, the futuristic though rather dismal stage for his superhero, Kane was likely influenced by the 1926 Fritz Lang film *Metropolis*. Interestingly, the city protected by competing superhero Superman is called Metropolis, but it is a much friendlier place than Gotham. Like the city in Lang's silent classic, Gotham is filled with huge, impersonal buildings and enormous machinery with gears the size of houses. Every scene is marked by deep shadow and the ominous feeling that something awful may happen at any moment.

Standing in the way of that something awful and of a host of outrageous criminals are the "dynamic duo" Batman and Robin. As everyone in the world now knows (the movies have spread Batman's fame far wider than the comics could ever have done) the man behind the black batmask is Bruce Wayne, a rich social gadfly. The "Boy Wonder," Robin—youthful now for more than fifty years—is Dick Grayson, an orphaned son of circus performers.

In the movies, Batman fights crime with an unlikely array of pseudoscientific, higher-than-high-tech gizmos that he has apparently invented and paid for himself. His rocket-propelled batmobile can blast through stone, climb the walls of skyscrapers, and maneuver through clouds like a B-2 stealth bomber. Weapons such as these are mostly beyond the reach of the Pentagon, the CIA, and the U.S. Treasury, so the movie Wayne's fortune must be very large indeed. The comic book Batman gets some of his punch from gadgets—a periscope that allows him to spy on his enemies practically anywhere in the city or a batmobile that looks a bit like a 1950s sweptwing Chevy—but most of the hard work of knocking down evil types is done with fists—sock!, pow!, and the like.

Alas, the duo almost never receive any credit for their efforts, and are in fact considered criminals themselves by the ungrateful citizens of Gotham. One wonders why they bother. Is Gotham, with all its greedy industrialists, corrupt politicians, and wrong-headed newspapermen, really worth saving? Oh yeah.

A copy of the Detective Comics Batman series published in 1939 would certainly have been worth saving. First editions that once sold for a nickel now bring thousands at auction. Maybe you can find one in some dusty old trunk up in the attic. The current version of the Batman comics can still be found at almost any newsstand or bookstore. And of course the legend has now reached its money-making zenith in Hollywood. Incidentally, the Batman movies are meant for the big screen and not for video, so if you haven't seen them already, try to catch a rerun at the theater. You'll find the movie version of Gotham City even darker and more foreboding than the original. The movie Batman is more inventive, perhaps, but not nearly so good with his fists as the comic book hero. Enjoy the flicks. Just keep in mind that the masked fellow dancing around on the screen is somebody else's Batman and not necessarily yours.

GO TO:
PAGE 73 FOR CARLSBAD CAVERNS
PAGE 189 FOR MAMMOTH CAVE
PAGE 308 FOR SUPERMAN (THE MAN WITH X-RAY EYES)

BEAN SUPPERS

With or Without the Beans

EACH WEEK in nearly every town and village in New England, the faithful gather in churches, granges, community centers, public parks, kitchens, garages, and even basements. Like emissaries carrying tribute to some foreign potentate, they bring apple and blueberry pies, chocolate cakes, cylinder-shaped loaves of sweet brown bread, and mounds of Toll House cookies. They arrive with bowls of leafy salad already dripping with pungent dressing, platters piled high with sliced ham and turkey, and steamy casseroles covered with crunchy toppings. And of course they deliver pots, pans, and crockery vessels of every description brimming with beans, beans, beans, and more beans. Long folding tables groan with the weight of it all, and before the evening is over, so will those in attendance.

Usually somebody sells tickets or takes up a collection. The money is not intended to cover the cost of the food—that is provided free through the consideration of the participants. Instead, the cash will go toward painting a church, buying a tire for an old fire truck, or sending some young person off to college.

In most parts of the country these affairs are called potluck dinners, but in New England they are known, for rather obvious reasons, as bean suppers. Frugal New Englanders like the idea of substituting the ubiquitous baked beans, for which they are rightly famous, in place of more expensive forms of protein such as turkey, ham, or roast. By eating beans they feel they are saving money for both themselves and their community, and this adds a note of Yankee righteousness to what might otherwise be an ordinary town hall feed.

Increasingly in recent years, plates of sliced turkey or ham have crept onto tables at some such community affairs, but these are considered an inferior variety of bean supper organized by people who don't know how to "do it proper." It is even possible nowadays to attend a bean supper with no beans. You see, it can happen that nobody thinks to bring beans. Or, for whatever reason, they just get left off the menu. This is, of course, a scandalous omission, not something to be mentioned in mixed company in, say, Dorset, Vermont; or Stonington, Maine; or Jackson, New Hampshire. For this reason, when such a thing happens, bean-supper-goers tend to ignore the absence of beans and satisfy themselves instead with tuna casserole, hot rolls, and a fat slice of rhubarb pie.

You can find a bean supper to attend at some point on the calendar in nearly every New England community. For news of them, turn the pages of small-town newspapers or check the bulletin boards of town halls. You'd have to be very unlucky not to find one, especially during the summer. Bean suppers are especially common in the tiny fishing and agricultural communities along the coast of Maine. One of the most down-home and delicious of these "Down East" feeds is held the second Saturday of each month, May through October, at the United Methodist Church in Penobscot, about forty-odd miles toward the Atlantic from Bangor. Supper is served in the hall behind the sanctuary by some of the friendliest people in the world. The first seating is at five o'clock sharp, and there is always a full house. But don't worry. If you miss the first seating, there is another at 6:30, and while you wait you can gaze out at Northern Bay, a nearly enclosed extension of the Atlantic more than twenty-five miles from the open ocean. Besides, the supper is worth the wait and many times over the price of admission. For a few dollars, you'll get salads, casseroles, vegetables, sinfully sweet desserts, and an hour or so in the company of some of earth's finest people. Your coffee cup will be steaming and bottomless, constantly replenished from large metal pitchers. And, of course, there are always plenty of baked beans.

GO TO:

PAGE 31 FOR ALL-DAY PREACHING AND DINNER ON THE GROUNDS

PAGE 44 FOR BAKED BEANS

PAGE 52 FOR BLUEBERRIES

PAGE 231 FOR QUIET SIDE (MAINE)

PAGE 282 FOR VERMONT

JACK BENNY

Now, Cut That Out!

PROBABLY AMERICA'S all-time favorite comedian, Jack Benny was much less a jokester than he was a straight man. The key to his success lay in the fact that he was the best—and the funniest—

straight man who ever lived. He could get a big laugh by just looking at the audience.

For nearly two decades beginning in 1931, Benny hosted the top-rated comedy show on radio. When the nation switched to television, Benny found an even more responsive audience there and managed to keep people laughing for another twenty years.

His on-stage persona was that of a vain, stingy, middle-aged man who was perpetually thirty-nine, played the violin with rasping ineptitude, kept his money in a dusty basement vault, drove an ancient 1927 Maxwell presumably because he was too cheap to buy a newer model, and paid his housekeeper, Rochester (Eddie Anderson), so poorly that he had to ask his own children for an allowance. These foibles made Benny the butt of nonstop gag lines delivered by the other characters in his skits, energetically portrayed by Don Wilson, Dennis Day, Frank Nelson, Artie Auerback, and Mel Blanc, as well as Anderson. For instance, Rochester would say: "I put gas in the car like you said, Mr. Benny, but a dime's worth don't go near as far as it used to." And Benny would react with one of his priceless deadpans, often lifting a hand to one cheek. The audience cracked up. A favorite Benny line, delivered when a gag had been milked for all the laughs it was likely to get, was: "Now, cut that out!"

Benny kept performing and kept audiences rolling in the aisles almost up to the day he died in 1977 at age eighty. He was survived by Mary Livingston, his wife for nearly fifty years. Livingston had been a regular on Benny's show.

The everyday-life Jack Benny was very different from the tightwad he portrayed on his show. A generous benefactor of numerous charities, he was in fact an accomplished violinist. But the stage Benny was so delightfully predictable and human that this is the way Americans best love to remember him. For most of us, he will indeed always be thirty-nine.

Episodes of the old Jack Benny television show can be seen occasionally on cable. However, to truly appreciate Benny's talents, one should hear his radio skits. How does a comedian do deadpan on radio? Benny pulled it off perfectly. For taped or CD copies of Jack Benny radio performances, see the website for Crabapple Sound, www.crabapplesound.com.

GO TO:
PAGE 107 FOR DAFFY DUCK
PAGE 242 FOR REVELL-MONOGRAM MODELS

BLUEBERRIES

Wild Taste, Purple Tongue

THERE ARE two types of blueberries: the plump, juicy ones that grow on cultivated bushes, and the smaller, tart ones that grow wild and much closer to the ground. While the former are what you most often see in stores, the latter are much more popular with bears, moose, and people. The plain truth is that wild blueberries are much tastier than the domestic kind. Of course, it takes a lot more of them to make a pie, but with all that extra flavor, who cares?

Among North America's most beneficent—and delicious—natural wonders, wild blueberries grow with little or no help. In fact, they all too often must grow in spite of human activities such as the rampant road construction and residential development. But grow they do, in prodigious quantities, on the boggy barrens of Maine and several other northern states. In August when the little berries ripen, rakers can scoop them up by the pound. (That is, if they can get to the fields ahead of the moose. The next time you see a picture of a moose or meet up with one in person, notice the shovel-like snout. There is a reason the snout is shaped like that.)

Raking wild blueberries is backbreaking work. The harvesting technique—using a close-tined hand rake—has changed little in the last two centuries. Usually one must crouch over the rake for hours at a time, but the rewards can be truly magnificent. A single acre of barren land can yield up to four thousand pounds of berries.

Maine is by far the largest producer of wild blueberries. About fifteen million pounds of wild blueberries are harvested in Washington County alone. Most of the state's harvest is frozen or canned by large distributors such as Jasper Wyman & Son of Milbridge. In recent years, however, a few fresh wild berries have begun to appear on grocery shelves, mostly in the Northeast.

Centuries ago, blueberries were an important staple of Native Americans, who saw them as a gift of the Great Spirit and found them especially useful as a sort of candy to quiet hungry children. Native tribes also used the blueberry root for brewing a medicinal tea.

Nowadays, people bake them in pies, muffins, cakes, and breads, add them to pancake batter, and make jams or preserves with them. Wild blueberries make a terrific addition to a green salad, especially when accompanied by a crisp lime vinaigrette dressing. Heaven on earth can be defined as a scoop of ice cream—preferably the soft vanilla kind—with a heaping handful of wild blueberries on top. But the best way to enjoy them is the same way the moose do— *au naturel.*

For information on wild Maine blueberries and where they can be purchased, contact Jasper Wyman & Son at P.O. Box 100, Milbridge, ME 04658, or call (800) 341-1758. During the summer, Wyman & Son offers hard work for the adventurous: an opportunity to rake blueberries by hand just the way the old-timers did it. The pay is not bad if you are quick and efficient. For some excellent blueberry chutney, conserve, vinegar, or syrup, write to Spruce Mountain Blueberries, P.O. Box 68, West Rockport, ME 04865, or call (207) 236-3538.

GO TO:
PAGE 48 FOR BEAN SUPPERS
PAGE 104 FOR CRANBERRIES
PAGE 218 FOR PAPER-SHELL PECANS

BLUEGRASS

That Old Throw'd-Away Music

WANT SOME music to get your legs and feet moving? Your toes, too? Then turn on to some bluegrass. If you can sit still in your chair through a full set of this stuff, somebody had better call an undertaker.

About as American as any music is likely to be, bluegrass is alive with youthful energy. Although to some ears it may sound a bit old-timey, the style itself is quite young, not much older than, say, pop-rock or heavy metal. True, it was inspired by traditional American folk music, and to trace the roots of that you have to go back hundreds of years to the first Scotch-Irish immigrants who brought long rifles and hot fiddles to the Appalachian mountains. You can trace it back farther, if you like, all the way to the days of the troubadours who strummed mandolins and broke the hearts of ladies in one medieval castle after another. But bluegrass as we know it today was born during the 1940s, the child of commercial recording companies and of a hillbilly picker from Kentucky. Making its appearance right about the end of the Golden Age of Radio, it got toes tapping in an America almost, but not quite, ready for television or the thumping electric rhythms of rock 'n' roll.

Perhaps more than any other musical movement, bluegrass was the idea of one man. Growing up in the western Kentucky bluegrass country, Bill Monroe was exposed to a wealth of traditional music, most of it the kind you might hear on the front porch of an unpainted mountain cabin. The modest country musicians Monroe loved best often said they played "those old throw'd-away songs."

When he launched his performing career during the 1930s, Monroe made up his mind to keep America's great old music from really being "throw'd away." He vowed to keep alive "the old southern sound," as he called it. For years, Monroe experimented with various instrumental and vocal arrangements that seemed to reproduce the old-time feeling of the music he had heard back home as a boy. By the end of World War II, he had hit on the right combination—what we now recognize as the basic bluegrass style. It featured high, plaintive vocal harmonies backed by an overdriven acoustic string band usually including a mandolin, guitar, bass, and banjo. Monroe called his band the Blue Grass Boys, and that is how the music got its name.

Before long, Monroe was appearing regularly on radio's *Grand Ole Opry*. His most popular tunes, such as "Blue Moon of Kentucky," often featured Lester Flatt on guitar, Earl Scruggs on banjo, and Monroe on mandolin. This new music with its old sound brought country folks to their feet all across America. Mountaineers clapped along and shouted. "Listen to that!" they said. "Listen to those danged fools play!" Suddenly, it was okay again to be a hillbilly. In fact, you could be danged proud of it. Front-porch pickers in mining towns and mill villages tuned up their worn-out guitars and started playing Monroe tunes. In this way bluegrass created its own folk tradition.

Other musicians caught up in the excitement over bluegrass soon followed Monroe up the steps to the Opry stage. Among the best of the early bluegrass groups were the Stanley Brothers, the Country Gentlemen, and the Foggy Mountain Boys, as well as Lester Flatt and Earl Scruggs, the flying-fingered guitar and banjo wizards who got their start playing alongside Monroe. These and a handful of other successful bluegrass bands won recording contracts and national recognition.

Not so, however, for many lesser-known bands. Bluegrass never won the broad commercial acceptance of mainstream country and western. During the 1950s, most bluegrass bands scratched out whatever living they could on the "rooster circuit," sleeping in cars and grabbing a few minutes of airtime on rural AM stations, usually around 6:00 a.m., when farmers were having breakfast and listening to the radio. If enough farmers tuned in, the band might get a gig at a local bar or dance hall. Otherwise, it was back to planting potatoes or mining coal. Eventually television, Elvis Presley, and the changing times put an end to the rooster circuit, but not to bluegrass music. It had plenty of life left in it and still does—more now than ever.

Now well past the age of fifty, bluegrass is still going strong. Over the years, it has attracted a steady stream of highly talented performers, all committed to Bill Monroe's goal of keeping alive that "old southern sound." Fresh blood keeps flowing into the bluegrass movement in the form of highly talented bands such as Radio Flyer, Northern Lights, and The Seldom Scene, and performers such as Doyle Lawson and Alison Krauss. And plenty of folks are listening. You should, too.

Bill Monroe's vintage recordings and those of other early bluegrass bands are available on CD, although you may find there is something a bit incongruous about listening to a digitized hillbilly ballad. Here are some CDs you might want to own: *Bill Monroe 1950–1958* (Bear Family BCD-15423); *Lester Flatt and Earl Scruggs* (Bear Family BCD-15472); *Stanley Brothers, Complete Columbia Recordings* (Bear Family BD-15564); *The Country Gentlemen, 25 Years* (Rebel CD-1102); *Doyle Lawson, Rock My Soul* (SH CD3717); *Alison Krauss, I've Got that Old Feeling* (Rounder CD-0275); *The Seldom Scene, The Best of the Seldom Scene* (Rebel CD-1101); *The Bluegrass Compact Disc* (Rounder CD-115202).

To hear some great live bluegrass, you have a choice of several dozen festivals. Among the best are the Grey Fox Bluegrass Festival, held each July in Ancramdale, New York (call [888] 946-8495); and the Merle Watson Memorial Festival, held in April at Wilkesboro, North Carolina (call [800] 343-7857). For a complete listing of these and many other bluegrass festivals, check the pages of *Bluegrass Unlimited,* a magazine published monthly in the Washington, D.C., area. To subscribe, write to Bluegrass Unlimited, P.O. Box 771, Warrenton, VA 20188, or call (800) BLU-GRAS ([800] 258-4727).

GO TO:

PAGE 91 FOR PATSY CLINE

PAGE 151 FOR JOHN HENRY: STEEL-DRIVING MAN

PAGE 189 FOR MAMMOTH CAVE

PAGE 117 FOR ELVIS PRESLEY

PAGE 291 FOR HANK WILLIAMS

HUMPHREY BOGART

Play It Again, Bogie

S URE, YOU could argue the point, but why bother? You would only embarrass yourself. Humphrey Bogart is the number one screen actor of all time. Today, more than four decades after he died of cancer in Hollywood, the name Humphrey Bogart remains familiar to nearly every American. People still line up to see his old black-and-white movies, many of them, like *Casablanca*, considered to be among the best films ever made.

Mention the name Bogart to almost anyone you meet, and they'll say, "Yeah, he was the greatest." People make that sort of comment about celebrities all the time, but in the case of Bogart, they really mean it.

No one would question Bogart's ability to act. He proved himself with solid performances in more than fifty feature films, carrying off without a hitch roles as demanding and diverse as the street gangster Baby Face in *Dead End*, the detective Sam Spade in *The Maltese Falcon*, and the old gin-sodden boatman Charlie Allnutt in *The African Queen*. However, Bogart's grip on the American imagination draws its strength not so much from his undeniable talent as an actor as from the masculine image he projected, that of a deeply romantic man who held a not-very-romantic view of the world. The Bogart persona, played out again and again on film as well as in the actor's own, very public personal life, was that of a no-nonsense individual occasionally fired by passions that were almost but not quite overwhelming. This is exactly how most American men would like to see themselves. Apparently, it was also how Humphrey Bogart saw himself.

Born in 1899, Bogart received a prep-school education, but when the U.S. entered World War I, he abandoned his college plans to join the navy. It was during his years as a sailor that Bogart received his trademark lip scar and accompanying lisp. Some say he was wounded by an exploding shell on his ship, the *Leviathan*. Others say the scar resulted from a confrontation with a court-martialed seaman being hauled off to Portsmouth Naval Prison. Supposedly, the young Bogart had been assigned to guard the prisoner who, taking advantage of a lax moment, slammed the sentinel across the mouth with his cuffed hands and ran. As the story goes, Bogart put a stop to the escape in truest Sam Spade fashion—with a well-aimed .45-caliber slug.

Following his discharge, Bogart landed a job as a stagehand with a New York theatrical production company. This led to a number of bit parts onstage and then to several eminently forgettable roles in the movies. As many eventually successful actors must do, Bogart toughed his way through years of revolving-door rejections and disappointments while honing his professional skills. Meanwhile, he was also toughing his way through a pair of unhappy marriages to actresses, both of them much closer to stardom than he.

Bogart was already thirty-five by the time he got his first big break, the part of a vicious killer named Mantee in the Leslie Howard movie *The Petrified Forest*. Afterward, he brought to life a rogues' gallery of criminals and hard-boiled types in a string of mostly grade-B pictures. Then, with the phenomenal success of John Huston's *High Sierra* and *Maltese Falcon*, Bogart emerged into the limelight as a top Hollywood box-office attraction. Even so, most producers still saw him in the role of a heavy—if not an out-and-out gangster, then a shady character like Spade. But cinematic history was about to be made.

In 1942, with battles raging all around the world, Warner Brothers launched a modestly budgeted movie based on an unproduced play called *Everybody Goes to Rick's*. The story of a star-crossed wartime love affair, its title was changed to *Casablanca*, and a veteran crew assembled to get it down on film. Shot in workaday studio fashion in little more than two months, it might have become just another standard Hollywood release, shown and then forgotten. But a lot of things went right for this picture. One of the things that went very right was the selection of Humphrey Bogart to play the lead role of Rick Blaine (Ronald Reagan had been the original choice). Studio executives had not thought Bogart could handle such a deeply emotional and complex character but, as it turned out, he was perfect for the part. Bogart poured all the pain of his failed marriages and the professional struggles of his youth into the role. When Ingrid Bergman as Ilsa asks her lover what he had been doing ten years earlier, Rick replies, "Looking for a job." Bogart could speak the lines truthfully, since that was precisely what he had been doing. In Rick Blaine, Humphrey Bogart had finally found himself.

And America had found Bogie. There would be no more job-hunting for this actor. During the next fifteen years, he starred in classics such as *To Have and Have Not, The Big Sleep, Key Largo, The*

Treasure of the Sierra Madre, The African Queen (for which he won his one and only Oscar), and a raft of other box-office hits.

At the same time, Bogart starred in another sort of passionate, high-profile role—that of a blissfully married man. While filming *To Have and Have Not,* an adaptation of the Ernest Hemingway novel, Bogie played beside a young actress named Lauren Bacall. Anyone familiar with the picture will remember the scene where Bacall tells Bogart how to whistle. "You just put your lips together and blow," she says. Apparently, Bogie took the hint. He married Bacall less than a year after the movie was released, and they would remain together until he died in 1957. After *To Have and Have Not,* the pair came together again on film in *The Big Sleep, Dark Passage,* and *Key Largo,* but for many Americans, their offscreen image was far more interesting than the characters they portrayed in the movies. Bogie and Bacall were seen as the ultimate couple—fiery, intimate, but not too close to douse the flames.

Likewise, many saw and continue to see Bogart himself as the ultimate man, a real-life version of Rick Blaine. Through Rick, Bogart identified the essence of American masculinity. From the beginning, American men have been obsessed with winning. Bogart's Rick discovered that a man could lose—even his greatest love—and win something even more important: his humanity. It is a dramatic statement that will live forever. And as long as it lives, so will Humphrey Bogart.

The Humphrey Bogart movies mentioned above can be rented at most video stores. Be wary, however, of "colorized" versions. These movies were meant to be shown in black and white, and that is still the best way to see them. Even better, catch them on the big screen. Local college or art theaters often bring back old Bogart films for two very good reasons—they are high-quality classics, and Bogie still has a lot of draw. You may even be lucky enough to come across a Bogart film festival. If so, expect to be spending a lot of time in the dark.

GO TO:
PAGE 83 FOR CASABLANCA
PAGE 112 FOR DRIVE-IN THEATERS
PAGE 211 FOR OLD HOLLYWOOD

BOSTON TEA PARTY

A Cup of Boston Harbor Water, Anyone?

OF ALL the revolutionary events that led this country to separate from Britain more than two centuries ago, none are more compelling or more peculiarly American than the Boston Tea Party. This bizarre, almost comical, act of defiance had a truly amazing impact on history. The battle of Lexington and the signing of the Declaration of Independence may be considered more important to our nation's founding, but it should be remembered that it was the Boston Tea Party that started us down the road to revolution in the first place.

Americans have never cared much for taxes, but they were even less friendly than usual to the British tax schemes of the early 1770s. This was true even though the revenues to be raised were intended not for the general coffers in England but for the defense of the colonies themselves. Saddled with a huge debt left over from the French and Indian War, fought mostly on this continent, the British were struggling to fund a soaring military budget. They thought it only fair that the colonials pay the cost of their own protection, but no one on this side of the Atlantic agreed. Every attempt to place a tax on goods or commodities used by Americans met with howls of protest from the colonists.

Particularly unpopular was a penny-a-pound tax on tea. Colonial opposition to the tax was stiffened by resentment over the tea monopoly Parliament had granted to Britain's own East India Company. On December 13, 1773, a group of Boston rowdies demonstrated their feelings in history's most famous act of tax resistance. Wearing paint on their faces and feathers in their hair, they forced their way onto a British ship and ceremoniously dumped its cargo of tea into the harbor. If the condition of Boston Harbor then was anything like it is today, the tea was certainly ruined.

Of course the Indian disguises fooled no one. Nor were they meant to. Actually, the Indian getups were intended as a sort of joke to take some of the sting and militancy out of what otherwise might seem a wanton act of destruction.

The British, however, were not amused. They retaliated by blockading Boston. Colonial legislatures responded in turn by calling emergency sessions and electing delegates to a Continental Congress. Before long, Paul Revere would be riding out into the night and minutemen would be forming up on Lexington Common. Just think, without all that tea polluting Boston Harbor, the world might never have heard of the "shot heard around the world," let alone George Washington, Yorktown, or Old Glory.

Other people at other times have defied authority and taken their destiny into their own hands. But only Americans would do so in such a spirit of good humor. The Tea Party raiders thought their Indian costumes were hilarious even if the British did not. Today in Boston, you can still share in the fun. Gift shops along the Boston waterfront often sell small, biodegradable bags of tea, which you are welcome to toss into the harbor. Indian costumes are optional.

For information on accommodations and activities in the Boston area, call the Boston Convention and Visitors Center at (617) 536-4100.

GO TO:

Page 26 for Samuel Adams
Page 86 for Celestial Seasonings Teas
Page 274 for U.S. Constitution (Bill of Rights)

BROOKLYN BRIDGE

Say, Buddy, You Wanna Buy Dis Ding

S avvy con artists have been selling the Brooklyn Bridge to gullible out-of-towners for generations. And why not? Anyone would be proud to own a structure that is so beautiful and useful to so many. The people of New York City have been its proud owners now for more than 110 years.

The first person known to have sold the Brooklyn Bridge was an engineer named John Roebling. He sold it to the New York State

Legislature in 1866, quite a trick since at the time, the bridge was nothing more than a dream he carried around in his head. Roebling owned a rope company. The tightly twisted hemp fibers of Roebling rope made it strong enough to lift a ship out of the water. Roebling believed that strands of steel wire could be similarly twisted to produce cables strong enough to hold up a bridge, even one large enough and long enough to span New York City's East River.

By the mid-1800s, Manhattan had become one of the world's greatest trading centers, but a lack of access to the mainland limited the size of the work force that could be employed on the island. Ferries could carry only a limited number of commuters, and it was difficult for people to work in the main part of the city and live elsewhere. In hopes of solving this problem, the legislature backed Roebling's plan to build what he called a "suspension bridge" linking Lower Manhattan to Brooklyn. Roebling's design called for the bridge's massive roadway platform to be suspended from two enormous towers by cables made from bundles of wire.

The project got under way in 1869 with construction of the huge open-water caissons that would provide platforms for the towers. The work had barely begun, however, when tragedy struck and Roebling literally gave his life for the Brooklyn Bridge. While he was out taking measurements for the bridge piers, his foot was crushed by a ferry as it pulled into Brooklyn. Roebling died of gangrene three weeks later.

Not knowing where else to turn, officials appointed Roebling's son to head the project. Only thirty-two years old when he took over as chief architect and engineer, Washington Roebling soon proved that he had inherited his father's vision and technical skills. The caissons were completed using a revolutionary pneumatic technique that the young Roebling had learned of during a recent trip to Europe. Air was forced into the caissons with pumps to pressurize them and keep water out while crews were laying foundations for the towers. With the foundations complete, the work progressed steadily. During the next fourteen years, Roebling would oversee construction of the towers themselves, the creation of thousands of miles of wire and cable, and placement of the two-tiered traffic deck. By 1877 the bridge was able to carry foot traffic, and six years later was officially opened.

During opening ceremonies in 1883, the Brooklyn Bridge was described as the "Eighth Wonder of the World." At the time this hardly seemed an overstatement, as it certainly represented one of history's most massive undertakings. Not only had it taken 85,159 cubic yards of masonry, 3,515 miles of wire, and 17 years to build, but it had cost the lives of 27 people—including that of the original architect. But the $15,211,988.29 price tag paid by the state was a bargain. It would probably cost billions to build the bridge today.

For many years after the bridge was completed, it ranked as the world's longest suspension bridge. No span would exceed its length by any notable margin for more than forty years. The first bridge to do so would stand at the opposite end of Manhattan. With a main span thirty-five hundred feet long, the George Washington Bridge—built by the Roebling Company—more than doubled the length of the old Brooklyn Bridge. But size is certainly not everything.

The Brooklyn Bridge is more than merely functional. It was meant to be beautiful, and people have always thought it so. Songs and even poems have been written in its honor. Featured in key scenes of hundreds of short stories and novels, it has been the subject of dozens of books and documentaries. Fine artists have painted it repeatedly, and it just may be the most frequently photographed man-made object on the planet. In the affections of New Yorkers and of Americans in general, the Brooklyn Bridge remains the greatest bridge in the world.

Here are some facts concerning the Brooklyn Bridge:
Length of the main span: 1,562 feet
Length of the bridge including approaches: 5,989 feet
Width: 85 feet
Height of the tower: 273 feet
Number of supporting cables: 4
Diameter of each cable: 15½ inches
Weight of the cables: 3,272 tons
Number of times bridge sold to tourists: not known

The Brooklyn Bridge is almost certainly New York City's best bargain. You can enjoy its pedestrian walkways for free and take in an unmatched view of the world's boldest city. On the Manhattan side, the pedestrian access is located on Park Row adjacent to the Municipal Building. On the Brooklyn side, pedestrians enter from Cadman Plaza or High Street. The bridge can be seen from many points along the city's Lower East Side.

If you have an online computer and a facility for messaging the Web, then an extraordinary treat is waiting. At any time of the day or night you can get a live picture of the Brooklyn Bridge through the following Internet address: www.romdog.com/bridge/brooklyn.html.

Curiously, the Internet also features an address offering to sell "stock" in the Brooklyn Bridge. They accept checks and take all major credit cards. Access this one, if you dare, at your own risk.

GO TO:

PAGE 206 FOR NEW YORK CITY BAGELS
PAGE 136 FOR GOLDEN GATE BRIDGE
PAGE 159 FOR HOOVER DAM

AMERICAN BUFFALO

Celebrating the American Bisontennial

A CENTURY ago, the American buffalo came about as close to extinction as any species ever gets without vanishing altogether. Once they had thundered across the Great Plains from Mexico far up into Canada in herds stretching for as many as fifty miles long and twenty miles wide. Their numbers are estimated to have exceeded forty million, but by the turn of the twentieth century, only a scattered few hundred remained.

In part, the plains buffalo were a victim of their own success. There were so many of them that the riflemen who wantonly slaughtered them during the late 1860s and 1870s could never have imagined the huge beasts might eventually disappear. Taking full advantage of the buffalo's abundance, greedy meatpacking companies shipped millions of carcasses eastward, often telling their cus-tomers they were buying beef. But it was not just the Winchester and the butcher that doomed the big bovines. The buffalo stood in the way of a lumbering and inevitable westward march of miners, rail-roaders, ranchers, and farmers. In time, they were simply squeezed off the plains by people.

Theodore Roosevelt shot one of the last free-range buffalo in 1883. By that time, blown away by the advance of civilization like puffs of brown smoke in a high wind, they had mostly disappeared from the plains. Vanishing along with them were the Native Ameri-cans who depended on the buffalo for food and hides.

That was little more than a century ago. Thanks to the efforts of conservationists, Theodore Roosevelt among the earliest and fore-most of them, things have changed dramatically. According to the National Bison Association, or NBA (not to be confused with the professional basketball league), there are now more than 150,000 buffalo in public and private herds throughout the U.S. and Canada. And it's great to have them back.

Unrelated to the true buffalo of Africa and Asia, the American buffalo—more accurately referred to as bison—are the distant kin of ordinary beef cattle. For the non-taxonomists among us, this rela-tionship is a bit hard to accept, since a plains buffalo is in no way suggestive of a gentle cow clanking and clambering into a milking barn. Bison are, in fact, the largest land animals on this continent. Bulls may stand more than six feet tall and ten feet long and weigh more than a ton. They are also easily annoyed, so if you should happen to see one, don't get too close.

One tried-and-true way to celebrate the American buffalo is the same way frontiersmen and the roaming tribes of the Great Plains did: by eating them. Buffalo meat is delicious, not in the least gamey, and is much better for you than beef. A buffalo steak has 85 percent less fat and 50 percent more thiamine than an equivalent cut from a beef steer.

Restaurants all over the country have begun serving bison, at least on special occasions. For some it is a staple. Bison entrées can be found on the menus of restaurants from New York to San Diego, Anchorage to Atlanta. A few entrepreneurial hamburger joints are now offering buffalo burgers. Try one, and you'll find that the meat dominates the bun rather than the other way around.

Those of you who might feel squeamish about eating an animal that once stood on the brink of extinction should consider that of the 150,000 buffalo now butting heads and breeding calves, nearly 80 percent are on private ranches. Without the burgeoning interest in healthy bison meat, the American buffalo would be much closer to oblivion than it is today. Besides, if the Sioux and the Cheyenne ate them, then why not the rest of us?

As with beef, the best bison steaks and burgers are likely to be the ones you grill in your own backyard. The problem, of course, is where to get the makings. Buffalo meat can be ordered from a number of specialty houses, most in the West. The Wyoming Buffalo Company offers a variety of bison cuts and products shipped fresh to your door. For a brochure, write to Wyoming Buffalo Meat, 877 Road 22, Powell, WY 82435. To order, call (866) 754-7277. You might also try Thundering Herd Buffalo Products at (800) 525-9730.

The return of the great American buffalo can and should be celebrated in a variety of ways. Bison can be seen in almost any zoo, but this is not really the way to appreciate them. These creatures were not meant for pens and cages. Impressive herds of wild buffalo can be viewed at the Theodore Roosevelt National Park in North Dakota. For more information, write to Park Superintendent, Box 7, Medora, ND 58645, or call (701) 623-4466. Buffalo also range free in Yellowstone National Park and in a number of state parks and wildlife preserves in Montana and the Dakotas.

GO TO:

PAGE 67 FOR BUFFALO-HEAD NICKEL
PAGE 68 FOR BUFFALO, NEW YORK
PAGE 294 FOR GRAY WOLF
PAGE 143 FOR GRIZZLY BEAR

BUFFALO-HEAD NICKEL

Five Cents' Worth of Freedom

ON ONE side was a romping plains buffalo and on the other an Indian brave. You could hardly imagine a pair of images more achingly American than these. Symbolic of the vanished western frontier, they reminded us of the bold nomadic impulses that have always pushed and tugged at the hearts of Americans. They represent the spirit of freedom itself. Taken together, of course, they were worth exactly five cents. Well, not anymore.

First minted in 1913, the famed buffalo-head nickel—made of the actual metal and not some plastic-like alloy—was produced until 1938. For at least two full generations, these shiny coins were treasured by little girls and almost as common in the jeans pockets of boys as lizards or slingshots. With a buffalo-head you could buy a frosty bottle of Coca-Cola, a Baby Ruth bar, or a Batman comic book. If you were lucky or industrious enough to own two, then you had something really worthwhile to rub together. In fact, you were just plain rich.

A buffalo-head nickel or two still might make you rich. Rare, high-quality specimens, especially those with flaws or other unique markings, can fetch thousands from coin collectors. Even garden-variety buffalo-heads in mint condition may go for up to fifty bucks—a thousand times the face value. With this in mind, you may want to break open that old piggy bank you've been keeping around, but if you turn up a buffalo-head, think more than twice before letting go of it. With one of these, you can hold a solid piece of America in the palm of your hand.

Buffalo-heads can, of course, be purchased from coin dealers, but expect to part with quite a few nickels if you want one.

GO TO:

PAGE 64 FOR AMERICAN BUFFALO (BISON)

PAGE 68 FOR BUFFALO, NEW YORK

PAGE 95 FOR COCA-COLA

BUFFALO, NEW YORK

Hot Time in a Cold Town

Buffalo gals,
Won't you come out tonight?
Come out tonight,
Come out tonight.
Buffalo gals,
Won't you come out tonight,
And dance by the light of the moon?

PRACTICALLY EVERYONE knows the words and the tune of this nineteenth-century party song. Adapted from a traditional minstrel ditty called "Lubly Fan," it brings to mind exuberant cowgirls square-dancing with their beaus at a rodeo fete somewhere out in Wyoming or Montana. The fact is, however, the title refers not to the Great Plains of the American buffalo, but to Buffalo, New York.

People enjoy comparing Buffalo to other places—nearly always in an unfavorable way. For instance, they may say, "Sure, our town isn't the greatest burg on the planet, but then, we could be living in Buffalo, New York."

Buffalo shows up frequently at the butt end of this sort of comment, mostly because of its reputation for terrible winter weather. Howling down the 240-mile length of Lake Erie and sweeping up moisture all along the way, winter's arctic winds find Buffalo a convenient dumping ground for prodigious quantities of snow. During December 9–10, 1995, for instance, Buffalo received thirty-nine inches of snow within a twenty-four-hour period, effectively burying the city for the better part of a week. Some winters are so bad and the accumulation of snow so great that vehicles left out in the open are entombed and cannot be retrieved until spring. People find themselves walking home over the roofs of their own automobiles.

Those who know and love the city, however, do not hold Buffalo's bold winter weather against it. In fact, the blizzards are part of the attraction. Winters here engender a cooperative spirit, and Buffalo's citizens live in relative harmony. Partly as a consequence, its neighborhoods are chock-a-block with mom-and-pop groceries and cozy ethnic restaurants. The one-hundred-year-old Broadway Market, with its old-world atmosphere, is a showplace of the city's diversity and cultural richness.

Perhaps more than any other American city, Buffalo is a mecca for lovers. Generations of loving couples have come here by train, bus, and plane on their way to Niagara Falls to be married, to spend their honeymoons, or to enjoy a romantic retreat within sight of the greatest spectacle on earth.

This is also a city of students, their ranks swelled by SUNY Buffalo, Buffalo State College, Canisius College, D'Youville College, and other fine educational institutions. It is a city of music, too, and not just because of the song. The world's first kazoos were made in nearby Eden in 1916. And player piano rolls are still manufactured in Buffalo by O.R.S. music.

Despite the weather, tropical fruits, palms, and even orchids flourish here—in the Botanical Gardens. Built during the 1890s, the gardens' main conservatory is an architectural gem, as is the city's splendid Frank Lloyd Wright house built for Darwin D. Martin in 1904. As if to outdo rival New York City, Buffalo has not one, but two Statues of Liberty standing guard over Main Street. And finally, for the benefit of those who own plenty of cold-weather gear (and who in Buffalo doesn't?), the city even has it own Mardi Gras or winter carnival.

Of course, sports fans are aware that Buffalo is the home of the Bills, who made it to the Super Bowl four consecutive times during the early 1990s. What New York City or Los Angeles team can boast that sort of record?

Sure, one could choose to live wherever, or in Buffalo, New York. The choice is worth more than cursory consideration.

For more information, call the Greater Buffalo-Niagara Visitors Bureau at (716) 852-0511. Or you can contact almost any travel agent. Because of all the tours and travel to Niagara Falls, Buffalo is a frequent and familiar stop.

GO TO:

Page 64 for American Buffalo (Bison)

Page 67 for Buffalo-Head Nickel

Page 299 for Frank Lloyd Wright

Page 208 for Niagara Falls

Page 254 for Statue of Liberty

C

CAPE HATTERAS LIGHTHOUSE

Old Man of the Outer Banks

OUT IN the Atlantic off the coast of North Carolina, the ocean is constantly at war with itself. Here the steamy Gulf Stream swirls up from the Caribbean to meet the cold Labrador Current, which has pushed down a thousand miles or more from the Arctic. These two rivers of seawater, each of them mightier than the Mississippi, slam into each other with a violence that can churn up hurricane-force winds, swallow up whole ships, and reshape entire coastlines.

Long ago, these titanic forces helped build the Outer Banks, that long, narrow string of sandy islands rising unexpectedly from the ocean seventy miles or so from the mainland. The same powerful currents that built the islands also tend to push ships much too close to them, with the result that the North Carolina Outer Banks have become a sort of maritime graveyard. At least twenty-three hundred major vessels have come to grief here along with many thousands more of their hapless passengers and crews. One such victim was the brig *Tyrell*, swept away with all but a single member of its crew in 1759. Another was the Civil War ironclad *Monitor*, which had only recently survived its point-blank cannon-to-cannon face-off with the Confederate warship *Virginia*.

Since 1803, one of the nation's most famous and important man-made structures, known to some nowadays as "the Old Man of the Atlantic," has fought back against the ocean's ship-killing natural

71

forces. Perhaps the world's best-known traffic light, it warns mariners to keep away from the Outer Banks, and its signal is observed and obeyed by ships' captains and navigators every night of the year. Soaring more than 190 feet above the beach, the black-and-white barber-pole-striped tower of the Cape Hatteras Lighthouse is recognized and loved by millions.

No drive along Route 12, the eighty-mile-long Outer Banks Highway, is complete without a stop at Cape Hatteras, where one still can enjoy the pleasure of looking up at the tallest and most impressive light tower in the country. Until recently, however, the old tower seemed about to vanish into history's attic of old post cards and nearly forgotten memories. The ocean's ceaseless sculpting had begun to undercut the tower's foundation, threatening to send it crashing down onto the beach like a giant redwood undone by a lumberman's saw. Fortunately, a $12 million government-funded relocation effort managed to save the structure by moving it nearly a third of a mile inland.

Losing the Cape Hatteras tower would have been a great shame, and not just because it is lovely and historic. Lighthouses in general, especially ones as venerable as this, are profoundly American in that they extend a welcoming hand to people from every part of the world. The Statue of Liberty is a lighthouse, and in a very similar way, every American lighthouse is an emblem of our national spirit.

For more information, contact the Cape Hatteras National Seashore at Route 1, Box 675, Manteo, NC 27945, or call (252) 473-2111. If you would like to learn more about this and other regional lighthouses, write to Outer Banks Lighthouse Society, P.O. Box 1005, Morehead City, NC 28557, or visit www.outer-banks.com/lighthouse-society.

Few structures are as historically and architecturally interesting as lighthouses. With their spectacular oceanfront settings and romantic evening glow, they are lots of fun to visit. To learn more about them, read *The Lighthouse Encyclopedia*, recently published by Globe Pequot Press of Guilford, Connecticut—ask for it at your favorite bookstore, or call (888) 249-7586. For help in locating the most scenic U.S. lighthouses, another good resource is *American Lighthouses*, also published by Globe Pequot.

GO TO:
PAGE 61 FOR BROOKLYN BRIDGE
PAGE 125 FOR EDMUND FITZGERALD
PAGE 177 FOR LAKE SUPERIOR

CARLSBAD CAVERNS

Journey to the Center of the Earth

ABOUT A hundred years ago, a New Mexico cowboy named Jim White noticed a column of black smoke rising from the scrubby desert rangeland where he herded cattle. Thinking he had spotted the beginnings of a dangerous wildfire, White rode at a full gallop to investigate. As he approached the source of the smoke, a magical thing happened. The billowing clouds of smoke became a swirling whirlwind of bats.

Countless thousands of the tiny leather-winged creatures swarmed upward through a yawning hole in the desert rocks. Peering into the hole, the curious cowboy could see only darkness, and a cold, moaning breeze struck him, as if the earth itself were expelling its chilly breath directly into his face.

White told the story of his bat cave experience to ranch hands, saloon keepers, country newspaper editors, and anyone who would listen. Before long, he had generated a groundswell of interest, especially from miners who wanted to exploit the cave's heavy deposits of guano, a nitrate-rich fertilizer made by the accumulation of bat droppings on the cave floor.

White signed on with a local company to help remove the valuable guano, but unlike his fellow miners, he did not always climb to the surface when the workday ended. Piercing the darkness with a crude kerosene lantern, he went exploring. Pushing farther and farther into the depths, he discovered astounding things, sights never before seen by human beings. There were brightly colored rocks, sparkling pools of cold water, hanging limestone formations bigger than any building White had ever seen, and enormous halls easily big enough to hold a town the size of nearby Carlsbad. The stories White told of these wonders eventually attracted the attention of conservationists, and in 1923, President Calvin Coolidge (see page 98) signed a proclamation establishing the national monument now known as Carlsbad Caverns National Park.

Today, you can see the cave much as White saw it, but you won't have to carry a kerosene lantern or earn your way mining guano. Early park visitors were lowered into the Caverns in rusty ore buckets and had to trudge over miles of treacherous trail to reach the most spectacular attractions. Nowadays you can accomplish the same thing by stepping into an elevator. The 750-foot elevator descent is a queasy plunge, not recommended for anyone with vertigo. It's a little easier to take if you try to think of it as a ride to the top of the Empire State Building, only in reverse. And just like the trip to the roof of the Big Apple, this one is darned well worth it. You'll end up in the Big Room, so named because you could fit a couple or three football stadiums in there with plenty of space left over for parking. But the best way to enjoy Carlsbad Caverns is to hike in through the natural entrance, following in the footsteps of White and other early explorers. Several times each day, rangers lead tours down through the cave mouth and along several miles of carefully marked and well-lighted trails.

During some tours, rangers pause in one of the corridors to turn out the lights. Most people have never encountered absolute darkness—there are just too many streetlights, stars, and other light sources up on the earth's surface. But way down in the depths of Carlsbad, it's possible. Many people are so moved by the experience, they refuse to talk about it afterward. The blackness has a tangible, almost liquid quality that seems to lift you off your feet.

For what in human terms could pass for an eternity, these caverns stood immersed in that same utter darkness, their secrets locked away in an opaque silence broken only now and then by the pitter-patter of dripping water. The story of Carlsbad Caverns began more than 250 million years ago in a failing ocean. Along its shallow margins, a reef teemed with tiny coral plants and animals. When these creatures died, their bodies became limestone, and the reef grew to a thickness of hundreds, even thousands of feet. Eventually, the ocean itself died and was replaced by an ocean of land, and sediments covered the reef, burying it beneath thousands of feet of sandstone. When the Rocky Mountains started rising about sixty million years ago, the violence of the uplift fractured the old reef. Water seeped into the cracks, bringing with it acids produced by decaying vegetation on the surface. Drip by drip, the acidic water carved out caverns and chiseled the fantastic sculptures we see today. Dissolved minerals in the seeping water left enormous deposits in the form of stalactites dropping down from the ceiling or stalagmites thrusting up from the floor. The process was excruciatingly slow. It might take a hundred years for a limestone deposit to reach the thickness of a coat of paint, perhaps one-fiftieth of an inch. Some of the Carlsbad formations stand sixty feet high. You do the math.

No one is certain how long the caverns have been open to the outside world, but we can be sure that for almost that long they have been home to a city of bats. The Mexican freetail bats that hang from the ceiling once numbered up to eight million. Insecticides in the environment—the most destructive of them being DDT—have reduced their numbers to about five hundred thousand. The freetail bats are impressive animals. Although they weigh only about half an ounce—about the same as a nickel—they have a wingspan of eleven inches, can fly at speeds of up to sixty miles per hour, and using their built-in sonar navigation to help them locate prey, will eat their weight in insects during a single night. The Carlsbad bat population can knock off five tons of insects in just a few hours. As Batman might say, "Sock! Pow! Take that, you crepuscular Lepidoptera!"

For more information on the caverns, bats, and other park attractions, write to Superintendent, Carlsbad Caverns National Park, 3225 National Parks Highway, Carlsbad, NM 88220, or call (505) 885-8884.

GO TO:

PAGE 45 FOR BATMAN AND ROBIN
PAGE 120 FOR EMPIRE STATE BUILDING
PAGE 189 FOR MAMMOTH CAVE

CARNEGIE DELI

And If You're Hungry After the Show

S URE, YOU can go out to a fancy New York restaurant, wait hours to eat, and spend about a million bucks. If you are really hungry, however, nothing beats an old-fashioned, old-world eatery, and among those, very few, if any, can top the Carnegie Deli.

In the business of feeding the famished since 1937, the Carnegie is located at Fifty-fourth Street and Seventh Avenue at the edge of the theater district. As the name suggests, it is just a block or so from Carnegie Hall. Every night at eleven or twelve o'clock, the concert and theater crowd comes trooping in, with the result that the deli is more crowded then than at the dinner hour. The explanation for this is simple. After hours of standing in line and watching beautiful, slim-bodied youths jump around onstage, people are starved nearly to death. And they all know they won't go away hungry from the Carnegie Deli.

Every table is supplied with plenty of deli-style pickles, but don't eat too many. Sandwiches at the Carnegie are weighed down with upward of a pound of savory, thinly sliced meat. If you really want to set your diet back a notch or two, you can add a plate of onion rings—there are always too many to eat. And are they good? You tell me. A featured item on the Carnegie menu—and this is no joke—is a three-pound turkey, corned beef, and Swiss cheese sandwich. Eat it all, and they'll give you another one on the house.

The Carnegie is also famous for potato pancakes, brisket, chopped chicken livers, and similar delicacies. The matzo ball soup is better than your mother used to make. (Don't tell her, though.)

And dessert is still to come. That should probably be the strawberry cheesecake, but there are plenty of other choices.

Walls are plastered with photographs of celebrities who have eaten and eaten and eaten at the Carnegie. You probably can't think of someone whose picture you won't see there. New York's old-time stand-up comics used to gather at the Carnegie after they had completed their nightclub acts. Sometimes they still do. The charming opening scene of the Woody Allen movie *Broadway Danny Rose* celebrates this tradition. Nowadays the Carnegie serves up a Broadway Danny Rose sandwich. It's a mountainous pastrami and corned beef combo, and is it good? You tell me.

The Carnegie seats its customers at long rows of tables in a highly democratic manner. You may end up sitting next to the mayor, but even if it's a truck driver, you won't feel you are among strangers. Anyone trying to wrestle a three-pound sandwich into submission always has plenty of friends. For information or reservations, call (212) 757-2245. Any New York cabdriver will know the location. Bring cash because they don't take credit cards.

GO TO:
PAGE 77 FOR CARNEGIE HALL
PAGE 109 FOR DAGWOOD SANDWICH
PAGE 206 FOR NEW YORK CITY BAGELS

CARNEGIE HALL
Cultural Delicatessen

IT WAS 1938, and the King of Swing had never seen a crowd quite like this one. When he looked out into the audience, he saw tuxedos, evening dresses, and, of course, lots of glittering jewels. He was concerned about how people here in America's unofficial palace of culture would react to his performance; so worried, in fact, that he had a popular comedian waiting in the wings just in case he got booed off the stage. But when Benny Goodman lifted his clarinet and started to play, his Carnegie Hall audience was magically transformed into a bunch of ordinary American folks. Just like everybody else in the country, they loved him.

Benny Goodman's 1938 Carnegie Hall performance was a turning point in American music and cultural history. It convinced concertgoers that America's popular musicians were not just entertainers, but artists. And it showed the nation's jazz-and-swing-loving masses that those high-culture symphony-and-ballet aficionados were not so rigid after all. Good music was good music, regardless of the style.

Carnegie Hall has been introducing people to fresh musical trends and new ideas for more than one hundred years. Its walls have echoed with applause for symphony orchestras and soloists, authors and crusaders, for John Philip Sousa and Leopold Stokowski, Fats Waller and Woodrow Wilson. Gustav Mahler performed there, and so did the Beatles. Clarence Darrow and Jack London both made passionate appeals from the Carnegie stage.

The concept of Carnegie Hall was born at sea on a transatlantic ocean liner, where a young conductor named Walter Damrosch, who had recently formed the New York Oratorio Society, met the multimillionaire Andrew Carnegie. No doubt over after-dinner port and cigars, Damrosch complained that New York had no first-class concert hall where his society could perform its oratorios (a hybrid composition including orchestra, chorus, and dramatic speech—sort of a highbrow version of rap music). Carnegie said he could fix that, and within months the effort to fund and build what is now known as Carnegie Hall was under way. By 1889 Carnegie had formed the Music Hall Company of New York, sold shares, and acquired eight parcels of land along Manhattan's then still-unpaved Fifty-seventh Street.

William Burnet Tuthill, a music-loving architect who belonged to Damrosch's oratorio society, was chosen to design the hall. He gave it the elegant combination of late Victorian and modernist elements admired by concertgoers to this day. But more important, he used his uncanny sense of acoustics—an art and science still not well understood—to ensure that songs, symphonies, and speeches could be heard with crystal clarity. As a result, the interior of the hall is somewhat like the inside of a piano—enriching rather than deadening the sound of musical instruments and the human voice.

Construction began in 1890 and was completed early in 1891, in time for a May 5 symphony performance with Peter Ilich Tchaikovsky himself conducting. One New York newspaper crowed: "Tonight, the most beautiful Music Hall in the World was consecrated to the loveliest of arts."

The list of performers who have appeared at Carnegie Hall reads like a music history text: Ignace Jan Paderewski, Sergei Rachmaninoff, Vladimir Horowitz, Arthur Rubenstein, Van Cliburn, Fritz Kreisler, Mischa Elman, Pablo Casals, Enrico Caruso, Maria Callas, Placido Domingo, and more than enough other recognizable names to fill several pages. By no means limited to the longhaired world of classical music, the list of notables who have filled the hall's seats to capacity also includes the likes of Louis Armstrong, Dizzie Gillespie, Ella Fitzgerald, Oscar Peterson, Miles Davis, Woody Guthrie, Pete Seeger, Judy Collins, Bob Dylan, Joan Baez, Ethel Merman, Nat "King" Cole, Lena Horne, Frank Sinatra, and the Rolling Stones.

Philosophers, scientists, and political advocates have also taken center stage at the hall. Prominent among them have been Winston Churchill, who spoke on the Boer War; Emmeline Pankhurst, who pressed for woman suffrage; and Booker T. Washington, who shared the stage with Mark Twain.

Perhaps it is not too much to describe Carnegie Hall as the focal point for culture in America. We tend to judge the acceptability of trends, movements, and artists by whether they have been invited to appear at the hall. Luckily for Americans, as well as for the world of arts, the Carnegie Hall stage door has been almost as open to the new, different, and marvelous as the nation itself.

Carnegie Hall celebrates not just art, but the spirit of America. So it was perhaps especially appropriate that Carnegie Hall was chosen for the world premiere of Anton Dvorák's *From the New World* symphony. One of the world's best-known and best-loved musical pieces, it was first heard here on December 16, 1893, when the hall was less than two years old. The symphony and the hall are now centenarians, and even more widely loved than when they were new.

For tickets or brochures, call (212) 247-7800. To subscribe for a season or to order tickets, write to Carnegie Hall Subscription Office, 881 Seventh Avenue, New York, NY 10019.

If you want to contribute money, contact Friends of Carnegie Hall, Carnegie Hall Society, Inc., 881 Seventh Avenue, New York, NY 10019-3210, or call (212) 903-9654. If you like, you can even have a seat named after you—call (212) 903-9809, or write to the same address as above, but address your letter to "Campaign Manager."

If you happen to be in Manhattan and don't have time for a concert, you should stop by Carnegie Hall anyway and visit the Rose Museum. In addition to hundreds of other notable cultural artifacts, the museum has on display the baton of Arturo Toscanini, the famed conductor remembered for many magnificent performances, as well as for audibly humming the tune of symphonic pieces as his orchestra played them. It also features the clarinet of Benny Goodman.

GO TO:

PAGE 76 FOR CARNEGIE DELI
PAGE 100 FOR AARON COPLAND
PAGE 138 FOR BENNY GOODMAN
PAGE 141 FOR MARTHA GRAHAM

GEORGE WASHINGTON CARVER

Wizard of Tuskegee

WITHOUT IT, a jelly sandwich would be unthinkable. Life would be a little less creamy and a lot less tasty. Peanut butter is a food fit for the gods, but eaten—in enormous quantities—by people short and tall. It is even good for you—that is, if you are otherwise careful with your fat intake.

Peanut butter, that wonder of the pantry shelf capable of giving meaning to a humble slice of bread or turning a simple graham cracker into a gourmet meal, was a gift to America from George Washington Carver. Born into slavery about 1860—nobody is sure of the exact date—he proved for all time that people's beginnings need not limit their accomplishments. A talented artist, scientist, chemist, agricultural expert, educator, philosopher, and humanitarian, he invented a world of delectable and delightful uses for peanuts and peanut butter. He gave us hundreds of new things to do with sweet potatoes and other crops and, by promoting the once-ridiculed idea of crop rotation, helped save the agricultural productivity of the entire South. Carver's name belongs on any list of American geniuses, right alongside that of Thomas Edison or Henry Ford, who, incidentally, was one of his friends. Another who was proud to call him friend and who fully understood what he had given the country was President Theodore Roosevelt.

When Carver was only a few weeks old, night raiders kidnapped his mother from the Diamond Grove, Missouri, plantation where he was born. The plantation owners managed to save the boy, raise him, and, following the Civil War, set him free. Young Carver remained at Diamond Grove until age ten and then struck out on his own to seek an education. Eventually, he managed to work his way through high school and Iowa State Agricultural College at Ames. He was fascinated by everything—art, literature, science—but his special interest was agriculture and the chemical properties of plants. With a master's degree in bacterial botany, Carver turned his attention to the problems of the nation's small farmers, many of whom, like himself, were former slaves.

Recognizing Carver's brilliance, Booker T. Washington offered him a job as head of the Tuskegee Institute agriculture program. Arriving at Tuskegee in 1897, Carver began a meticulous analysis of southern soil conditions. He soon concluded that the south's old-plantation economy, based on the production of a single, nutrient-hungry crop—cotton—had thoroughly depleted the soil throughout much of the region. To address this problem and improve yields, Carver developed a crop-rotation system that alternated cotton with nitrate-producing legumes such as peanuts. Finding a market for the peanuts was another problem, but by 1906 he had solved that problem, too. Shazam! Peanut butter! Nowadays, this melt-in-your-mouth spread fuels a national industry with annual sales in the billions. More than half the nation's peanut harvest, amounting to approximately four billion pounds annually, is turned into peanut butter.

Carver went on to invent hundreds of other uses for the peanut and the sweet potato, another successful rotation crop, all of which earned him recognition as the "Wizard of Tuskegee." No doubt, Carver could have earned millions on the products he invented and the processes he developed, but he never tried to cash in on them. "It's not the clothes one wears," he said, "neither the kind of automobile one drives, nor the amount of money one has in the bank. These mean nothing. Service is the only measure of success."

Sadly, it is hard to imagine anyone saying something like that today, but Carver would have stood out from others in any era. He died in 1943 having made the world a richer place for a lot of otherwise very poor farmers. He had also made it a much more wonderful place for hungry children in search of a tasty afternoon snack. His epitaph reads: "He could have added fortune to fame, but caring for neither, he found happiness and honor in being helpful to others."

The edible seed of a vine called *Arachis hypogaea,* peanuts are known in different parts of the country as goobers, goober peas, ground nuts, and monkey nuts. They are known everywhere as good eating—and not just in the form of peanut butter and jelly sandwiches. For instance, what would a ball game be without a bag of hot roasted peanuts? Here is a recipe for a delicious dish known as:

TUSKEGEE SOUP

5 scallions, chopped	½ cup cream
2 tablespoons butter	1 quart oysters, with juice reserved
2 tablespoons flour	Salt and pepper
2 cups chicken stock	Dash of sherry
½ cup peanut butter	

In a skillet sauté the scallions in the butter until tender. Add the flour and make a light mixture. Cook for about 3 minutes. Add the stock and the peanut butter and stir until smooth. Add the cream and the oyster juice and simmer on low heat. Add salt and pepper to taste. Pour in oysters and simmer until edges of oysters begin to curl. Add a splash of sherry to each bowl. Serve immediately.

The George Washington Carver National Monument in Diamond, Missouri, celebrates the life and genius of the inventor. For information on the monument, museum, and surrounding 210-acre park, write to Superintendent, George Washington Carver National Monument, 5646 Carver Road, Diamond, MO 64840, or call (417) 325-4151.

GO TO:

PAGE 21 FOR HANK AARON

PAGE 115 FOR THOMAS EDISON

PAGE 151 FOR JOHN HENRY: STEEL-DRIVING MAN

CASABLANCA

Here's Looking at You, Kid

SOME CONSIDER *Casablanca* to be the best movie ever made, but that may be a stretch. Just think of the competition—*Citizen Kane, Gone with the Wind, Cat on a Hot Tin Roof, The Graduate,* or *One Flew Over the Cuckoo's Nest,* to name only a few. Anyway, does it really matter whether *Casablanca* is *the* best? Certainly it is one of the best. A more interesting question is why, more than sixty years after its release in 1943, does this dusty, old black-and-white picture continue to delight Americans like no other? Ask anyone you know, and they will likely tell you it is their favorite film, even though they may be a lot younger than the movie itself.

Part of the explanation for *Casablanca*'s long-lived popularity must lie in its extraordinary quality. It was a product of the now-defunct Hollywood studio system, a massive creative engine able to focus the right talent on the right projects and get the job done. *Casablanca* is an example of studio moviemaking at its best: The dialogue is crisp, the scenes rock-solid, and the timing flawless. It brought together a stellar cast including Humphrey Bogart, Ingrid Bergman, Claude Rains, Peter Lorre, Dooley Wilson, Paul Henreid, Conrad Veidt, and Sydney Greenstreet, most of them near the peak of their acting careers. And it received a powerful emotional boost from one of the silver screen's greatest songs, the Cole Porter-like

"As Time Goes By." Add up all these pluses, and you have one heck of a motion picture, but like most things mentioned in this book, *Casablanca* is more than the sum of its parts.

There is something inescapably American about this movie. That is true even though every instant of the action takes place far from Broadway or Main Street. With the exception of a brief flashback to Paris, the entire picture is set as the title suggests, in the ethnically tumultuous African port city of Casablanca (of course, the whole bit was filmed on a Hollywood lot).

At the center of the movie is its American protagonist, Rick Blaine (Humphrey Bogart), who has fled not only the U.S.—for dark and mysterious reasons—but Nazi-occupied France as well. To some extent, every American is at heart an expatriate, alienation being a requirement of citizenship. Living in exile, Rick is more alienated than most, but no matter how far he runs, he can never leave America entirely behind. Rick tries to bury his American nature deep inside, along with the heartbreak he suffered in Paris, but he ends up parading both around like a flag. Revealingly, the classy jazz joint/gambling parlor he owns in Casablanca is called Rick's Cafe Americain.

Bogart's performance as Rick is a wonder to behold. So, too, is that of Dooley Wilson as Sam, the black jazz pianist who serves as Rick's only friend and guardian angel. So are all the performances. Peter Lorre is even more lugubrious than usual as Ugarte, the thief who steals the "letters of transit" that provide the focal point for the plot. Claude Rains delivers his delicious quips with perfect timing as Captain Renault, a corrupt police official who trades exit visas for the right to take his pleasure with attractive, young refugees. The 280-pound Sydney Greenstreet weighs in with typical substance as Señor Ferrari, owner of a cantina that competes with Rick's. Paul Henreid is uplifting as the underground leader and freedom fighter Victor Laszlo, and Conrad Veidt is convincingly sinister as the Nazi Major Strasser, who is determined to trap Laszlo and pack him off to a concentration camp. And Ingrid Bergman as Ilsa, Rick's former Paris flame and Laszlo's wife? With her on the set, they could have filmed the movie without lights.

Casablanca is so well loved that memorable lines from the movie have worked their way into public discourse as well as our everyday lives. In editorials, speeches, and ordinary conversation, you frequently hear things like "Round up the usual suspects" . . . "Here's lookin' at you, kid" . . . "I think this is the beginning of a beautiful friendship." All that and more is from *Casablanca*.

One of the movie's best lines and certainly its highest comic moment comes when the Nazis force Captain Renault to close Rick's saloon/casino. Rick demands to know why his place is being shut down, and Renault, while pocketing his own winnings from the roulette tables, replies, "I am shocked, shocked, to learn that gambling is going on in this establishment!" Nowadays, two-faced politicians who feign surprise at some supposed outrage are accused of being "shocked, shocked!" to learn of it.

Here is a selection of *Casablanca* trivia:

- Warner Brothers paid $20,000 for the rights to *Everybody Comes to Rick's* (later renamed *Casablanca*), an unusually high figure for that time.

- Warner Brothers had originally slated Ronald Reagan to play the role of Rick. Bogart was the third choice.

- The script was not completed until shooting was already under way. Unsure of whether the movie should have a happy or a tragic ending, writers gave it several alternative concluding scenes. In some Ilsa ended up with Rick, and in others with her husband, Victor Laszlo.

- In one rewrite, Laszlo is killed in the climactic airport scene, leaving Ilsa free to rejoin Rick.

- Listen closely to the dialogue, and you'll discover that Rick never actually says, "Play it again, Sam."

- Dooley Wilson's role as Sam was originally intended for a female singer.

- (Here is a real zinger!) Dooley Wilson received only $150 for playing the role of Sam and delivering one of the most memorable performances in cinematic history. Incidentally, Wilson was the only member of the cast who had actually been to Casablanca. A few years earlier he had played there with a jazz band called the Red Devils.

An interesting historical note: Two weeks before the movie pre-miered at the Hollywood Theater in New York City in November 1942, the Allies landed in North Africa and quickly captured the city of Casablanca. Because the movie only went into general release several months later in 1943, it was eligible for the 1944 Academy Awards. *Casablanca* took Best Picture, Best Director, and Best Screenplay.

If you have not seen *Casablanca*, see it. If you have, then see it again. It should be available at any video store, but be sure to rent the original black-and-white rather than the colorized version. This movie should be experienced as originally intended—in black and white. If you are lucky, you can catch it on the big screen at a theater hosting a classic movie festival. You also might enjoy the Woody Allen movie *Play It Again, Sam,* which uses the Bogart persona as a takeoff point for the usual, high-camp Allen comedy set up.

GO TO:
PAGE 56 FOR HUMPHREY BOGART
PAGE 211 FOR OLD HOLLYWOOD
PAGE 215 FOR OZ

CELESTIAL SEASONINGS TEAS

Hot Cup of Heavenly Herbs

WHEN AMERICANS want to warm their innards, they're better off sipping tea than giving themselves the jitters by guzzling coffee—at least, that's what the Celestial Seasonings Company has always believed. Founded in 1970, Celestial Seasonings has reawakened, for almost the first time since the Boston Tea Party, our national passion for tea. This has been accomplished not with traditional Chinese varieties but with a colorful array of herbal tea options that are refreshing, delicious, and may even be good for you. Raspberry Zinger, anyone?

In case you imagine herbal tea drinking to be a quirky habit acquired—along with some much quirkier ones—by subculture types in the 1960s, think again. Celestial Seasonings sold more than a billion bags of tea in 1995 and sales topped $70 million. This despite fierce competition from a half dozen or more big-name tea and coffee corporations. True enough, when the Colorado-based company started selling their nontraditional brews back in the 1970s, few Americans had ever heard of herbal tea, let alone tried it. Today, however, thanks largely to Celestial Seasonings' pioneering efforts, herbal tea has found a place on the menu of nearly every restaurant and in the kitchens of a majority of American homes. The Celestial Seasonings box usually sits on the shelf right next to the Lipton and the coffee cans.

Like many big, successful businesses, this one started small. At first its only tea was Mo's 24, a pungent, potpourri-like blend created by Mo Siegel, one of the founders. The ingredients were natural, hand-picked herbs gathered and packaged near Boulder, the exuberant university town where the company still makes its home. Mo's 24 sold steadily, mostly in health food stores and a few groceries in Boulder and the nearby Denver metropolitan area. But Celestial Seasonings might never have been much more than a local business had it not been for an exciting new product called Red Zinger. Loaded with citrusy tang, Red Zinger was caffeine-free, and as with many health food products, there was even some likelihood that it was good for you. In an increasingly health-conscious national food and beverage market, the new red-tinted tea quickly found a niche. Obviously, it had just the zing Americans wanted.

Over the years Celestial Seasonings has introduced dozens of additional varieties, including a Lemon Zinger and a relaxing late-night tea called Sleepytime. Recently the company has even ventured into the more traditional black tea market, and they are gaining on the competition. If the British were still running this country today, you can bet they would try to tax Celestial Seasonings back to the Stone Age—either that or give in and start drinking Red Zinger with their crumpets at afternoon tea.

Celestial Seasonings teas can be found on the coffee and tea shelves of nearly every grocery store. For more information on the company's herbal teas and other products, write to Celestial Seasonings, Inc., 4600 Sleepytime Drive, Boulder, CO 80301, or call (800) 351-8175. The Celestial Seasonings plant in Boulder is open to visitors six days a week.

GO TO:

PAGE 31 FOR ALL-DAY PREACHING AND DINNER ON THE GROUNDS

PAGE 48 FOR BEAN SUPPERS

PAGE 60 FOR BOSTON TEA PARTY

PAGE 95 FOR COCA-COLA

PAGE 110 FOR DR PEPPER

CHICAGO, CHICAGO

Emerald City of the Plains

MUCH AS with the fabled city of Oz, the impression you get of Chicago depends on how you look at the place. Sure, this is the town where Al Capone murdered and bootlegged his way to the top of the syndicate, where thousands once died of cholera, where a river got so polluted that it threatened to poison all of Lake Michigan, where politics can get so crooked that it's often impossible to tell the good guys from the bad. On the other hand, Chicago is also the city that gave us Ernest Hemingway, Benny Goodman, Carl Sandburg, Saul Bellow, Gwendolyn Brooks, Nat "King" Cole, and more Nobel Prize winners than any other place in the country. This is the city that made Frank Lloyd Wright famous—much of his best architecture can still be seen in Chicago and its environs. Roller skates were invented here. So were zippers, Cracker Jack, window envelopes, Hostess Twinkies, and McDonald's hamburgers. Chicago is the home of the Field Museum, the Bulls, the Bears, the Blues, and the tallest building on the planet—the Sears Tower.

Like many frontier towns, Chicago started out as a military post—Fort Dearborn was established here in 1804. The fort saw action during the War of 1812, and much of the local population was massacred by Indians when the army tried to evacuate the garrison. But just as it has repeatedly done over the last two centuries, Chicago bounced right back from the disaster. Strategically located on the far southwestern shore of Lake Michigan, with all the lush and resource-rich Midwest spread out before it, Chicago was a city with a destiny.

Even the great fire of 1871, started supposedly by a cow kicking over a lantern, could not slow down the city. The blaze swept across three square miles of homes and businesses, consuming 17,450 buildings in all. In the downtown area, only a water tower and pumping station remained standing. However, according to John Wright, one of the city's many famous—and pompous— pundits, "nothing of the least consequence" was destroyed. The ninety thousand people left homeless by the blaze may have disagreed, but in one sense Wright was—well, right. The fire served the purpose of initiating a massive urban-renewal project allowing Chicago to completely rebuild itself. The flurry of construction provided a huge amount of work for laborers, and immigrants streamed into the city in ever greater numbers. By the time the Columbian Exposition brought the world to Chicago's doorstep in 1893, it was considered the most modern city in the world, and with 1.25 million residents, it was also one of the largest. The crush of visitors who attended the big fair (twenty-six million admission tickets were sold) gawked at Chicago's steel-frame skyscrapers and elevated trains, the first of their kind in the world.

Of course, there was a high price to pay for all that growth. The Chicago River became an enormous open sewer, pouring pollution into Lake Michigan and threatening the city with disease. To deal with this smelly problem, engineers concocted a plan typical of big-thinking Chicagoans: They reversed the course of the river. Since 1900, Lake Michigan has drained into the Chicago River rather than the opposite, making it the only river on earth that flows backward.

There was also a social price to pay. Whenever commerce runs at a gallop and loads of money are being carted around, you can bet gangsters will come rushing in. This was certainly the case in

Chicago, home of history's most infamous bad guy: Al Capone. A notorious New York mob enforcer, Capone was known to his enemies as Scarface because of a nasty razor slash he had received in a Brooklyn bar brawl. While still in his twenties, Capone moved west to Chicago, where he energetically set about giving the 1920s a little extra roar. By the age of thirty, he had made millions selling beer to thirsty Chicagoans who more or less ignored Prohibition. By the age of thirty-two, he was already out of business and in federal prison. Before he was imprisoned, Capone pulled off one of the bloodiest gangland hits ever when a raiding party of his henchmen, dressed as policemen, machine-gunned seven members of a rival gang in the gory St. Valentine's Day Massacre. The Tommy gun was not Capone's favorite method of dispatching enemies, however. He liked to whack them over the head with a baseball bat.

Speaking of baseball, Chicago has two major-league teams—the true mark of a major-league city. One of these clubs, the Cubs, can lay undisputed claim to the title of "America's Team" for having institutionalized the underdog status. The Cubbies haven't won a World Series since 1908 and haven't appeared in one since the end of World War II. Since all true Americans pull for the underdog, it's hard to claim citizenship without being a Cubs fan. On the other hand, Chicago's American League franchise, the White Sox, haven't fared much better. The Sox haven't won the World Championship since 1906 and are probably best known for the 1919 "Black Sox" Scandal, when they tried to lose the Series and succeeded in doing so.

Chicago is a superlative city not just in terms of commerce, architecture, inventiveness—or World Series futility—but in a host of ways.Birthplace of the Tootsie Roll and Brach's Confections, Chicago is the sweet tooth capital of the world. The Art Institute of Chicago displays the largest collection of impressionist paintings this side of Paris. Chicago can boast not only the world's tallest building, the Sears Tower, which soars 110 stories and 1,450 feet, but also its largest commercial structure, the Merchandise Mart, with ninety acres of floor space. Chicago has the world's largest public library, with more than two million books, and its largest cookie factory, where Nabisco turns out sixteen billion crunchy and delicious

Oreo cookies every year. It offers more than six thousand restaurants, 150 theaters, forty museums, twenty-nine miles of lakefront, fifteen miles of beaches, and seventy-seven distinct neighborhoods. What is more, Chicago is perhaps the most ethnically rich city on earth. Nearly as many Poles live here as in Warsaw. There are also large African-American, Irish—they dye the Chicago River green on St. Patrick's Day, and to heck with the pollution—Italian, Jewish, and Lithuanian populations, and a smattering of folks of nearly every known national origin. Of course they are all Americans now, and that makes it all the more fun. If you want to eat ethnic here, you can try a different restaurant every night for a month and never repeat the same cuisine.

What all this comes down to is that Chicago is one great old city. Some might say it is *the* American city. Of course, some are of the opinion that Mrs. O'Leary's cow had the right idea. But before you make up your mind about the place, give Chicago a closer look. Pay the city a visit and have some fun here. You can have more fun in Chicago than almost any other place on earth. You just have to open your eyes and your heart to it.

For travel information, write to Chicago Office of Tourism, Chicago Cultural Center, 78 East Washington Street, Chicago, IL 60602, or call (877) CHI-CAGO ([877] 244-2246).

GO TO:

PAGE 138 FOR BENNY GOODMAN
PAGE 215 FOR OZ
PAGE 299 FOR FRANK LLOYD WRIGHT

PATSY CLINE

Sweet Dreams for a Country Gal

Perhaps the most compelling voice that ever called to Americans from the country and western stage was that of Patsy Cline. While her sound was rich in country tradition, it appealed to people with a wide variety of musical tastes—in fact, to almost everyone. It still does.

In many ways, Cline's background and career resembled that of Hank Williams. Born Virginia Patterson Hensley in 1932 at the height of the Great Depression, she grew up poor in Winchester, Virginia. Displaying an aptitude for music at a very early age, she had learned to play her family's used piano by the age of eight. Inspired by her idol, child film star Shirley Temple, she also taught herself to sing and dance. But whatever hopes she may have had of a more formal musical education were dashed when her father abandoned the family. At sixteen she was forced to drop out of school and help support her mother and siblings by working at a poultry factory and behind the counter of a downtown drugstore.

Her talents would not go unrecognized, however. Members of a local band called the Melody Playboys heard her sing and hired her as their female vocalist. She and the Playboys traveled constantly, playing in roadhouses and VFW halls throughout the South. The power and emotional depth of her voice attracted attention wherever she went, and soon she was singing for radio and television audiences on country music programs such as the *Ozark Jubilee* and the *Louisiana Hayride* (also an important way station in Hank Williams's rise to stardom).

During the early 1950s, she was briefly married to a man named Gerald Cline. It was as Patsy Cline that she appeared on Arthur Godfrey's *Talent Scouts* in January 1957. Performing for the first time before a nationwide television audience, she sang "Walkin' After Midnight," a number that would become her trademark. Soon, "Walkin' After Midnight" was soaring near the top of both the country and mainstream popular music sales charts. Later Cline hits such as "I Fall to Pieces," "Leavin' On Your Mind," "Crazy," and "Sweet Dreams" would do the same. Few country artists have achieved such a broad appeal, and the fact that she could reach across the barriers of genre and culture so easily was, perhaps, the surest sign of her greatness.

Eventually, Cline and her second husband, Charley Dick, moved to Nashville, where she bore two children and continued to record hits. Like that of Hank Williams, however, her career would tragically be cut short. On March 5, 1963, she sang at a Kansas City benefit concert to raise money for the family of a local radio personality who had been killed in a car crash. Late that evening, the small plane carrying her back home to Nashville ran into a thunderstorm and crashed on a Tennessee mountainside, killing all aboard. At the time she died, Patsy Cline was only thirty years old. Had she lived, she would be well past seventy now, but people still listen to her songs as if they had been sung just yesterday.

At least fifteen Patsy Cline albums are still available from MCA Records Nashville, a division of MCA, Inc., and they can be found in the country section of most record stores. To join the Patsy Cline Fan Club, write to Always Patsy Cline, P.O. Box 2236, Winchester, VA 22604.

GO TO:

Page 53 for Bluegrass
Page 34 for Appalachian Country Stores
Page 117 for Elvis Presley
Page 291 for Hank Williams

TY COBB

Nobody's Peach

He was not what you might call a "peach of a guy," but who says you have to be nice to be great? They called him the "Georgia Peach," likely a nickname made up by some press agent or sports journalist. But Tyrus Raymond Cobb was nobody's peach.

Born in the mountains of North Georgia in 1886, when the major leagues were only about ten years old, Ty Cobb jumped into professional baseball as a teenager. By 1906, he was playing for the Detroit Tigers and pounding balls around American League parks almost at will. For the next twenty-four years, he tormented major-league pitchers, who found it almost impossible to strike him out. In all, he cracked 4,191 hits for a lifetime batting average of .367. More than half a century would pass before Pete Rose finally topped Cobb's mountainous record for total hits. Nobody—absolutely nobody— will ever eclipse Cobb's lifetime batting average—not over a comparable number of seasons. Nowadays, anyone who hits over .300 for a few years running is considered Hall of Fame material. But .367 over twenty-four years? No way. It will never happen again. Anyone who understands the game or knows anything about baseball statistics will inevitably reach the conclusion that Ty Cobb was the greatest player who ever lived.

He was also the meanest. He taunted and insulted his opponents mercilessly, for it was his object not just to beat them but to humiliate them as well. For Cobb, baseball was war. It is said that before each game, Cobb would sit outside the Tiger dugout, sharpening his spikes so that opposing players could see what he had in mind for them. Those razor-sharp spikes were bound to make an impression, since Cobb was notorious for sliding into bases with his feet held high—no doubt in hopes of slashing the baseman's legs. When charging toward home plate, he bowled over catchers as if they were tackling dummies.

"The great American game should be an unrelenting war of nerves," said Cobb, and apparently even his own teammates and the fans were not to be spared the scars of battle. Other Tiger players had little use for Cobb or his tactics, and most kept their distance. This is understandable, considering they were almost as likely to be verbally or physically pummeled by him as opposing players. It is said that Sam Crawford, who played in the outfield with Cobb for years, never exchanged a civil word with him. Once, when a fly ball dropped between them, Cobb and Crawford stood arguing over who should have made the catch while the ball lay there on the ground and the batter circled the bases for an inside-the-park home run. After the game, Cobb got into a fistfight with his own pitcher over the incident.

Fans, too, were likely targets of Cobb's rage and abuse. In one famous episode, Cobb jumped into the stands to confront a man who had been razzing him. Cobb beat the man senseless.

Despite Cobb's all-out style of play and relentless pursuit of victory, he never won baseball's ultimate prize: a World Series title. From 1907 through 1909, he and the Tigers played in three straight

Series but never took the world championship. Still, anyone who ever watched Cobb on the field knew they had seen a man play baseball—for real.

Ty Cobb was the first player elected to the National Baseball Hall of Fame when it was established in 1936. Halls of fame are now so numerous that they are almost a cliché, but the Baseball Hall in Cooperstown is, like Cobb himself, the real thing. Everyone who loves baseball should pay it a visit at least once in their lifetime. For information, write to National Baseball Hall of Fame Museum and Library, Main Street, P.O. Box 590, Cooperstown, NY 13326, or call (607) 547-7200.

GO TO:
PAGE 21 FOR HANK AARON
PAGE 313 FOR YOGI [BERRA]
PAGE 132 FOR GEORGIA PEACHES

COCA-COLA

A Niagara of Coke

IF YOU'VE ever seen the Niagara Falls up close (and if you haven't, see page 208), you know that it is an impressive, almost overwhelming sight. There is a lot of H_2O coming over those falls—more than a million gallons a second. If all that water were distributed evenly to each person around the world, no one would ever go thirsty. Now consider this: If all the Coca-Cola ever sold could be dumped into the Niagara River, there would be enough to keep the Falls going for nearly three days. We're talking 2.4 trillion bottles, 240 billion gallons, or a lake of Coca-Cola ten miles long, eight feet wide, and twelve feet deep.

Atlanta's Dr. John S. Pemberton could not possibly have guessed what he started when he mixed the first Coca-Cola in 1886. He had intended his new drink, flavored with extracts of the coca leaf and cola nut, as a health tonic. It is very easy to imagine him naming it "Dr. Pemberton" and even a little surprising that he didn't; Dr Pepper had been invented only the year before. No doubt the two "doctors" would eventually have gone head-to-head in the marketing wars, and wouldn't that have been a fine howdy-do? Instead, as everyone on the planet knows, Pemberton chose the name Coca-Cola. Interestingly, the first time the name appeared in Pemberton's records, it was written in the flowing script still seen today on the sides of Coca-Cola bottles and cans. The advertising wizards shouldn't get credit for everything. They can take credit for a lot, however.

Coca-Cola has been one of the most heavily advertised products in history. The company's slogans have been pushed so hard that Americans know them almost as well as their own names. Here are just a few of the more familiar ones: "Always Coca-Cola" (introduced in 1996), "Coke Is It!" (1982), "Coke Adds Life" (1976), "It's the Real Thing" (1970), "I'd Like to Buy the World a Coke" (1971), "Be Really Refreshed" (1959), and "The Pause That Refreshes" (1929). Of course, there were also a few clinkers along the way. For instance: "Red, White & You" (1986), "Ice-Cold Sunshine" (1932), and "The Great American Temperance Drink" (1906). Dr. Pemberton and his friends probably had the right idea back in 1886 when they kicked things off with the straightforward "Drink Coca-Cola." The latter is still used in advertisements today, and it still works.

More than seventy million servings of Coca-Cola products are quaffed each day by thirsty folks around the world. No one knows how many times a deep "Ahhhh!" of satisfaction is heard when the drinks are finished. Such sounds were not heard very often back in 1886, Dr. Pemberton's first year of marketing Coca-Cola. He sold only twenty-five bottles of syrup for a grand total of $50. Since he spent more than $70 on supplies and advertising, the good doctor lost money.

Within a few years the business was doing a little better, however, and in 1891, Atlanta pharmacist Asa Chandler bought the company—the whole kit and caboodle—for $2,300. It would take a bit more than that to buy the company today. Ernest Woodruff bought it for $25 million in 1919, and nowadays Coca-Cola is one of those stocks Wall Street pundits refer to when they use the term "blue chip." What is the Coca-Cola Company really worth today? Many billions. Entire nations could be bought or sold for less.

You wouldn't have thought it possible to make so much money from a product that for more than seventy years sold for just five cents. It was during the 1950s—recently enough for many of us to remember—that stores started charging six cents for a 6.5-ounce bottle of Coke. Some vending machines were fitted with a special box where customers were supposed to put a penny. A buffalo-head nickel would still get you your Coke, but if you were honest, you dropped in the extra copper. Those penny boxes didn't stick around for very long to challenge people's integrity, however, since the price of refreshment soon became a dime. Before long, it was a quarter. Today, some vending machine Cokes cost as much as a dollar—a 2,000 percent increase in the original price.

Soft drink bottlers like to point out that their half-gallon containers sold in grocery stores often go for prices that put the cost per serving back where it was almost forty years ago. That is true, but it is also true that people are drinking carbonated beverages in far greater quantities than they once did. Nowadays, soft drinks, especially Coca-Cola, are much more popular than water.

Coca-Cola has made an indelible mark on American culture. The traditional fluted Coca-Cola bottle and hand-script logo are national icons as familiar to many as Old Glory itself. Museums, antique shops, and collectibles galleries around the country celebrate the role Coca-Cola has played in American life during the last century. To visit any one of them is to step back in time to a more relaxed era, when summer afternoons were warmer and Coke was just a nickel.

The World of Coca-Cola in Atlanta is one of the largest and best soft drink museums in the country. Here you can walk through a century of Coca-Cola and American history, from the Gibson Girl posters of the 1890s to the dancing polar bears of the 1990s. Located at 55 Martin Luther King Jr. Drive, beside Underground Atlanta, The World of Coca-Cola charges admission and accepts reservations for group tours. Call (404) 676-5151, or write to the museum at 55 Martin Luther King Jr. Drive, Atlanta, GA 30303. For additional information on the Coca-Cola Company or its products, call (800) 438-2653.

GO TO:

PAGE 86 FOR CELESTIAL SEASONINGS TEAS

PAGE 198 FOR MOXIE

PAGE 208 FOR NIAGARA FALLS

PAGE 110 FOR DR PEPPER

CALVIN COOLIDGE

The President with Moxie

REMARKING ON the characteristically sour expression of President Calvin Coolidge, humorist Dorothy Parker (some hold that it was Tallulah Bankhead) said he looked as if he had been "weaned on a pickle." That may have been closer to the truth than even the razor-witted Parker believed. Coolidge was born in a room at the back of a country store in tiny Plymouth Notch, Vermont. No doubt, there was an ample supply of pickles on hand in the place.

Coolidge was an old-time New England Republican with strong hands and rock ribs, and he made a very old-fashioned sort of president. His philosophy of life and government simply put was this: "Pay your own way and expect others to do the same." There was absolutely no nonsense about the man, and he smiled so seldom that on those rare occasions when he did, it made the newspapers. Humorist Will Rogers swore he could bring a smile to Coolidge's lips and was one of the few who ever accomplished the feat. When introduced to the president, Rogers said "Sorry, I didn't catch the name."

Coolidge's tightfisted stodginess had its roots in the country store his father rented for $40 a year. Surrounded by chilly, windswept hills, it was a small and orderly establishment that provided for the modest shopping needs of the few dozen residents of Plymouth Notch. Its customers were unwilling to pay for frills, and they received none.

Young Calvin grew up sweeping floors, stocking shelves, and offering efficient but unsmiling service to customers. However,

Coolidge had set his sights higher (some would say lower) than a career as a storekeeper. He took a law degree in Massachusetts, entered politics there, and was eventually elected governor of the state. His star rose quickly, and in 1920, he earned a spot as the vice-presidential candidate on the Republican national ticket with Warren G. Harding. Wielding a political broom as effectively as he had a straw whisk at the family store back in Plymouth Notch, Coolidge helped sweep the Democrats out of office in Washington.

Plagued by one scandal after another, Harding proved something of a disappointment to the nation. Most historians would agree he was among the least-competent men ever to sit in the Oval Office. Harding's multiplying troubles ruined his health, and on August 2, 1923, he died in what newspapers described as "a stroke of apoplexy."

The sad news of President Harding's death reached the vice president in the middle of the night at Plymouth Notch, where he was vacationing at his father's house. The older Coolidge had given up his retail business many years before and moved into a house just across the street from his former general store. As frugal as he was conservative, he had no telephone or electricity. A telegraph operator had to drive the long, winding road from the neighboring town of Bridgewater and bang on the front door to deliver word that John Calvin's son was now president of the United States.

Calvin Coolidge climbed out of bed, put on a black suit and tie, and crossed the road to the store, now run by an indomitable woman named Florence Cilley. The store did have a phone, and Coolidge was able to call Washington, D.C., and speak to the attorney general, who gave him the exact wording of the presidential oath of office. A while later, in the sitting room of his father's house, he took the oath. It was administered by John Calvin himself, a justice of the peace, and witnessed by Vermont Congressman Porter Dale, a reporter, and several other men who had raced through the night to Plymouth Notch to be on hand for the ceremony.

It was a sultry summer evening. With the oath taken, President Coolidge suggested they all go across the dirt road to the old store and break the heat with a refreshing bottle of his favorite elixir. Gathered in the front room of the Cilley store, the small party toasted the nation's new leader with six-ounce bottles of Moxie

Nerve Food. At this point, Coolidge made clear his vision of the presidency. He slapped a nickel on the counter to pay for his own bottle of Moxie—and then invited everyone else to do the same.

If you would like to raise a bottle of Moxie to help you "Keep Cool with Coolidge," a good place to do so would be the Florence Cilley Store. Now part of the Plymouth Notch Historic District operated by the state of Vermont, the store is open daily from late May to mid-October. The Moxie, however, will cost you more than a nickel. Besides the store, a stone visitors center, and the house where the swearing-in ceremony took place, Plymouth Notch consists of a dozen or so clapboard buildings, all looking much as they did when Coolidge was born here in 1872. Nearby is a cheese factory that features a Cheddar so sharp, a small bite will leave you with a sour expression, perhaps not unlike the one President Coolidge often wore. The surrounding hills are unspoiled and beautiful, and it is easy to see why Coolidge vacationed here so often. Incidentally, he spent more time on vacation than any other American president. For more information, write Plymouth Notch Historic District, Plymouth Notch, VT 05056, or call (802) 672-3773.

GO TO:
PAGE 282 FOR VERMONT
PAGE 219 FOR DOROTHY PARKER
PAGE 198 FOR MOXIE

AARON COPLAND

Fanfare for an Uncommon Man

WHEN YOU think of composers, the names that usually come to mind are those of long-dead Austrians, Russians, or Italians—people like Mozart, Tchaikovsky, and Rossini. Americans don't write that kind of music. Or do they? To the less sophisticated among us, orchestral music is almost by definition old and foreign. No matter how familiar we are with the classics, they often sound distant. Some-times, when we hear them—for instance, during the interludes between fundraising drives on public radio—they sound far off, as if they were being played by an orchestra on a hill about a mile away, as if they were separated from us not just by distance, but by time. Well, it doesn't have to be that way. Not if you listen to the right composers.

One of the greatest composers who ever lived was an American. What is more, both he and his music were thoroughly modern (he died little more than a decade ago and lived every day of his ninety-year life in the twentieth century). Whether you know it or not, you have already heard and enjoyed most of his best music, as he did a lot of composing for the movies. But none of this keeps him from being one of the greats—right up there with Bach, Beethoven, or Brahms. However, you will find his name listed under the Cs, not the Bs.

Aaron Copland was born in 1900 in Brooklyn, New York. He studied music during the early 1920s in Paris, where he wrote some brash, ultramodernist pieces that sound a little wild even today. But when it came time to do some serious work, he returned home. Here in America, Copland drew on the rich musical resources of his own country and began to incorporate folk tunes and jazz into his orchestral scores. This made pieces like *Billy the Kid* (1938), *Rodeo* (1942), *El Salon Mexico* (1946), and *The Tender Land* (1954) more accessible to Americans. Copland also wrote the sound-track music for many well-known movies: *Of Mice and Men* (1939), *Our Town* (1940), and *The Red Pony* (1948), to name a few. In time, Copland was able to convert a wide audience to the happy habit of listening to orchestral music—we all tune in to the classics occasionally, even if we don't like to admit it.

With the exception of one other piece (see *Appalachian Spring* on page 36) Copland may be best remembered for the magnificent *Fanfare for the Common Man*. As the title suggests, it is a celebration of ordinary people, just as America itself is a celebration of the individual. In 1964, Aaron Copland was awarded the medal of freedom by the U.S. government.

Copland's music can be found on tapes and CDs at any fully stocked record store. If you are unfamiliar with *Fanfare for the Common Man*, be sure to give it a try. Filled with booming kettle-drums and horns, it is the sort of classical piece likely to appeal to even the most die-hard bluegrass fan. If you don't like it, you'd better have your ears checked.

GO TO:

PAGE 36 FOR APPALACHIAN SPRING
PAGE 53 FOR BLUEGRASS
PAGE 141 FOR MARTHA GRAHAM
PAGE 77 FOR CARNEGIE HALL

COYOTE

Call of the Wiles

To NATIVE Americans, he is a god and a devil, one of the "dawn creatures" who helped bring the world into existence. To the Navajo, he is "Little Brother," a friend and an enemy, an incarnation of the fate lying in wait for us just behind the next rock. To children, he is "Wile E. Coyote," the unlucky but tenacious pursuer of the ever-so-speedy Road Runner. To western ranchers, he is an annual financial loss and a constant menace to lambs, calves, and other livestock. To those who love wilderness and wild things, he is a passionate cause. To state and federal officials who run predator control programs, he is, like hurricanes, earthquakes, and erupting volcanoes, one more proof that some forces in nature cannot be held back or legislated into submission. To the rest of us, he is a mysterious, beckoning howl in the dark—put in other words, the call of the wild.

Those who have never seen a Road Runner cartoon may miss the meaning when kids go "Beep Beep," giving these seemingly nonsensical words a heavy, nasal intonation. Chuck Jones and Michael Maltese created the cartoon series for Warner Brothers in 1948, and it has been a favorite of children and adults ever since. Supplied by the multispecies voice of Mel Blanc, the "Beep Beep" line belongs to a propeller-footed bird named Road Runner, who can outrun fast cars, locomotives, jet planes, and coyotes. Forever on Road Runner's trail is the devious Wile E. Coyote.

Although Wile is undeniably the star of the cartoon, he has no lines. He has nothing to say because he is always too busy constructing elaborate, Rube Goldberg-style contrivances aimed at one, and only one, purpose: to kill the Road Runner and make a quick meal of him. Of course Wile never succeeds. His bombs blow up in his face. His missiles miss the Road Runner and turn back in his direction. His cannonballs fly up and straight back down again onto his head. His secret trapdoors—meant for the Road Runner—fly open under him instead. Should he take to the air himself, his helicopter blades are sheared off, his parachute catches fire, and with a sheepish grin he plummets to a canyon floor far below. We hear a crash and see a puff of smoke. For Wile E. Coyote, every day is "one of those days."

The real, living, breathing, and howling coyotes in the wilds are much more successful than their cartoon cousin. In fact, the doglike coyote stands happily among the least threatened creatures in America. Despite being hunted, trapped, poisoned, run to ground by greyhounds, and shot from airplanes in fantastic numbers (the U.S. Fish and Wildlife Service alone killed more than four million in recent decades), coyotes have prospered. Today, they are more numerous than ever. They roam every state east and west of the Mississippi and even the suburbs of major cities. They patrol Los Angeles subdivisions in search of unwary cats and small dogs. When pets disappear in Albuquerque, owners blame coyotes, which often can be seen trotting along streets in the middle of town. The familiar coyote howl has been heard in the suburbs of Boston, Atlanta, and Chicago.

The key to their success is that coyotes are incredibly adaptable. As wolves have been killed off and driven out of the woods throughout most of America, the coyote has moved in and taken over as the top-dog predator. While coyotes are great hunters, working alone, in pairs, or in highly organized, cooperative packs, they will eat almost anything. Depending on the circumstances, their diet may include deer, antelope, jackrabbits, prairie dogs, fish, frogs, lizards, bats, poisonous snakes, mice, small birds, cranes, crickets, berries, grass, potatoes, squash, chickens, turkeys, lambs, goats, calves, and livestock of all kinds. A coyote will not turn up its nose at roadkill, and will drive off the neighborhood raccoons in order to scavenge through the garbage cans (if he doesn't eat the raccoons themselves).

The coyote is a very American animal. Refusing to respect limits and boundaries set by others, he constantly expands his range. In cartoon language, "Beep Beep" means "Sorry, but I really must be on my way." The coyote's nocturnal howl, whether heard in the wilds or in the hills just outside a new suburban development, means something all together different: "I am Coyote, and I am here to stay."

While the haunting howl of coyotes is heard on rare occasions in states east of the Mississippi, you are more likely to encounter it in the West. Any moonlit evening in Wyoming will be punctuated by the animal's calls. For more information on the coyote and its place in the natural environment, contact the U.S. Fish and Wildlife Service at 4401 North Fairfax Drive, Arlington, VA 22203, or call (703) 358-2171. Another source of information—one likely to offer you a slightly different view of the animal—is the Defenders of Wildlife, which can be reached by mail at 1101 Fourteenth Street NW, #1400, Washington, DC 20005, or by telephone at (202) 682-9400. Warner Brothers Wile E. Coyote and Road Runner cartoons can be found at nearly any video store. If you are familiar with the series, there is a self-administered personality quiz you can take. Just ask yourself: Do I or do I not secretly hope to see the coyote throttle that darned bird some day?

GO TO:

PAGE 107 FOR DAFFY DUCK
PAGE 143 FOR GRIZZLY BEAR
PAGE 294 FOR GRAY WOLF
PAGE 184 FOR LOON

CRANBERRIES

Relishing an American Tradition

BECAUSE CRANBERRIES are so closely associated with Thanksgiving, we tend to think of them as uniquely American. But these crimson berries grow wild in Europe as well as North America and have been puckering the mouths of children on both continents for as long as people have gathered the bounty of the land. Only in this country, we make such a fuss over them when holiday meals are served. We all are firmly convinced that no plate of turkey and dressing could ever be complete without an ample serving of cranberry sauce. If on Thanksgiving the cranberry sauce should—horror of horrors—go missing, you can bet someone in the family will be dispatched on a quixotic search for an open market. And good luck to him.

Most American families seem to prefer the jellied—as opposed to whole-berry—type of cranberry sauce. In fact, the jellied variety is so ubiquitous that some young children may be unaware that it is made from real berries; maybe they think that maroon stuff is some kind of Jell-O. But of course it is not.

Our favorite holiday sauce is made possible by a low, trailing vine found in the bogs of New England and the Great Lakes region. The plant takes its name from the odd shape of its blossoms, suggestive of the crook in the neck of a crane. Early Pilgrim farmers may have been the first to make the connection between the tiny vine and the big wading birds so often seen in the same marshy areas. Even today, cranes can be seen stilting through the giant bogs where the scarlet berries are found in such abundance. Incidentally, the berries have been known by other names. Some rural Massachusetts folks call them bounceberries, since they bounce when ripe.

Cranberries are cultivated primarily in Massachusetts and Wisconsin, although a few commercial growers can be found in Washington, Oregon, and parts of Canada. As is the case with blueberries, cultivated cranberries are quite different from their wild cousins. Cultivated cranberries are plump and juicy, while the wild ones are smaller and pack more flavor punch.

Unlike most other fruits and berries, people do not commonly eat handfuls of raw cranberries, either the wild or the cultivated kind— they are just too darned tart. But that same lip-puckering quality makes them a hit in muffins, cakes, and cookies. It makes cranberry juice exceptionally refreshing as a mixer or an afternoon wake-me-up. And it helps explain why cranberry sauce is widely appreciated at Thanksgiving and Christmas: It puts a little life in meals otherwise dominated by the rather bland flavors of turkey and dressing.

The first Thanksgiving dinner was held in coastal Massachusetts, so it is fitting this same area is today the center of the cranberry universe. The world's largest producer and most enthusiastic promoter of things cranberry is a cooperative known as Ocean Spray Cranberries, Inc., and it operates out of Middleboro very near Plymouth, the place with the rock. Visitors are more than welcome at the Ocean Spray Plymouth facility, which offers a boardwalk tour of cranberry bogs and a museum filled with informative displays on cranberry harvesting and processing. The gift shop is loaded with cranberry honey, wine, vinegar, and other such items. For information, write to Ocean Spray Cranberries, Inc., One Ocean Spray Drive, Lakeville-Middleboro, MA 02349, or call (800) 662-3263. Ask about the Massachusetts Cranberry Festival held each Columbus Day Weekend.

Harwich, Massachusetts, on Cape Cod hosts its own Cranberry Harvest Festival each year about the second week of September. Events include nature walks, bean suppers, pancake breakfasts, fireworks, and so on. If you are lucky, you may be able to pick a few wild cranberries. For information, write to Cape Cod Cranberry Harvest, 33 Rocky Way, Harwich, MA 02645, or call (800) 848-8862.

GO TO:

PAGE 48 FOR BEAN SUPPERS
PAGE 52 FOR BLUEBERRIES
PAGE 270 TOLL HOUSE COOKIES

D

DAFFY DUCK

All-American Quack

A HUNTER steps out of the woods and points his double-barreled shotgun at a big black duck. Does he bag his prey? No way. Instead, he watches in amazement as the duck flies into an insane routine, tumbling through the air, crashing back to earth, skidding on his heels, running around in wild circles, doing handsprings and back-flips, splashing across a lake, and crying out all the while, "Hoo, hoo, hoo, hoo, hoo, hoo!" No doubt about it, here was the craziest duck ever, so crazy that the only possible name for him was Daffy.

In 1937, the world got its first look at an entirely new type of cartoon character when Daffy Duck first appeared in the scene described above. Daffy was the creation of Tex Avery and his Warner Brothers Looney Tunes production team. A sportsman, Avery thought it would be fun to see a hunted animal avoid its fate by behaving in a completely unexpected and wacky way.

Before going ahead with a cartoon project, Avery and his associates would act it out as if it were a stage drama, taking on the roles of voraciously hungry crows, conniving housecats, not-so-innocent canaries, befuddled pigs, and even "wascally wabbits." When they tried out the hunter-and-crazy-duck scenario in this way, they were not sure it would work onscreen.

"But it did," said Bob Clampett, who animated the cartoon. "When it hit the theaters, it was like an explosion."

Daffy Duck became a star almost overnight. So did Bugs Bunny, another Avery character, who bounced onto the screen about a year after Daffy. To keep up with Bugs, his more talkative sidekick, Daffy soon learned to say a lot more than just "Hoo, hoo." In fact, he acquired the personality of a frenetic, fast-talking schemer, forever impatient with slow-witted screen companions such as Porky Pig or Elmer Fudd. "You're despicable!" he would spit at them.

Here are a few of Daffy's most famous lines:

"I had to go and open my big beak."

"Devilishly clever."

"All right, enough is enough."

"Look, Mac, just what's going on around here?"

"Well, I wish you would explain it to me sometime, buster."

"I can't help being a greedy slob; it's my hobby."

"I've never been so humiliated in all my life."

"Brother, what a way to run a railroad."

These spitting and spewing lines were actually delivered by Mel Blanc, "the man with a thousand voices." Blanc supplied Daffy's voice, not to mention those of Bugs Bunny, Porky Pig, Elmer Fudd, Sylvester the Cat, Tweetie, and many others. When Blanc died in 1989, silencing an entire pantheon of fantastic cartoon creatures, Porky's most famous line was used for his epitaph: "That's all, folks."

Despite the extraordinary success of Daffy, Bugs, Porky, and Looney Tunes, Tex Avery worked for Warner Brothers only six years, leaving in 1941 to join MGM. He went on to invent Droopy, Chilly Willy, and many lesser-known cartoon figures. Then, when color cartoons began to disappear from movie houses during the late 1950s, Avery entered the television advertising field, where he brought to life the Frito Bandito and a host of other fanciful salesmen. Avery died in 1980, leaving behind an enormous quantity of animation generated during a career spanning more than half a century. Most would agree, however, that Daffy, Bugs, and the other characters he created during his relatively brief stay with Looney Tunes were the heart of his legacy.

People have always wondered how Avery got his offbeat ideas. For instance, what was his inspiration for Daffy? Avery never said, but we can guess. As a young hunter he would often have encountered a large dark bird known as the common loon—seen much more frequently then than today. Not many ducks are black like

Daffy, but when observed from a distance, loons appear to be mostly black. What is more, loons have strange hooting calls not unlike the sounds Daffy made in his first film. It is interesting to note that Warner Brothers cartoons are called *Looney Tunes.* And there is one more piece of fairly convincing evidence: Because of its unusual call, old-timers in New England often refer to the loon as—you guessed it—the daffy duck.

Daffy Duck and other Looney Tunes cartoons and movies can be found in any video store.

GO TO:

PAGE 211 FOR OLD HOLLYWOOD

PAGE 184 FOR LOON

PAGE 219 FOR DOROTHY PARKER

DAGWOOD SANDWICH

How to Build a Tasty Skyscraper

$\mathbb{T}$ HE DAGWOOD sandwich ranks among this nation's most profound culinary innovations. Inspired by the omnivorous appetites of American males, they are made possible by the fact that most American families fill their large refrigerators to overflowing with leftovers. A properly made dagwood puts all those leftovers to use and makes the morning garbage detail less onerous.

As anyone who has ever read the funnies is sure to know, the dagwood sandwich takes its name from Dagwood Bumstead. He is the hero of *Blondie,* the immortal comic strip created by Chic Young in 1930. At night, usually after everyone else in the comfortable suburban Bumstead home is fast asleep, Dagwood descends to the kitchen in his pajamas to architect and inhale a skyscraper sandwich. Usually, he does this after a difficult day of being henpecked by his wife, Blondie, conned by his children, bamboozled by his neighbor Herb, or fired by his boss, Mr. Dithers. To help him forget his troubles, Dagwood piles his sandwiches impossibly high. He always seems to leave a string of linked sausages hanging out the side.

The dagwood sandwiches made in most real-life kitchens are usually not so ambitious, but they are, nonetheless, delicious. The important rule to remember when making a dagwood is that there are no rules, and no recipes either. You just have to make sure that everything you put in the sandwich is edible and untainted. However, it is generally agreed that a true dagwood should be at least eight inches high and contain at least five different meats and ten different vegetables and cheeses. *Bon appétit.*

For a visual serving suggestion, check the Blondie panels in the Sunday color comics section of your local newspaper. When eating dagwoods, be sure to keep an ample supply of antacids on hand.

GO TO:

PAGE 76 FOR CARNEGIE DELI
PAGE 120 FOR EMPIRE STATE BUILDING
PAGE 146 FOR ALL-AMERICAN HAMBURGERS
PAGE 247 FOR CHARLES M. SCHULZ
PAGE 264 FOR TABASCO

DR PEPPER

Doc Morrison's Tonic at 10, 2, and 4

MANY PEOPLE believe Coca-Cola is the oldest of America's brown-and-bubbly carbonated beverages. Not so. By a very narrow margin—a matter of months—Dr Pepper is the world's senior bottled soft drink. A young Texas pharmacist named Charles Alderton served up the first Dr Pepper in 1885, less than a year before Atlanta's John Pemberton—also a pharmacist—brought Coca-Cola into the world.

At the time, Alderton worked at Morrison's Old Corner Drug Store in Waco, where one of his duties was to concoct new soda flavors to tempt customers. One of his formulas quickly became a favorite, especially among parched locals who had just stepped out of the harsh Texas sun. Many years earlier, the store's owner, Wade Morrison, had gotten his start in the pharmacy business by working in a rural Virginia drugstore owned by one Dr. Charles Pepper. Things had gone along well, until the good Dr. Pepper caught the young Morrison romancing his daughter and promptly sent him packing. Either as a joke or to honor Morrison's former mentor—no one is sure which—Alderton suggested they call the new drink Dr Pepper.

Because of its name, Dr Pepper has often been mistaken for over-the-counter remedies and tonics. However, the Dr Pepper Company, the nation's oldest and fourth largest soft drink manufacturer, makes no medicinal claims for their star product. They just say, "It refreshes," and that it does. The famous Dr Pepper slogan "10, 2, and 4" comes from an old company advertisement: "Drink a bite to eat at 10, 2, and 4." Other advertisements have touted Dr Pepper as "Old Doc," the "King of Beverages," and as the nation's "most misunderstood soft drink."

Dr Pepper fans agree it has a distinct taste that sets it apart from Coca-Cola and Pepsi. Another thing that sets Dr Pepper apart from the other two is its sales volume. The good Dr has a way to go to catch up.

To learn more about the Dr Pepper Company and its products, call its consumer affairs department at (800) 696-5891. You may also want to visit the company website at www.drpepper.com. The Dr Pepper Museum (and Free Enterprise Institute) in Waco is certainly worth a visit. All sorts of Dr Pepper posters, ads, bottles, trays, and equipment are on display. For information, write to Dr Pepper Museum, 300 South Fifth Street, Waco, TX 76701, or call (254) 757-1024. More than in most other parts of the country, Dr Pepper is an institution in Texas. The nation's oldest Dr Pepper bottling plant is in Dublin, Texas, and every year the town hosts a wild Lone Star State-style celebration on the anniversary of its founding. For information, call (800) 9-DUBLIN ([800] 938-2546). If you are a Texas-sized fan of Dr Pepper, consider joining the 10-2-4 Club. It publishes a quarterly newsletter and hosts an annual convention and swap meet.

GO TO:

PAGE 86 FOR CELESTIAL SEASONINGS TEAS

PAGE 95 FOR COCA-COLA

PAGE 34 FOR APPALACHIAN COUNTRY STORES

PAGE 218 FOR PAPER-SHELL PECANS

DRIVE-IN THEATERS

Last Triple Feature at the Bijou

IT HAS been said that a drive-in movie theater is "the closest you are likely to get to heaven without making a lot of work for an undertaker." Why are drive-ins so wonderful? That's an easy one. They combine two of America's best and most beloved innovations: movies and automobiles. Movies are the stuff of dreams, and cars can represent the fulfillment of those dreams.

There has probably never been a better way to spend a Saturday evening than at a drive-in. Relaxing in your own car, you are free to really enjoy a movie. Twisted into the seat of one of those multi-screen shopping mall theaters, behind the lady with the big hair and right beside the guy with the tubercular cough, you are only able to endure it.

At the drive-in, you can lounge in your car seat, make as much noise as you like—as long as the windows are up—and eat anything you want. You can chow down on fried chicken, potato salad, and munchies brought from home or on deliciously high-calorie and even higher-fat hot dogs and popcorn bought at the snack bar. You and your companions can talk, too, about the movie or about other things. Unless you get really rowdy—in which case you are likely to be chased out of the theater—you won't disturb anyone outside your own car. Drive-ins make a trip to the movies what it was always meant to be—a social occasion. And you don't have to worry about parking, since that comes with the price of admission, which in turn is nearly always more than reasonable.

Please do not imagine that you can get all or even most of the same advantages by watching a movie at home on video. Seeing a movie on television is like reading the comic book version of a classic novel such as *Gone with the Wind.* You get the plot and the characters, but otherwise, it just ain't the same. Incidentally, the movie *Gone with the Wind*, with its giant-screen cinematography, four-hour length, and intermission, is the perfect drive-in flick.

Drive-in movies did not just happen. Like so many other everyday things we take for granted, they were invented by a genius. The inventor of the drive-in was a New Jersey auto parts salesman named Richard Hollingshead, and he actually held a patent (number 1,909,537) on the concept. To perfect his idea, Hollingshead experimented in his own driveway using a 1928 Kodak projector and a bed sheet for a screen. To simulate the rain showers likely to stop the show on occasion, he pressed into service the family lawn sprinkler. Together with three local investors, Hollingshead opened America's first drive-in theater at Camden, New Jersey, in June 1933. The charge was twenty-five cents a person, or a dollar per carload.

Hollingshead's drive-ins did not catch on quickly. By 1940, the same year *Gone with the Wind* swept the Academy Awards, there were still only about twenty drive-ins in the entire country. By 1948, however, their numbers had swelled to more than eight hundred, and a decade later to a phenomenal peak of more than four thousand theaters nationwide. During the 1950s and 1960s, the drive-in theater was America's entertainment of choice.

About two decades ago, drive-in theaters fell on hard times. Beset by high land prices (they require a couple or three acres of prime real estate), the proliferation of multiscreen cinemas, and, worst of all, the advent of the home video, they fell into decline, and their numbers steadily dwindled. In recent decades they have disappeared at such a rate that the government should list them as an endangered species. Ironically, no more drive-in theaters remain in New Jersey, the state where they were created. Today, the drive-ins in most towns are choked with weeds, their projection buildings vandalized and their screens sagging or fallen. These forlorn and abandoned reminders of joys past suggest ruins left behind by some once-vibrant but now-vanished culture.

Take heart. There are still several hundred drive-in theaters in operation throughout the U.S., Canada, and Australia. Most states, although not New Jersey, still have a few big outdoor screens. There may even be one near you. If it's not too dark yet, you may still have time to catch the show—maybe *Gone with the Wind* or some great old cowboys-and-Indians thing. For a list of still-operating outdoor movie theaters, write to Drive-in Theatre Fanatic Fan Club, Mark Bialek, President, P.O. Box 18063, Baltimore, MD 21220.

GO TO:

PAGE 56 FOR HUMPHREY BOGART

PAGE 83 FOR CASABLANCA

PAGE 95 FOR COCA-COLA

PAGE 107 FOR DAFFY DUCK

PAGE 211 FOR OLD HOLLYWOOD

PAGE 146 FOR ALL-AMERICAN HAMBURGERS

E

THOMAS EDISON

Wizard of Menlo Park

As EVERYONE who was ever a child in this country knows, the Wizard of Oz gave people special glasses so his "Emerald City" would appear green to them. The world Thomas Edison helped create would have looked very different from the one that came before it, no matter what color lenses the observer wore. Whatever else might be said about the man, Edison certainly changed things.

When he was a child, Edison had no interest whatever in seeing things through filtered lenses. What he wanted was answers. Why are clouds white and the sky blue? Why do tree trunks grow straight? Why does lightning seem to dance in the air and break into forks? Why this? Why that? It was as if he never outgrew that stage very young children go through when they ask why all the time. Edison drove his parents and everybody who knew him crazy with his questions. Legend has it that he sat on an egg out in the family chicken coop to see if he could hatch it. (The legend is not clear on the point of whether or not he succeeded!)

What is known for certain is that by the time he had reached manhood, Edison had hatched a plan to spend his life creating new and useful whatchamagadgets and thingamajigs. And so he became history's first professional inventor. It would have been easy to dismiss him as a half-crazed eccentric—maybe a little wacky—had it not been for the fact that Edison realized his ambition. Did he ever! He received his first patent in 1868, and by the time he died in 1931 had registered 1,092 more. No other inventor has even come close.

Among the inventions Edison concocted—and decided the world just couldn't do without—were the printing telegraph, gal-

vanic battery, address machine, magnetic ore separator, AC genera-
tor, electric motor, electric meter (he set up the country's first electric
company, which was later known as the General Electric Company),
phonograph, film for motion pictures, and countless other things
you may or may not find familiar. And yes, of course, he invented
the first practical light bulb. Think you might make use of one of
those today?

Many of Edison's inventions came out of his Menlo Park, New
Jersey, workshops—America's first industrial laboratory—or the lab
he later established in Orange, New Jersey. To help him, he had a staff
of machinists, carpenters, glass blowers, clock makers, and mechanical assistants. Working together, often at all hours of the night, Edison
and his helpers ran a smoothly operating invention factory.

The world's first phonograph was created at the Menlo Park
facility. Its ability to store and retrieve sound—especially the human
voice—so astounded people that they were soon calling Edison the
"Wizard of Menlo Park." New York newspaper editors speculated
endlessly about possible uses for the new device. One editor suggested that a speaking Statue of Liberty—the silent version of the
lady was then under construction—might be one of the truly "awful
possibilities" of the phonograph. Edison himself suggested some
much more practical uses: writing and dictating letters, recording
the human voice to make books for the blind, making clocks that tell
time or children's toys that talk, and, of course, recording music. The
phonograph and other recording devices have long since been put
to all the uses Edison had planned for them.

Late in life, Edison met young Henry Ford and convinced him to
power his automobiles with gasoline engines. The two became fast
friends, and Ford later built a replica of the Menlo Park lab at his
Dearborn Michigan Museum. There, in 1929, Edison reenacted his
invention of the light bulb. By then, the products of his genius had
been brightening American homes and cities for almost fifty years.

To learn more about Edison, you can visit one or more of the
museums dedicated to his life and work. Perhaps the best is the
Henry Ford Museum & Greenfield Village. For information, write to
Henry Ford Museum, 20900 Oakwood Boulevard, P.O. Box 1970,
Dearborn, MI 48124-4088, or call (313) 271-1620.

The well-preserved West Orange, New Jersey, laboratory and nearby Edison home are open to the public. For information, write to Edison National Historic Site, 12 Honeysuckle Road, West Orange, NJ 07052, or call (973) 736-0550.

Also worth visiting are Edison's birthplace in Ohio and his winter home in Fort Myers, Florida. For information on the former write to Thomas Edison Birthplace Museum, 9 Edison Drive, Milan, OH 44846, or call (419) 499-2135; on the latter, write to Edison Winter Home and Museum, 2350 McGregor Boulevard, Fort Myers, FL 33901, or call (239) 334-7419.

If you are an inventor or would like to be one, you may want to contact the U.S. Patent and Trademark Office at P.O. Box 1450, Alexandria, VA 22313-1450, or call (800) 786-9199. You don't yet have an invention ready for the patent office? No sweat. Just keep in mind what Edison once said: "Genius is 1 percent inspiration and 99 percent perspiration."

GO TO:

PAGE 29 FOR ALADDIN LAMPS
PAGE 193 FOR MODEL T FORD
PAGE 285 FOR VICTROLA
PAGE 215 FOR OZ

ELVIS PRESLEY

All the King's Hits

ELVIS PRESLEY the man and Elvis Presley the king of rock 'n' roll are two different phenomena. One was a shy young musician from Memphis, Tennessee, with an extraordinary ability to sing and move an audience. The other was—and remains today, nearly thirty years after his death—a cultural cult hero with a following larger than that of any public figure in modern times.

Born in Mississippi in 1935, Presley moved to Memphis with his family as a teenager. It was there that he began to sing and exercise his natural-born talent for throwing young audiences into a riotous rhythmic celebration. However, he was earning his living as a truck driver rather than as a musician in 1954 when Sam Phillips, a local record producer, spotted him. Phillips had been searching for what he described as "a white man with the Negro sound." In Presley he thought he had his man. The Elvis Presley version of the blues tune "That's All Right, Mama" became a local hit, and then the rockabilly number "Mystery Train" carried the as yet obscure Memphis singer to the top of the country and western charts.

Presley then came to the attention of Colonel Tom Parker, the legendary promoter who had what might be called "a genius for genius." Almost immediately, Parker recognized in Presley the makings of a superstar. What impressed Parker the most was the young performer's ability to spark emotion and spontaneous movement in an audience. His stage act included a sort of dance, a mesmerizing gyration of the hips that caused pundits to call him "Elvis the Pelvis." Young girls responded to Presley with screams of adoration much as their mothers had responded to Frank Sinatra some years earlier.

Parker milked the Presley stage magic for all it was worth, booking him to perform before live audiences whenever and wherever possible. By 1957, with "Heartbreak Hotel," "You Ain't Nothin' But a Hound Dog," and a dozen or so other Presley hits rocking the national charts, Parker landed his client the ultimate booking: an appearance on Ed Sullivan's "Really Big Shoe." Most of the tens of millions who tuned in that night were probably unaware that they were witnessing a moment of history, but those who could sit still long enough to think about it might have been tipped by the audience reaction. As Presley throttled the microphone, the screaming grew so loud that it was practically impossible to hear the words "One for the money, two for the show."

A new and exciting movement was under way in America. Rock 'n' roll in general, and Elvis Presley in particular, had given the post-World War II generation a sense of itself. The word *teenager,* which had once been only a descriptive term, now became a badge of identity. Actor Jimmy Dean and singers such as Chuck Berry and Little

Richard probably played a more important role in this process than Presley. Some would say they were better performers as well. But while Presley's talent may or may not have put him in a class by himself, the way it was packaged and received by the public was certainly unprecedented. "Blue Suede Shoes," "Teddy Bear," "All Shook Up," and similar releases became not just hits, but megahits. Presley sold vinyl platters in numbers that made recording industry accountants dizzy.

Then the unthinkable happened—Elvis Presley was drafted. Some believe the authorities chose to make an example of Presley, the point being that "even the most rebellious of youth must conform." Others think his call from Uncle Sam came in the normal course of events. In any case, it was considered unseemly for Presley not to comply. Beginning in 1958, he spent two years in uniform, serving mostly in Germany.

When Presley got out of the army in 1960, he returned to a very different America than the one that had gobbled up his "Jailhouse Rock" singles only a few years before. There were other big stars on the rock stage now, and there was a whole new feeling pervading the country. Oddly enough, the Elvis Presley phenomenon had gone on without him. His recordings had continued to sell as well or even better than before. He was able to step back into his entertainment career without missing a beat. Still, things were not the same, and Presley himself had changed—the wiggle had gone out of his hips.

It was at this point—about the time when Elvis Presley became just "Elvis"—that his story muddies. Usually, Elvis's story includes his middle-of-the-road 1960s hits such as "It's Now or Never" or "Are You Lonesome Tonight," his movies (he was one of the worst actors who ever lived), his eventual marriage to Priscilla, their divorce, his Graceland mansion, his revolving-door appearances in Las Vegas, the obesity, the drugs, and his death in 1977 in a Las Vegas hotel room. But no matter how the story is told, we lose sight of the young man who once drove a truck in Memphis. That is because long before he died, probably even before he got out of the army, even his closest friends had ceased to know him as anything but "The King."

Is it possible to recover anything of the real Elvis Presley? Of course not. It's no more possible than for any of the countless Elvis imitators to do a convincing Presley number on stage. However, for a refreshing taste of the original, pre-Elvis Presley, see if you can find one of his old vinyl singles from the 1950s—and a record player that can handle 45s—and give a listen. Between the cracks and pops, you may hear something surprisingly good and begin to understand the forces that in time would turn the most famous man in the world into one of its loneliest people.

GO TO:

PAGE 53 FOR BLUEGRASS
PAGE 91 FOR PATSY CLINE
PAGE 138 FOR BENNY GOODMAN
PAGE 291 FOR HANK WILLIAMS

EMPIRE STATE BUILDING

A Climb Fit for King Kong

PEOPLE CALLED it the "Eighth Wonder of the World" when it was completed in 1931. Moviegoers knew it was tops when they watched King Kong clamber up its 102 stories in 1933, carrying a petrified Fay Wray along for the ride. And we know it today: The Empire State Building is still the greatest.

Soaring 1,250 feet over the heart of Manhattan Island, it reigned as the tallest building on the planet for more than twenty years and remains to this day one of the earth's loftiest structures. Built in high art deco style, it is also one of the most beautiful. Its many tiers faintly suggest the steps of a Mayan temple. At night, columns of colorfully illuminated water give it the look of a gigantic, mystical fountain.

Planned during the real-estate boom of the 1920s, it would be the last of the old-style New York skyscrapers to be built. Construction began in January of 1930 and proceeded swiftly, with four new stories of steel framework added each week. More than thirty-four hundred people were employed on the project. Considering that the building itself was envisioned as the very image of modernity, it was incongruous and perhaps a touch poignant that horses and mules were used to muscle blocks of stone and other heavy materials around the construction site. Work continued around the clock seven days a week for more than a year, with one new story completed about every three days.

In all, thirty-seven million cubic feet of steel and masonry, including many thousand tons of Indiana limestone and fine Italian marble, would go into the building. So, too, would seven million man-hours—not to mention horse and mule hours—of labor. The price tag for all this was expected to exceed $50 million, but because the depression had made materials and labor dirt-cheap, the actual cost was less than half that much—$24,718,000. Even when the cost of the land (the site of the old Waldorf Astoria Hotel) was thrown in, bringing the price tag to $41 million, the owners must have thought they were getting a tremendous bargain.

In a flashy ceremony on May 1, 1931, President Herbert Hoover pressed a button in Washington, D.C., turning on the lights of the gleaming new Empire State Building. No doubt, he and other Americans looked on the event as a sign that the country's moribund economy was moving again. Unfortunately, it was not. The developers could find no tenants for their sparkling new tower, and soon journalists were calling it the "Empty State Building." Without the ticket income from sightseers streaming to the observation deck, the owners would have been unable to pay taxes on the building.

Even so, Americans saw the new building as a promise of better things to come. What other building could the Hollywood dream-makers have chosen for King Kong to climb? Produced by Merian C. Cooper and Ernest B. Schoedsack, the monster classic starred Fay Wray, a ravishing brunette who appeared in a blonde wig. The twenty-four-foot-tall ape was, like many other love-struck males, actually a dummy. No one who has ever seen the movie will forget Kong hanging from the radio tower at the top of the Empire State Building and swatting at the biplanes sent to machine-gun him. The biplane pilots were none other than Cooper and Schoedsack, making cameo appearances in their own movie.

In an extraordinarily incident suggestive of the movie, a World War II B-25 bomber slammed into the building in 1945, striking it at the seventy-ninth floor. Little structural damage was done, but fourteen people were killed. This was not the role the building was supposed to play in aviation history. Its designers had something more auspicious in mind. The tower at the top was originally intended as a mooring dock for dirigibles and the eighty-sixth floor as a lounge for passengers. The plan, a little too science fiction-like even for the future-minded 1930s, proved impractical, however. The flaming destruction of the dirigible *Hindenburg* over a New Jersey field in 1937 ended all chance that the Empire State Building would become Manhattan's first and only downtown airport.

Those who go up in the old building nowadays may feel they are taking a ride in an airplane or a dirigible. But for anyone who wants to see New York—really see it—the Empire State Building observation deck is still the right vantage point. You can see almost forever from up there; that is, unless some big ape is standing in front of you obstructing the view.

The Empire State Building remains one of New York City's most popular attractions. For this reason, you may have to stand in a long line to catch an elevator ride to the top, but the experience is well worth the wait. On a clear day, you can see for approximately eighty miles in every direction. To avoid the crush of tourists, consider making your trip to the top in the evening. Not only is it less crowded, but you will be rewarded with a spectacular nighttime view of the city. The observation tower is open from 9:30 a.m. until midnight.

The Empire State Building is located at 350 Fifth Avenue and Thirty-fourth Street, right in the heart of midtown. For information, call (212) 736-3100. For an extraordinary live picture from the seventieth floor of the Empire State Building, log on to the Internet and access the following website: www.realtech.com/webcam/.

Any worthwhile video store will have a copy of the 1933 Fay Wray version of *King Kong*. If you haven't seen it, do so. If you are a true American, you'll be pulling for the ape all the way.

GO TO:

F

FALLINGWATER

The Most Beautiful House on and of the Earth

IN 1935, Edgar J. Kaufmann, a wealthy department store owner, picked up a telephone and called Frank Lloyd Wright, the famous architect. Would Wright design a house suitable for a lovely, wooded Pennsylvania tract Kaufmann owned about sixty miles from Pittsburgh? Wright, who at sixty-seven was past the retirement age for most regular folks, eagerly accepted the commission.

Kaufmann appreciated beauty, both in nature and in buildings. He wanted a lovely home, but one that would take full advantage of the wonderful scenery on his property. What he had in mind was a comfortable country house with an expansive view of a waterfall he and his family had long adored.

Wright explored the property and visited the waterfall, noting its many tiers, ledges, and pools. Then he set to work on a design. This was to be no ordinary house.

When he first learned of what Wright was planning, Kaufmann was befuddled and more than a little disappointed. He had asked for a house with a view of the falls. Wright was giving him a house directly *over* them. How could he enjoy his beloved waterfall if he was living right on top of it? Then it struck him. Frank Lloyd Wright intended the waterfall to be an integral part of the house and the house to be part of the fall. Nature and architecture would be joined.

Some say Fallingwater is the most beautiful house in the world, and who can argue? Rooms open onto graceful cantilevered balconies that extend out over the walls and into the spreading foliage of surrounding trees. The mass of the building clings to rocky ledges, while its living areas seem to float on air over the still-living fall. The interior celebrates the setting, with natural rocks pushing up through the floor and incorporated into the decor. Wright even designed the furnishings. As with most Frank Lloyd Wright homes, this one has a huge stone fireplace in the living room. A special "stairway to nowhere" leads down to the surface of the stream not far from where it cascades over the rocks.

Fallingwater is an American treasure. Said one visitor: "Fallingwater is a great blessing. . . . all the elements are combined so quietly that . . . although the music of the stream is there . . . you listen to Fallingwater the way you listen to the quiet of the country."

The Kaufmanns enjoyed Fallingwater for many years, but their lives were often disrupted by the enormous attention the house attracted from architects, scholars, and the public. As the owner of another house designed by Wright once said: "There are only two things wrong with a Frank Lloyd Wright house. People will hardly let you get it built, and will hardly let you live in it once it is done."

Today, Fallingwater is part of a Pennsylvania state park. It is open to the public, but there is an admission fee, and you must call ahead for reservations. Hours vary throughout the year. For information, write to Fallingwater, P.O. Box R, Mill Rum, PA 15464, or call (724) 329-8501.

GO TO:
PAGE 88 FOR CHICAGO, CHICAGO
PAGE 200 FOR JOHN MUIR
PAGE 208 FOR NIAGARA FALLS
PAGE 299 FOR FRANK LLOYD WRIGHT

EDMUND FITZGERALD

Saga of a Doomed Lake Freighter

IF YOU like radio (and who in America doesn't?) you are certainly familiar with Gordon Lightfoot's immensely popular *Ballad of the*

Edmund Fitzgerald. Sounding a bit like one of the chanteys sailing men used to sing as they hauled on the lines of a schooner, the ballad, as with so many traditional songs of the sea, tells of a ship and crew in trouble. But the next time you hear it, listen carefully to the words. This is not some seaman's yarn about a seventeenth-century man-o'-war sank by a hurricane down on the Spanish Main nor some *Flying Dutchman* fantasy. It is a true story. The *Edmund Fitzgerald* was a real ship, a modern freighter almost two city blocks long. One stormy November evening in 1975, she and her crew of twenty-nine vanished—from the middle of a lake.

Launched in 1958, the 729-foot Great Lakes freighter *Edmund Fitzgerald* was at that time the world's largest freshwater ship. Because of its long, narrow dimensions, some called her the "Big Canoe," but the crew came to affectionately know the freighter as the "*Big Fitz*." And big it was, displacing almost fourteen thousand tons of lake water when empty and able to carry a train-sized, twenty-six-thousand-ton cargo of reddish iron taconite. During the ship's seventeen years of service, it shuttled back and forth hundreds of times between the loading docks of upper Michigan or Minnesota and the Bessemer furnaces of the lower Midwest, delivering enough ore to make steel for millions of trucks and cars. When the *Fitz* left Duluth on November 9, 1975, and headed out onto Lake Superior with yet another load of taconite, it was considered still to be in its prime. The freighter's career, however, was about to be tragically cut short.

Around midday on November 10, a mighty gale swept across the lake and began to batter the *Fitz* with thirty-foot waves and seventy-mile-per-hour winds. The storm howled all afternoon and by early evening had done notable damage to the ship. The wind and waves had snapped deck cables, smashed ventilation covers, and wrenched open critical hatches. What was worse, there were signs the ship had started taking on water, having begun to show a list. But the *Fitz* was in the highly competent hands of Captain Ernest McSorley, who, like his ship, was a veteran of many voyages on the Great Lakes. He had weathered storms like this one in the past and was confident he could shepherd his big freighter through the mountainous waves and into safe water at the south end of the lake.

As a precaution, Captain McSorley put out a call to the masters of nearby vessels, asking them to keep a close watch on the *Fitz*. Only a few miles to the north, the freighter *Anderson* was fighting its way through the same storm. The officers on the *Anderson*'s bridge had their hands full with problems of their own, but knowing that McSorley's ship had been damaged, they kept an eye on the radar screen, where the *Fitz* showed up as a sizable green blip. Eerily, when the waves mounted up high enough to block the radar signal, the blip would flicker and disappear. Then, as the *Fitz* climbed up the side of the next huge wave, it would reappear on the screen.

Shortly before 7:00 p.m., an officer on the *Anderson* radioed the *Fitz*. "How are you making out?" he asked.

"We are holding our own," replied Captain McSorley.

These were the last words heard from anyone aboard the *Edmund Fitzgerald*. A few minutes later, something happened that no one on the *Anderson* that day will ever forget. The *Fitzgerald*'s ghostly radar image faded from the *Anderson* screen, just as it had done so many times throughout the afternoon. But this time it did not return. Seconds passed, then minutes, and still there was no sign of the *Fitzgerald*. Incredibly, a modern ship as long as a sixty-story building is tall had vanished in the blink of an eye.

How did it happen? We may never know. No survivors were ever found, and a concerted search by air and water turned up only a few scattered bits of debris: a wooden stool, a propane bottle, a shattered lifeboat, and little else. Many months would pass before the wreck itself was located. According to a Coast Guard survey of the site completed in the spring of 1976, the *Fitzgerald*'s broken hull lay in two pieces among mounds of rusting taconite some five hundred feet below the surface of Lake Superior. Some believe the *Fitzgerald* was broken in half by a pair of huge waves that struck it simultaneously at the bow and the stern. Others think the ship took on too much water, slid down the side of a wave, and plunged to the bottom, where it was broken apart by the impact.

In 1980, a number of divers from Jacques Cousteau's famous research ship *Calypso* braved the lake's deep, blood-freezing waters to visit the *Fitzgerald* in her grave. Since then, at least two robot submarines have taken photographs of the wreck. But none of these expeditions have shed much light on the cause of the disaster. To this day, the *Fitzgerald* continues to guard its secrets jealously. All we know for certain is that the *Fitz* was sunk by one of Lake Superior's furious late autumn storms—what Great Lakes seamen sometimes call "the Witch of November."

The disaster that claimed the *Edmund Fitzgerald* has become a legend in our own time. Much has been written about it, and the wreck is occasionally mentioned in television documentaries. However, the most appropriate, and certainly most enjoyable, place to learn about the *Fitz* is on the banks of the same large lake that swallowed it. At Grand Marais, in Pictured Rocks National Lakeshore on the Upper Michigan Peninsula, the National Park Service maintains an excellent maritime museum. Here you'll find displays and artifacts from many Great Lakes shipwrecks, including that of the *Fitzgerald*. Even the museum's restrooms are historic. The *Fitzgerald*'s last messages were picked up by a radioman in a communications room once housed in this building. The room has now been subdivided into men's and women's toilets, where signs inform visitors, "You are now seated in almost the same spot where the last message from the *Fitzgerald* was received." During the summer, rangers offer a three-hour lakeshore walking lecture titled "Shipwrecks and Lighthouses." For more information, write to Pictured Rocks National Lakeshore, P.O. Box 40, Munising, MI 49862, or call (906) 387-2607.

A poignant *Fitzgerald* memorial ceremony is held each November at Split Rock Lighthouse in Minnesota. Built high on a cliff overlooking Lake Superior, this is one of the most beautiful lighthouses in the world. While its once-powerful light is no longer used to guide ships, it is relit each November 10 in honor of the *Fitzgerald* and the twenty-nine seamen who died aboard the freighter. Unfortunately, the lighthouse, now part of Minnesota's Split Rock State Park, is not open to the public at that time of year. However, you can visit this historic lighthouse during the day from May 15 through October 15. The panoramic, hundred-mile lake view through the windows of the lantern room gives you an idea of what those who brave the waters of this lake must face. The Split Rock Lighthouse is located just off U.S. Highway 61, about fifty miles from Duluth. For information, call (218) 226-6372.

GO TO:
PAGE 177 FOR LAKE SUPERIOR
PAGE 71 FOR CAPE HATTERAS LIGHTHOUSE

FRISBEES

Identified Flying Objects

LOOKING FOR UFOs? You can see brightly colored disks spinning through the air in almost any city park nearly every Sunday afternoon of the year—or Monday through Saturday, for that matter. But these are Identified Flying Objects (IFOs), and no one has ever yet been hauled up into one on a beam of light to be dissected, examined, and pieced back together by alien surgeons. An unwary observer may be whacked in the head by an errant IFO, but except for this danger, they are wholly unthreatening.

Like so many worthwhile objects nowadays, these are made of plastic. They usually take the shape of a slightly concave disk with a rolled edge, and they come in every color of the rainbow. Their identity is well known: They are Frisbees.

While IFOs carry no passengers, alien or otherwise, their owners often seem not-of-this-world. Shirts, shoes, and haircuts have never been mandatory for Frisbee-throwers. Neither is skill, although many throwers are amazingly adept. With a barely perceptible flick of the wrist, a Frisbee expert can send his plastic airship sailing gracefully over impossible distances, cause it to dip, dance, and boomerang on the wind, or make it hang over one spot as if its anti-gravity engines were running full throttle.

The Frisbee's remarkable flying ability is due to its shape. In much the same way as an airplane wing creates lift, the Frisbee's curvature produces less pressure *above* the disk than *below* as it slashes through the breeze. Literally floating on a continuous column of air, the Frisbee can remain aloft for as long as it retains its forward momentum. If it catches a handy updraft or puff of wind at just the right moment, it may hover magically above the ground, waiting for some person or Labrador retriever to snatch it from the sky. Gyroscopic forces lend the rapidly spinning Frisbee its extraordinary stability.

How did the Frisbee get its name? Back during the 1920s, the Frisbie Pie Company (founded by one William Russell Frisbie) had a factory near the Yale University campus. The tasty Frisbie pies were a favorite among famished Yalies, who, in their typically inventive fashion, also found a use for the sturdy pie tins. During breaks in classes or on Sunday afternoons, they filled the air above New Haven parks and university playing fields with the silvery, disk-shaped missiles. Throwers warned unsuspecting passers-by with calls such as "Look out for the Frisbie!" or just plain "Frisbie!" The name, if not the spelling, stuck.

The inventor of the modern plastic Frisbee was a California carpenter named Walter Morrison, who called his disk the "Lil Abner," perhaps because he sold it at country fairs. As part of his sales pitch, Morrison claimed to guide the Lil Abner along its flight path with a length of invisible string. With the willing suspension of disbelief typical of fairgoers everywhere, customers bought the magical string and received the Lil Abner as a free gift.

In 1957, Morrison sold his "Lil Abner" to the slingshot manufacturer Wham-O, which introduced it to America as the "Pluto Platter." The toy was an immediate hit, especially with barefoot teenagers in parks, who were soon referring to their Pluto Platters as "Frisbees." Within a year, Wham-O gave in and changed the name. That is why you don't need a ball and glove anymore to play catch or a shot of hard liquor to do some flying. All you need is a Frisbee.

You can buy Frisbees or Frisbee-like throwing disks at almost any toy store or five-and-dime. However, it is not always necessary to have your own. On any nice day, there are usually plenty of them zipping through the air at parks, especially those with open expanses of grass. Just kick off your shoes, and you will almost certainly be welcomed to join in the fun.

Nowadays, official Frisbee-brand disks are manufactured by the Mattel Toy Company, makers of the renowned Barbie Doll. For information on new and improved models, call (800) 524-8697.

An interesting recent development in the Frisbee world has been the rise of a sport called *disc golf.* Players negotiate prepared courses in much the way regular golfers do. The object is to maneuver a disk down the course and get it into a basket in a minimum number of throws. Believe it or not, there are now dozens of disc golf courses around the country and even a Professional Disc Golf Association. If you failed to make the cut at the U.S. Open this year, maybe you should store your golf clubs and try your hand at disc golf. You can find out all you need to know about the sport and the upcoming tournament schedule at www.pdga.com.

GO TO:

PAGE 95 FOR COCA-COLA
PAGE 110 FOR DR PEPPER
PAGE 242 FOR REVELL-MONOGRAM MODELS

G

GEORGIA PEACHES

Thomas Jefferson's Juicy Treat

YOU CAN slice them up into a bowl and add milk or cream. You can cut them in half and whop a scoop of ice cream down into the place where the pit used to be. You can bake them in pies and cobblers. You can add a little raspberry sauce to them and enjoy a fancy melba dessert. Best of all, you can let one sit out in the sun to steep for a while before you bite into it, then let the juice drip down your chin and the pleasure drip down into your soul.

Nothing in this world tastes better than a ripe and fuzzy Georgia peach. Of course, it has to be a *Georgia* peach. So what if many of the best Georgia peaches come from California, Texas, or South Carolina nowadays? It's the idea and the taste that count.

The Spanish first brought peaches to the New World hundreds of years ago, and Native Americans liked the juicy things so much that they planted huge groves all over North America. The father of the American peach industry, however, was none other than Thomas Jefferson. He imported the first commercial varieties in 1802 and later vigorously promoted their commercial production. Jefferson managed this agricultural coup—he also gave tomatoes a big push—despite the part-time distraction of being president of the United States.

It is not entirely clear how peaches came to be so closely associated with Georgia. Today, the state ranks seventh in production of the savory fruit, behind California, New Jersey, Pennsylvania, Virginia, and North and South Carolina. But, as we all know, Georgia is *the* Peach State. It says so right there on the state's peach-tinted auto license plates. Back during the 1950s, the plates were emblazoned with a golden peach, but the legislature considered the practice too expensive and discontinued it.

There is a Peach County, a region thick with peach orchards, smack in the middle of the state. It is a beautiful area to visit, especially in March when all its millions of peach trees are in bloom. Middle Georgia's largest city is Macon, which at one time was the home of a minor-league baseball team called the Peaches (now, alas, the Braves). Pete Rose got his start in professional ball with the Peaches back during the early 1960s. Coincidentally, Rose often has been compared to baseball great Ty Cobb, who was known as—you guessed it—the Georgia Peach.

Then there is Atlanta with its Peachtree Street, Peachtree Boulevard, Peachtree Avenues, Ways, Circles, Drives, and more than two hundred other similarly named thoroughfares and alleys. This obsession with naming things "Peachtree this" or "Peachtree that" has resulted in an Atlanta street map being about as useful as a wet finger in the air.

While the fruit itself ranks among the wonders of the world, it is hard to understand why the folks in Atlanta think so highly of peach *trees*. As trees go, they are not very impressive. Illustrations in a state history book once widely distributed to Georgia elementary schools depicted them as about the size of oaks and bearing fruit that looked a lot more like big red grapefruits than peaches. Obviously, the New York City artist who illustrated the book had never been much farther south than Thirty-seventh Street. Actually, peach trees are gnarled and twisted things that never grow much more than ten or twelve feet tall. Instead of wasting energy on growing tall and straight, they throw all their natural exuberance into the production of the most delicious fruit on this, or likely any other, planet.

A note on canned peaches: Forget them. They may be an appropriate additive for some syrupy fruit salad, but keep in mind that they are not real peaches. A real peach must have fuzz; that is, unless it is a nectarine.

Fort Valley, the county seat of Georgia's Peach County, hosts a Peach Festival every year around the middle of June when the fruit is ripening. For information, call the Peach County Chamber of Commerce at (912) 825-3733. The Lane Packing Company in Fort

Valley ships ripe peaches through the mail and offers gift boxes containing a baker's dozen of the area's juiciest. Fort Valley visitors are welcome to tour the Lane Company packinghouses, enjoy a light lunch at the Peachtree Restaurant, and browse the Just Peachy Gift Shop. Write to Lane Packing Company, Highway 96 East and Land Road, Fort Valley, GA 31030, or call (478) 825-3592.

Of course, other states are justifiably proud of their peaches—South Carolina especially. If you want to find out why, you might order a box of South Carolina's Big Smile premium peaches. For information or to order, call (800) 267-3224 (that's 26P-EACH). Just don't tell these folks you're interested in Georgia peaches.

GO TO:

PAGE 52 FOR BLUEBERRIES
PAGE 93 FOR TY COBB
PAGE 218 FOR PAPER-SHELL PECANS
PAGE 289 FOR WHITE MOUNTAIN ICE-CREAM FREEZERS

RUBE GOLDBERG

And His Wacky Machines

HOW DOES a Rube Goldberg stamp-licking machine work? First, a dwarf robot overturns a can of ants onto the gummed side of a sheet of stamps. Then a starving anteater licks them off, moistening the stamps in the process. You may think the Goldberg approach is not much of an improvement on the simpler, old-fashioned method of licking the stamps yourself, but don't scoff. The U.S. Postal Service only recently improved on the original technique by introducing self-adhesive stamps. Goldberg put forward his suggestion almost a century ago.

The anteater-powered stamp-licking machine is only one of the thousands of wacky devices Goldberg proposed during his fifty-five-year career as a cartoonist. Goldberg's ridiculous inventions, usually attributed to a harebrained character named Lucifer Gargonzola Butts, satirized the needless complexities of modern life. Born in 1883, Goldberg received an engineering degree from the University of California in 1904, but never practiced the profession. Instead, he drew cartoons and comic strips, first for the *San Francisco Chronicle* and then for the *New York Evening Mail*. He eventually won a Pulitzer Prize for his political cartoons, but it is for his outrageous, though perfectly logical, machines that he will always be remembered. In fact, his name has been enshrined in the language. *Webster's Dictionary* defines *Rube Goldberg* as "accomplishing by extremely complex, roundabout means what seemingly could be done simply."

Nowadays, high schools and universities offer prizes for students who can devise the best Rube Goldberg machines, and these contests have proved wildly popular. The Rube Goldberg Machine Contest hosted by the Theta Tau engineering fraternity is Purdue University's largest annual media event. Winners are likely to find themselves on the *Today Show* or shaking hands with David Letterman.

However, the sad truth is that we don't need engineering students to invent our Rube Goldberg machines. We have them all around us. Probably you can list a dozen or so in the next couple of minutes, beginning, if you wish, with the IRS Form 1040, your company's method of tracking accumulated vacation time, or your spouse's method of balancing a checkbook. Ain't the twenty-first century wonderful?

To learn more about Rube Goldberg, his life, his art, and his wonderful cartoon machines, write to Rube Goldberg, Inc., 40 Central Park South, Suite 7E, New York, NY 10019-1633, or fax (212) 371-3761. Rube Goldberg is a registered trademark. Also check your local library for *Rube Goldberg vs. the Machine Age*.

GO TO:

PAGE 45 FOR BATMAN AND ROBIN

PAGE 102 FOR COYOTE

PAGE 107 FOR DAFFY DUCK

PAGE 115 FOR THOMAS EDISON

PAGE 247 FOR CHARLES M. SCHULZ

GOLDEN GATE BRIDGE

Door to the West

IF THERE is a universally recognized symbol for the American West, surely it must be the Golden Gate Bridge. This magnificent span, often pictured rising out of the Pacific mists, represents our golden dream of the frontier, which Americans have always seen as a bridge to a better, happier future. Could any structure built by human beings ever match such a lofty image? If not, the Golden Gate Bridge, nevertheless, rises very close to it.

The twin towers of the Golden Gate soar almost 740 feet above the waves. They can be seen from ship decks dozens of miles out in the Pacific. Even before they catch their first glimpse of land, mariners often spot the instantly recognizable outline of the bridge. It beckons to them, welcoming them to America and the West. The bridge calls to people on the landward side as well. Every day, more than one hundred thousand vehicles cross over it, and the people of San Francisco look to it as the symbol of their city and their aspirations.

The Golden Gate Strait is a door opening the San Francisco Bay to the Pacific. It allows the bay and California's central river system to be used as a highway for ships and vessels of every description. Ironically, for generations that same vital two-mile-wide stretch of water hindered construction of a land highway linking San Francisco with the Marin Peninsula and the vast coastal resources to the north.

The notion of building a bridge across the strait dates to the earliest days of the gold rush, but it was not seriously discussed until railroad magnate Charles Crocker put forward the idea in 1872. Even then, more than a generation would pass before any action was taken. In a series of newspaper editorials in 1916, journalist James Wilkins revived interest in the concept and attracted the attention of city engineer Michael O'Shaughnessy and designer Joseph Strauss. Detractors argued that the bridge would cost $100 million, an unthinkable sum at the time, but O'Shaughnessy and Strauss countered with a radical plan they said would cost less than a third of that amount. They would span the strait with a suspension bridge similar in principle to New York's Brooklyn Bridge.

It took more than sixteen years to raise the necessary funds—mostly from locally secured bonds—to get the project moving. At last, in January 1933, construction got under way with Strauss as chief engineer.

Working hundreds of feet above the ocean, construction crews were often exposed to high, unpredictable winds and practically blinded by thick fog. To keep accidents to a minimum, Strauss insisted on rigorous safety precautions. Workers wore goggles and hard hats, the first ever used on a bridge-building project, and they maintained special diets to help fight dizziness. To save the lives of those who inevitably slipped and fell, an enormous safety net was stretched beneath the bridge from end to end. In all, nineteen men would be snatched from death by the net and, once they were rescued, join the exclusive "Half-Way-to-Hell Club." In four years of construction, the project recorded only one fatality. Then, in February 1937, a scaffold collapsed and broke through the net, dumping ten men into the ocean hundreds of feet below. None survived.

The Golden Gate Bridge opened to pedestrian traffic on May 27, 1937, and to vehicles on the following day. Its final cost, excluding the lives lost, was $35 million. In time, it would prove to have been one of America's greatest bargains. Annual toll revenues now exceed $55 million. Total toll revenues since the bridge opened amounted to $776 million as of June 1995.

Here are some other fun facts concerning the Golden Gate Bridge:

> Total bridge length including approaches: 1.7 miles
> Width of the bridge: 90 feet
> Clearance above high water: 220 feet
> Weight of the bridge and approaches: 887,000 tons
> Height of the tower above high water: 746 feet
> Height of the towers above the roadway: 500 feet
> Diameter of the main cables: 36⅜ inches
> Length of the cables: 7,650 feet
> Number of separate wires in each cable: 7,572
> Number of vehicle crossings in 1995: 40,715,000

Average weekday vehicle crossings: 115,870
Total vehicle crossings since the bridge opened: 1,436 billion
Southbound toll: $3.00
Northbound toll: free

Touring San Francisco without driving or, better still, walking across the Golden Gate Bridge is an even worse omission than a visit to Chinatown without having dinner. When you go, stop by the historic Roundhouse gift shop and visitor center on the southeast side of the toll plaza. Nearby are a statue of Joseph Strauss and a cross section of one of the bridge's massive cables.

Probably the best way to see the bridge and the fine view of the city it affords is to walk across. Pedestrians can enter the east sidewalk from 5:00 a.m. until 9:00 p.m. seven days a week. Take your camera and maybe something for a queasy stomach.

You can also see the bridge from water level by taking one of several scenic ferry trips. For Golden Gate Ferries departing from the end of Market Street, call (415) 332-6600. For Red and White Fleet ferries departing from Fisherman's Wharf, call (415) 673-2900.

GO TO:
Page 40 for Art Deco
Page 61 for Brooklyn Bridge
Page 159 for Hoover Dam

BENNY GOODMAN

King of Swing

ONE OF the many remarkable things to note about Benny Goodman is how young he was when he introduced the world to the one-of-a-kind voice of his jazz clarinet. Born in 1909, he was only thirteen years old when he first appeared onstage with the Benny Meroff Orchestra in Chicago. Soon after, he was playing regularly with the

Ben Pollack Orchestra at the Venice ballroom in Los Angeles. By age seventeen, he had recorded his first solo, a number called "He's the Last Word." It was an appropriate title, because Goodman was about to completely rewrite the lexicon of American music by bringing jazz to the radio, dance floor, and even stuffy, old Carnegie Hall.

One of twelve children of a Russian immigrant tailor, Goodman grew up in a shabby Chicago ghetto. His escape—both psychologically and literally—from the poverty he saw all around him was music. He received his first musical training at a local synagogue and then studied under Franz Schoeppe, a Chicago music professor who drilled him incessantly in the classics. But jazz was Goodman's first love, and he learned it by jamming with Dave Tough, Bud Freeman, and other members of a highly talented group of Chicago youths known as the Austin High Gang. Goodman had barely reached his teens when his father died and he was forced to go to work to help support the family. The toolbox of his trade would be his clarinet case.

From the beginning, nearly everyone who heard him recognized that Benny Goodman was bringing a whole new sound to music. His style brought together the polish and discipline of formal musical tradition and the freewheeling exuberance of jazz. It also brought people to their feet.

After several years with the Pollack Orchestra, Goodman joined the Red Nichols Band, then worked as a journeyman studio musician in New York City. In 1934, Goodman decided to form his own band. He had picked an excellent time to do it. After four years of economic depression, Americans were tired of, well, being depressed. What is more, young people were listening for a new sound they could call their own. Benny Goodman would give it to them.

The NBC Radio show *Let's Dance* signed Goodman's band for a series of five-hour concerts broadcast nationwide on Saturday nights. When the radio concerts proved a success, Goodman decided to try his luck by taking his band on the road for a coast-to-coast tour. After only a few weeks, it became painfully obvious that the tour was a flop. Everywhere they went, Goodman's band played in front of empty seats and uncrowded dance floors. The tour had started in New York, and by the time it reached the Rocky Mountains, the financially pressed Goodman was ready to call it quits. One of his musicians took the bandleader aside. "You can't stop now, Benny," he said. "Not until you see what's on the other side of those mountains."

Goodman decided to cross the Rockies, but the band's reception on the far side of the Great Divide was little better than it had been in the East. That is, until they reached Los Angeles. There, on August 21, 1935, in the very last concert of the tour, Goodman's career took a sharp turn and so did music history. When they arrived for the concert, band members could not believe their eyes. People were lined up for blocks to get into the Palomar Ballroom. Most of those who crammed the ballroom that night were teenagers, the 1930s version of bobbysoxers, and when the rubber-faced Gene Krupa drummed Goodman out onto the stage, they went wild. Kids were dancing in the aisles. They were still dancing when Goodman brought the band back to the Paramount Theater in New York, and afterward they danced everywhere Goodman and his musicians went.

Goodman's band touched off an entertainment phenomenon not unlike those later generated by Frank Sinatra, Elvis Presley, and the Beatles. He and his band, which included jazz greats such as Krupa, Harry James, Lionel Hampton, and Ziggy Elman, had invented the jitterbug, or swing, as it is often called. Whether they danced or not, everyone wanted to hear the new music. Swing records sold right off the charts. Astonishingly, Goodman would even be asked to perform in that temple of musical tradition, Carnegie Hall. Goodman's concert at the Carnegie in 1938 is seen by many as one of the major mileposts in American music history.

The so-called "Big Band Era," which Goodman helped launch, lasted until well after the end of World War II. When it finally came to an end about 1950, Goodman returned to his musical roots and became a classical clarinet soloist, playing with many of the world's greatest orchestras. Even so, Goodman still jammed occasionally with his old jazz buddies.

Goodman died in 1986 at the age of seventy-seven. By then, the onetime boy wonder from the Chicago ghettos, the young man who had sent so many teenage feet flying, had long been recognized as an elder statesman of American music.

Look for Benny Goodman tapes and CDs at any record store. Among his best recordings are *The Birth of Swing* (1935 RCA), *After You've Gone* (1937 RCA), *Avalon* (1939 RCA), *Benny Goodman Sextet* (1952 CBS), and *Benny Goodman and Friends* (1984 Decca).

GO TO:

PAGE 77 FOR CARNEGIE HALL
PAGE 88 FOR CHICAGO, CHICAGO
PAGE 100 FOR AARON COPLAND
PAGE 179 FOR LINDY HOP

MARTHA GRAHAM

She Could Have Danced All Century

MARTHA GRAHAM was born in the spring of 1894 and died in the spring of 1991, just a few weeks shy of her ninety-seventh birthday. During most of the years between, she danced—danced as no one has ever danced before or perhaps ever will again.

In a profession from which most retire before the age of twenty-five, Martha Graham proved ageless. Pirouetting through several entire generations of ballet performers, she was still delighting audiences with her grace and agility well into her seventies. Even after she stopped dancing onstage in 1970, she continued to play a vigorous role in the world of dance, choreographing ballets and running her world-famous Martha Graham Dance Company. At the time she died, Graham was hard at work on *The Eye of the Goddess*, a ballet to be performed at the Barcelona Olympic games.

Unlike most of today's dancers, whose parents hurried them off to ballet classes when they were children, Graham did not receive formal training until her mid-teens. She chose the art for herself. When she was sixteen, her father, a Santa Barbara doctor, bought her a dark gray dress, a hat, and a corsage of violets and sent her to the Mason Opera House to see Ruth Saint Denis, the internationally acclaimed ballet star. That night, watching Saint Denis leap and whirl across the stage, Graham decided that she wanted no other life but that of a dancer.

Soon Graham was studying at the Denishawn School of Dance—not coincidentally run by Saint Denis—and firing the emotions of audiences, just as her mentor had fired her own passion for dance. Her passions were not limited to art, however. She soon fell in love with composer Louis Horst and moved with him to New York, where she became world famous as a performer.

Over the years, Graham starred in literally hundreds of ballets and choreographed dozens of others, but it was as a teacher that she was to have her most wide-ranging influence. She began teaching dance at the Eastman School in Rochester, New York, in 1926. In time she would teach the children, grandchildren, and even great-grandchildren of her original students.

Here are a few highlights from the career of Martha Graham:

1927—She founded the Martha Graham School of Contemporary Dance. During the depression that soon followed, money was so tight that her ballets were performed without sets, and she made most of the costumes for her dancers herself.

1936—She was invited to perform at the Munich Olympic Games, but refused because of Nazi persecution of artists and intellectuals. "I would find it impossible to dance in Germany at the present time," she said.

1937—She danced for Franklin and Eleanor Roosevelt in a garden at the White House. She would eventually perform for seven other presidents.

1944—She choreographed and then danced Aaron Copland's ballet *Appalachian Spring.*

1948—She married dancer Erick Hawkins after an eight-year romance, but their relationship soon fell apart. "Never try to hold anything too closely," said Graham.

1973—She created *The Scarlet Letter* and *Lucifer* with Rudolf Nureyev and Margot Fonteyn in the lead roles. Of Nureyev she said, "He is a god of light."

1984—She received the Legion of Honor from the French government.

While she was certainly among the world's most respected artists, Martha Graham often scoffed at those who saw classical ballet and modern dance as high-toned bastions of a wealthy establishment. In 1980, a fundraiser suggested that her most effective fundraising tool was her respectability. "Respectable!" she spit back at him. "Show me any artist who wants to be respectable."

To learn more about America's all-time greatest dance artist, you may want to read *The Life and Work of Martha Graham* by Agnes de Mille (Random House, 1991). No doubt, Graham would have preferred, however, that Americans remember her by going out to see a dance performance. Try one. You won't be sorry.

GO TO:

PAGE 36 FOR APPALACI IIAN SPRING
PAGE 77 FOR CARNEGIE HALL
PAGE 100 FOR AARON COPLAND
PAGE 179 FOR LINDY HOP

GRIZZLY BEAR

Ursa Major, King of Grrrr

IT IS big and mean, the King Kong of the American outdoors. Few animals have growled their way into more legends or loomed more frighteningly in the imaginations of children and adults alike than the grizzly bear. Also known as the brown bear, the grizzly is not as large as his close cousin, the Kodiak, or his more distant relative, the polar bear. He is, nonetheless, a very impressive critter. Full-grown male grizzlies may stand more than eight feet tall and weigh up to eight hundred pounds.

People are fascinated by these hefty, brownish-gray bears. In our minds, as in legend, we see them rearing up and roaring, and to most of us they represent the sheer irresistible force of nature. For the public, the grizzly has a lot of what might be called the "grrrr factor." They are about the closest thing we have nowadays to the tyrannosaurus rex, another American predator with lots of *grrrr.*

Much of the grizzly's fearsome reputation is well deserved. When startled, angered, or hungry, grizzlies have been known to overturn vehicles, knock down the walls of cabins, and demolish entire storage buildings. It should be noted, however, that bears are not generally man-eaters. Unless, of course, somebody happens to get in their way. Don't you be one of them!

The experts point out that bear attacks on humans are extremely rare. You are much more likely to be struck by lightning than to be killed by a bear. When maulings do occur, it is usually in a national park such as Yellowstone, Glacier, or Yosemite, where ordinary people and large, dangerous bears do sometimes encounter one another. Even in parks, bear maulings are so uncommon that rangers calculate the likelihood of these unhappy incidents as a ratio per million visitors. For instance, there is one bear attack for every 2.2 million park visitors nationwide. You are much more likely to be mugged in New York City's Central Park than to be mauled by a bear in Yellowstone.

Back when the country was still a frontier and the human arsenal consisted mostly of spears, arrows, flintlocks, and bowie knives, people must have dreaded the grizzly more than any other creature. A knife offers very little protection from a seven-foot-tall bear. It is impossible to say how many early American trappers, frontiersmen, and Indians ended up as meals for grizzlies—probably more than a few. In the end, however, the grizzlies were the ones who lost out. In 1800, the year Thomas Jefferson was elected president, the region that would eventually become the lower forty-eight states was inhabited by as many as fifty thousand grizzly bears. Today, fewer than one thousand remain. But in Alaska and parts of western Canada, the grizzly is still king. The Canadian grizzly population is estimated at more than twenty thousand, while up to thirty thousand grizzlies live in Alaska, where they take full advantage of the abundant berries and salmon and, on occasion, make life exciting for hikers and fishermen.

Believe it or not, grizzlies are at heart shy creatures who keep mostly to themselves. You are unlikely ever to see one in the wild except perhaps in Alaska or in Yellowstone National Park, where about 250 grizzlies roam. For more information on observing wildlife in Alaska, contact the Alaska Division of Tourism, Department 401, P.O. Box 110801, Juneau, AK 99811-0801, or call (907) 465-2010. For information on Yellowstone, write to Yellowstone National Park, P.O. Box 168, Yellowstone National Park, WY 82190-0168, or call (307) 344-7381.

Like other wild predators, grizzly bears are best enjoyed from a considerable distance. Never, under any circumstances, approach a wild bear or attempt to feed one.

Those interested in conservation may want to join the Yellowstone Grizzly Foundation, a nature group dedicated to preserving grizzlies and their habitat. Write to YGF, 104 Hillside Court, Boulder, CO 80302-9452, or call (303) 939-8126. The YGF offers one-week summer study sessions that provide participants with a unique opportunity to observe grizzlies in the wild.

GO TO:
PAGE 164 FOR IDITAROD
PAGE 184 FOR LOON
PAGE 102 FOR COYOTE
PAGE 294 FOR GRAY WOLF
PAGE 311 FOR YELLOWSTONE PARK

⊞

ALL-AMERICAN
HAMBURGERS

With Pickles, Mustard, Onions—the Works!

AFTER A few weeks in Europe, an American tourist will work up a raging hunger that cannot be satisfied by fish and chips, *jambon* sandwiches, or *schnitzl mit salat*. Visions of fresh buns, slices of tomato, onion, and pickles, and charcoal-grilled beef patties will float through the traveler's mind, robbing the ability to properly appreciate the elegance of the Champs Elysées, the pomp of the changing of the guard at Buckingham Palace, or the cobblestoned quaintness of Old Heidelberg. What is needed, of course, is a good, old-fashioned hamburger. Only trouble is, finding such a delicacy on the other side of the Atlantic can be next to impossible. On occasion, European hotels, restaurants, or hospitable families attempt to please their American guests—and perhaps save them from starvation—by serving up what they believe to be a hamburger, but the result is nearly always a disaster. Europeans don't know how to make hamburgers—and never will—just the way they don't know how to play baseball—and never will.

Ironically, the hamburger takes its name from the German city of Hamburg, where butchers have always pounded the dickens out of their beef with mallets to make it tender. Apparently the Hamburgers even made sandwiches with their abused beef. It was in America, however, that butchers began to grind beef, and the hamburger sandwich took on the catsup, mustard, pickle, and onion flavor and unmatched juicy savoriness that have made it our one true contribution to the world of haute cuisine.

146

It is difficult to imagine America without hamburgers. What on earth would everybody eat? According to government statistics, people in the U.S. eat about five billion fast-food hamburgers each year. Add to that a billion or so more that were pan-fried, broiled in the oven, or charcoal-grilled at home, and you've got a lot of hamburgers—somewhere between fifty and one hundred of them per year per American.

Why do we eat so many hamburgers? Why have we made them what potatoes are to Ireland, rice dishes are to China, curries are to India, and rolled tortillas are to Mexico? They are darned good eating. That's why.

Of course, some burgers are better than other burgers. Some are fat, juicy, and delectable, while others are undernourished and highly suggestive of cardboard and plastic. But the author of this book—who eats perhaps three times the national burger average—is of the opinion that all hamburgers are good. All of them. The Nobel Prize-winning author William Faulkner once said, "I like any drink but Scotch—and I'll drink Scotch." In the same way, some burger aficionados have been known to say, "I like any hamburger but a White Castle, and I'll eat a White Castle." Or a dozen.

The White Castle hamburger is not just a hamburger; it is an all-American institution. This is true despite the fact that the White Castle chain is not a universal phenomenon like, for instance, McDonald's, Burger King, or Wendy's. But those unlucky people who live in areas without a White Castle franchise can often remember the last time they ate a White Castle hamburger and where they ate it. Eating one—or a dozen—of these little steam-grilled burgers is a memorable experience. Schools and charitable organizations in Castle-less places sometimes raise money by having truckloads of frozen White Castles shipped in to be sold in cases to contributors.

All this—and the entire fast-food hamburger business—began in Wichita, Kansas, with a young burger flipper named Walt Anderson. In a converted trolley-car diner with five stools, Anderson started selling his revolutionary burgers with small, flat patties served on light buns fresh out of the oven. A single buffalo-head nickel would buy one. Real-estate investor E. W. "Billy" Ingram ate a plate full of Anderson's burgers and found them so tasty that he suggested the two form a partnership to sell them. With $700 in borrowed capital, they opened several outlets in Wichita. Each tiny restaurant had parapets along the roofline to suggest a castle and a sparkling coat of white paint to suggest cleanliness.

The idea caught on, and over the years more and more White Castles were opened and more and more burgers served. By 1961, White Castle was selling upward of one billion hamburgers every year.

Anyone hungry for a hamburger nowadays can nearly always find one close at hand in one of the ubiquitous franchises spawned by the success of White Castle, which, incidentally, remains much smaller than the big three: McDonald's, Wendy's, and Burger King. There are also dozens of less-well-known hamburger chains and thousands of independent restaurants dedicated to the great American repast. Some sell fat burgers, others sell thin burgers, and a few sell those gimmick burgers with the redundant middle bun. But to a famished American, especially one who has been out of the country for a while, all these burgers will taste the same—delicious.

While it is nearly always possible to buy a great burger, the tastiest hamburgers are the ones you fix at home. For the best results, use only top-quality ground beef. If possible, fire up the old charcoal grill, and don't be afraid to experiment with spices and seasonings.

Here is a suggestion: To about 1¼ pounds of ground beef, add about ½ teaspoon of salt, ¼ tablespoon of black pepper, 1½ tablespoons of dried onion, and a pinch or two of garlic. With this basic mix, you can grill up four or five burgers good enough to make you kick your grandmother out of the kitchen.

Also, by adding a few extra ingredients, you can create the following exotic burgers:

South of the Border Burgers: Add 1 heaping tablespoon of crushed red pepper.

South Seas Burgers: Add ½ teaspoon of dry mustard, ¼ teaspoon of nutmeg.

Tyrannosaur Burgers: Add about ten dashes of Tabasco.

Very Beefy Burgers: Sprinkle granulated bouillon on top of the patties.

Dilly Burgers: Add ½ tablespoon of crushed dill seed.

Dagwood Burgers: When the grilling is done, pile on the fixings.

Hollywood Burgers: Serve with bean sprouts and sliced radishes.

Want a great, old-fashioned griddle burger just like they used to serve at those wondrous roadside honky-tonk places in the 1940s? The world's best, or close to it, can be found at Winstead's in Kansas City, Missouri. You can have it with fries and a malt so thick you'll have to eat it with a spoon. And yes, they do have onion rings. If you like, you can enjoy all this good eating while leafing through a copy of the *Kansas City Star.* That's the newspaper Ernest Hemingway started with as a cub reporter (although in his day, they didn't have Winstead's). If you happen to be in KC, be sure to make a Winstead's stop; there are four locations. Call (816) 753-2244.

GO TO:

PAGE 95 FOR COCA-COLA
PAGE 109 FOR DAGWOOD SANDWICH
PAGE 110 FOR DR PEPPER
PAGE 162 FOR IDAHO POTATOES
PAGE 264 FOR TABASCO

HARLEY-DAVIDSON

The Bike with Lots of Vroom

DESPITE THE "tough guy" or "tough girl" mystique sometimes associated with them, Harley-Davidson motorcycles are about as American as the Washington Monument or the Statue of Liberty. After all, freedom is what "Harleys" are all about, and it's been that way since they were first made almost a century ago.

Back at the turn of the twentieth century, bicycles were all the rage. There were some riders, however, who thought pedaling them was too much hard work, especially when going uphill. What is more, for people who wanted a thrill or who had wanderlust in their blood, they were just too darn slow. A pair of young Milwaukee factory mechanics named William Harley and Arthur Davidson decided that a motor was needed to give the bike a little extra zip and to take the work out of riding. Beginning in 1901, they experimented with a single-stroke, three-horsepower engine and a hefty, steel bicycle frame. Soon they had assembled their first motorcycle. Gleaming with pinstriped black enamel, it would have been recognizable even today as a Harley.

In 1903, Harley and Davidson founded the business that still proudly bears their names, but it did not get off to a roaring start. During its first full year of operation, the Harley-Davidson Motor Company produced and sold exactly three motorcycles. As a hedge against failure of the enterprise, the young partners kept their factory jobs for several more years. By 1906, they had sold a grand total of only fifty machines, but during the following year, they filled orders for more than three times that many. In 1908, 450 new Harleys rolled out the door. In 1909, one thousand more hit the streets, and by 1913, annual production and sales had soared to nearly thirteen thousand motorcycles. Americans had discovered something they liked.

So had the U.S. military. Harleys first saw combat duty in the Mexican border skirmish with Pancho Villa in 1916, and nearly twenty thousand were purchased for use in World War I. An army of more than ninety thousand Harleys would later churn up the dust on five continents during World War II.

The Harley-Davidson was so useful to the military because of the same qualities that eventually made it a favorite of peacetime road warriors: It was rugged, reliable, versatile, and, best of all, fast. With the introduction of the dual-cylinder engine in 1909, the Harley had evolved into a very powerful machine, able to outrun all but a few four-wheeled vehicles. It was also the two-cylinder engine that gave the Harley the deep-throated, masculine roar for which it is still known and loved.

Today, Harley-Davidsons are outsold by a phalanx of high-powered, high-performance Japanese motorcycles. Nonetheless, the Harley remains the "ride" of choice for motorcycle aficionados.

Harley riders are considered by many to be a breed apart, and that is how they think of themselves. But while the commonly held image of the Harley rider is that of a loner, often of the rough-and-tough variety, he or she usually has plenty of good company.

Harley-Davidson motorcycle clubs (usually called Harley Owners Groups or HOGs) can be found in every state, and on almost any weekend their members can be seen rumbling up and down the highways. There are HOGs for businessmen, HOGs for retirees, and yes, HOGs especially for women.

The club initials HOG have led some Harley owners to call themselves *hogs* or, more often, *hawgs.* Sometimes they call their Harleys hawgs as well. For instance, a Harley with an especially muscular engine is likely to draw comments such as, "That hawg has a lot of grunt."

To find out about the HOGs and other motorcycling organizations in your area, check with your local Harley-Davidson dealership, or call (800) 258-2464 ([800] CLUB-HOG). You can obtain a wealth of fun Harley facts along with a list of nearby dealerships by calling the Harley-Davidson Information Center at (800) 443-2153 or by visiting the official website (www.harley-davidson.com). For additional information on the company and its latest production models, write to Harley-Davidson Motor Company, 3700 West Juneau Avenue, P.O. Box 653, Milwaukee, WI 53208, or call (414) 343-4056.

GO TO:
PAGE 53 FOR BLUEGRASS
PAGE 193 FOR MODEL T FORD
PAGE 202 FOR ALL-AMERICAN MULE
PAGE 254 FOR STATUE OF LIBERTY

JOHN HENRY

Legendary Steel-Driving Man

YES, HE was a real man. John Henry was a black laborer who worked for the C&O Railroad during the early 1870s. In 1873, the company decided to straighten out a serpentine stretch of track along the Greenbrier River by cutting Big Bend Tunnel through a

West Virginia mountain just outside the little town of Talcott. At first, the work was done in the backbreaking old-fashioned way: with hammers, pick axes, steel rods, and muscle. Then a steam drill was brought in to speed up the process.

Their livelihoods threatened by automation, the manual laborers of the tunnel crew pitted a human champion against the mindless, tireless machine in a race meant to show that men could do the work just as well as a steam drill. Their man was John Henry.

According to the ballad "John Henry," here is what happened:

> John Henry said to the captain,
> A man ain't nothin' but a man.
> But before I let that steam drill beat me down,
> I'll die with this hammer in my hand, Lord,
> I'll die with this hammer in my hand.

John Henry lifted his hammer, and the race began. After hours of pounding away at the stone, smoke was rising from both man and machine. When it was over, John Henry had won the race. But his valiant efforts had burst his mighty heart. As the ballad puts it:

> He laid down his hammer and he died, Lord, Lord.
> He laid down his hammer and he died.

The John Henry ballad is one of America's best-known and best-loved folk songs. It celebrates the construction of America's railroad system, the hard work of laborers who built this country, and the struggle of working people to defend their humanity in the age of the machine.

There are hundreds of versions of "John Henry." Here are a few of the best, along with the recordings on which you can find them: Cephas, Bowling Green John and Wiggins, Harmonica Phil, on *Dog Days of August* (Flying Fish, 1984); Leadbelly, *Leadbelly's Last Sessions* (Folkways/Smithsonian); Johnny Cash, *Blood Sweat and Tears* (Columbia CS 8730); Woody Guthrie, *Worried Man Blues* (Collec-tables); Muddy Waters and Memphis Slim, *Blues Masters Volume 1* (Capital Blues Collection); Doc Watson, *Songs for Little Pickers* (Sugar

Hill). Uncle Dave Macon's classic banjo version may be the best, but it is very hard to find. You may come across it on a collection of Uncle Dave's music (he was one of the earliest Grand Ole Opry performers). If so, grab it!

The railroad tunnel where John Henry is said to have raced a steam drill was abandoned many years ago. The nearby town of Talcott still exists, although, like many tiny Appalachian communities once dependent on coal and the railroads, it is hanging on by the slenderest of threads. A drive along State Highway 12, which runs through the town, will give you a feeling for the sort of rugged country that produced the John Henry ballad and legend. In fact, so would a drive along almost any stretch of West Virginia road.

During the summer, rides are available on scenic trains that run through country much like that along the Greenbrier River where John Henry drove his steel. For information, contact the Potomac Eagle at P.O. Box 657, Romney, WV 26757, or call (304) 424-0736.

GO TO:

PAGE 53 FOR BLUEGRASS
PAGE 34 FOR APPALACHIAN COUNTRY STORES
PAGE 181 FOR LIONEL MODEL RAILROAD
PAGE 291 FOR HANK WILLIAMS

JOHN HENRY

Stretch-Driving Horse

DURING THE mid-1990s, a thoroughbred stallion with the unlikely name of Cigar thrilled horseracing fans by winning sixteen major races in a row. Only the great Citation had equaled this feat, and he had done so running against less-impressive competition in the late 1940s. Even after Cigar's amazing streak was broken and he suffered a string of three defeats before being retired in 1996, many were calling him the greatest racehorse that ever lived. They were wrong, though. So are those who point to the mighty Secretariat, winner of racing's fabled Triple Crown in 1973, and call him the greatest. There are still a few old-timers around who say the legendary Man o' War was, is, and always will be the greatest. But they are wrong, too.

The greatest racehorse that ever lived never won the Triple Crown (the racing championship for three-year-old horses that includes the Kentucky Derby, Preakness, and Belmont Stakes). He never even ran in a Triple Crown race. He never won sixteen races in a row, although he certainly won far more than his share—more than forty. And, unlike Man o' War, he will not be remembered for generations. Although he did his winning—and winning and winning—only twenty or so years ago, most sports fans already seem to have forgotten him. But some will never forget.

You see, he was a fast horse—really fast. And he was tough and mean. And he never gave up. And he had a name that was pure magic; no racehorse ever had a better one. They called him John Henry.

John Henry was born in Kentucky on a cold March morning in 1975. Nobody who was anybody in the horseracing world took any notice of his arrival, and why should they? His mom and pop (that's dame and sire in horse lingo) were a couple of nobodies named Once Double and Ole Bob Bower. In fact, John Henry was descended from a long line of losers. It is a safe bet that collectively they finished last in more races than they won. A lot more.

The little thoroughbred didn't look like much either. He was so spindle-legged and gimpy that his original owners were sure he would never race. In fact, they were so unimpressed with him that they sold the colt at auction for $1,100. Farmers have been known to pay more than that for a decent mule.

Over the next year and a half, John Henry was bought and sold several more times. It was evident that nobody wanted him. He was passed around so often that one Louisiana horseman ended up owning him three separate times, and never once was he glad to have the colt. For one thing, John Henry was no fun to have around. He trampled feed buckets. He kicked down the door of his stable. And he bit people. Giving John Henry a carrot was a tricky and dangerous business.

Somebody decided to enter John Henry in a race, and, amazingly, he won. But then he began to lose and lose and lose. It seemed hopeless.

Enter a man named Sam Rubin. Rubin's life had been a hard one. The son of Jewish immigrants from Russia, he had started out in business on the Lower East Side of New York City, driving a laundry wagon. For a while he owned a small laundry, and then he became a salesman. Decades passed before he finally hit it big in the bicycle business. In 1977, he decided to spend a little of the small bicycle fortune he had accumulated on a racehorse. Fate brought Rubin to Louisiana, where he looked at John Henry and recognized a kindred spirit. He paid $25,000 for the horse, which on the surface appeared to be no bargain. The seller took Rubin's check to the bank and cashed it, grinning like a cat who had just swallowed a canary.

Rubin brought John Henry to New York's Aqueduct Race Track and entered him in a claiming race. As the lowest level of thoroughbred competition, claiming races attract herds of has-beens, never-weres, and never-will-bes. To keep things fair, owners must put their horses up for sale for a stated price, in this case $35,000. On the day he ran the race, anyone in the world could have walked in and "claimed" John Henry for $35,000. No one did, and John Henry won the race by fourteen lengths. He could have won by twenty. Needless to say, he was never entered in a claiming race again.

After his first big win in New York, John Henry was a changed animal. Not that he was any nicer. He still trampled buckets, kicked walls, and bit handlers, but on the racetrack he had suddenly begun to run like an out-of-control freight train. He breathed fire and brimstone and left other horses in the dust. He won major races in the East and the West, on grass tracks and on dirt, on dry courses and in the mud.

His running style was maddening both to those who wished him well and to other owners who wished he would lose or at least go away. He lumbered along far back in the pack, often dead last, until the leaders began their final charge for the finish. Then, when no one, often not even Rubin, thought he had the slightest chance to win, John Henry would put his hammer down. And away he would go. He usually didn't win by much—just enough to notch the victory. Said one horseman, "He would win by a whisker. He would win by the snot on his nose. But he would win."

And he kept right on winning. Most thoroughbreds are finished with racing and put out to pasture by the time they are five or six. Secretariat retired before he turned four. Cigar raced until age six. But John Henry just kept on going. When he was six, the sportswriters said that would be his last good year. When he turned seven, they said *that* would be his last year. They said the same thing when he turned eight. Long before the end of his ninth year, they had stopped writing that sort of thing about him. He had already won better than $6 million in purses, more than any horse in racing history up to that time. In 1981 alone, he won eight of the ten races he entered and a whopping $1,798,030—quite a performance for a horse that once sold for $1,100.

John Henry finally retired in 1985 at age eleven. Even then there was talk of his going on, but it was time to quit. Considering his more than extraordinary performances, he might have retired much earlier to be happily employed as a stud, but, ironically, he had been gelded at the age of two. What a shame. It would have been nice to know a Little John or Henrietta—and watch them run.

For those interested in horses and horseracing, the closest thing to heaven on this earth is the Kentucky Horse Park near Lexington, Kentucky. Situated on 1,032 lush acres in the heart of Kentucky Bluegrass horse country, the park celebrates the long and close relationship between the human and equine species. There are dozens of museums, films, and demonstrations to enjoy. John Henry himself lives at the Horse Park, or at least he did as of January 2004 when he turned age twenty-nine. Old John seems determined to outlive all other horses just as he once outran them. Incidentally, Man o' War is buried on the grounds, and there is a special memorial for Secretariat, who died during the late 1980s. (It has been said that "if you had a device that could measure a horse's strength and speed and you hooked it up to Secretariat, smoke would come out of the machine.") For more information, write to the Kentucky Horse Park, 4089 Iron Works Pike, Lexington, KY 40511, or call (800) 678-8813.

While in Lexington, don't miss out on the opportunity to drive through the gorgeous surrounding countryside with its many horse farms and famous stables. White wooden fences and galloping future champions are everywhere. For information and a self-guiding map, call (800) 845-3959.

Also of interest to fans of champion racehorses is the National Museum of Racing and Hall of Fame located near the historic Saratoga Race Track in Saratoga Springs, New York. Write to the museum at 191 Union Avenue, Saratoga Springs, NY 12866, or call (518) 584-0400.

GO TO:
PAGE 53 FOR BLUEGRASS
PAGE 151 FOR JOHN HENRY: LEGENDARY STEEL-DRIVING MAN
PAGE 202 FOR ALL-AMERICAN MULE

HOMINY GRITS

Who Can Say How Many?

AMONG THE glories of southern cooking—there are too many of them to count—grits stand out as the dish most closely identified with the region. Perfectly acceptable and devilishly delicious plates of southern-style, home-fried chicken can be had in Kansas City or, if you are lucky, even in Boston or Seattle. But walk into a restaurant in any of those places and order a side of grits with your toast, eggs, bacon, and coffee, and you are likely to get a blank stare from your waitress. Or worse—and this is a real danger nowadays—you'll be served instant grits.

The old joke goes like this. A southerner orders breakfast at a diner in New York.

> "I'd like a side of grits with that, please."
> "A side of what?"
> "Hominy grits."
> "What'd you care hominy? We don't have'm."

Northerners making their first trip to the Southland are amazed to see glops of grits on their breakfast plates, usually where they would expect to see potatoes. These folks are easy to spot in southern restaurants. They are the ones with the uncertain expressions on their faces, trying very hard to inconspicuously scrape the grits over to the sides of their plates, away from their eggs and ham. What a waste.

There is, or should be, no mystery about grits. They are just good old basic stuff. Hominy is hulled corn with the bran and germ removed. When the hominy is ground to the consistency of coarse sand, you have grits.

Grits usually are prepared by boiling. Here is how to do it:

TRUE GRITS

2 cups water
½ cup grits (preferably stone-ground)
Salt and pepper
Plenty of butter

Pour the water into a 2-quart pot, bring to a boil, and stir in the grits. Once the water and grits return to a boil, turn the heat to low and cook for about 10 minutes or until they reach the desired consistency (thick, runny, or in between). Then add the salt and pepper, and butter to taste. Makes about 4 servings.

Grits are served in an endless variety of ways: as a side dish at lunch or dinner (they always go great with ham), as a late-night hunger-buster, or, of course, on the plate with breakfast. Occasionally, aficionados will press cooked grits into a sort of cake to be sliced, fried, and eaten on bread as a sandwich.

You can add almost anything to grits: cheese, onion, cinnamon, nutmeg, pepper sauce, whatever. But the best way to have them is as above with salt, pepper, and butter. There is only one fixed rule when serving grits: Always keep enough on hand for seconds.

Note: Instant grits may or may not be better than no grits, but this author's recommendation is to avoid them if at all possible.

Super-delicious grits can be enjoyed in any worthy southern restaurant. They usually can be found even on the cereal shelves of northern supermarkets. The world's best grits, the stone-ground variety, are harder to find, however. Here are a couple of sources: The 117-year-old Nora Mill in Sautee, Georgia, sells grits that have been stone-ground by waterpower. Write to Nora Mill Granary, P.O. Box 41, Sautee, GA 30571, or call (800) 927-2375. The 120-year-old Falls Mill near Lynchburg, Tennessee, home of Jack Daniel's Whiskey, turns out delectable white-corn grits. Write to Falls Mill and Country Store, 134 Falls Mill Road, Belvidere, TN 37306, or call (931) 469-7161.

GO TO:

PAGE 31 FOR ALL-DAY PREACHING AND DINNER ON THE GROUNDS

PAGE 109 FOR DAGWOOD SANDWICH

PAGE 264 FOR TABASCO

HOOVER DAM

Pyramid of the Great Depression

HOOVER DAM is 726 feet high, 660 feet thick at the base, and 1,200 feet wide at the top. Containing more than 3,250,000 cubic yards of concrete, or about as much material as in one of the larger Egyptian pyramids, it is a sizable structure by any measure.

The farmers of Egypt built the pyramids, applying their energies to the task when the Nile was in flood stage and they could not tend their fields. American farmers and laborers built Hoover Dam when a flood of another sort—the Great Depression—left them without the fields or work they needed to feed their families.

The big dam in the lower Colorado River's Boulder Canyon was not originally intended as a depression-era relief project. Instead, the idea was to provide water for southwestern cities and agriculture and electrical power for the entire region. President Calvin Coolidge signed the bill providing funds for the dam in December 1928, almost a year before the stock-market crash signaled an end to the prosperity of the Roaring Twenties era. Actual construction did not begin for more than three years, however, and by the time it got under way in 1931, the nation's economic engine had almost stopped running.

People everywhere were out of work, and most of the unemployed had no prospect of any sort of job. City dwellers lost their homes, and country folk lost farms that had been in their families for generations. Many of those who had no place to go and nowhere else to turn for help looked to the dam in Boulder Canyon as their last hope. Thousands packed their families and possessions into their broken-down Model T Fords and headed for the Southwest.

Paid for with $31 million in federal money, the dam was the most expensive and extensive single project the U.S. had ever undertaken. Even so, the construction effort was managed not by government agencies but by a consortium of private contractors known as the Six Companies. In all, they employed more than five thousand American workers, most of whom could not have found jobs elsewhere.

The work was hard and it was dangerous. "We had five thousand men down in a four-thousand-foot canyon," said construction superintendent Frank Crowe. "The problem was to set up the right sequence of jobs so they wouldn't kill each other off."

More than a few workers lost their lives in accidents or fell prey to the tremendous heat. Like the pyramids, Hoover Dam was built in the middle of a desert. "For a month during the summer, the thermometer never went below a hundred, day or night," said laborer Neil Holmes. "It was from that on up to 138."

Few complained, however. To have a job—any job—at the height of the Great Depression had, as one worker put it, "a definite cooling influence." Such attitudes helped make the dam the centerpiece of Roosevelt administration efforts to revitalize the economy, and in the minds of many it came to symbolize the New Deal. Ironically, in the late 1940s, years after the dam was in place and generating electricity, Congress would name it after Herbert Hoover, whose administration had overseen the early stages of construction. But many of those who labored in Boulder Canyon during the 1930s saw it differently. In their view, they were working on Mr. Roosevelt's dam.

The dam in Boulder Canyon took more than four years to build. When completed in 1935, it was the largest and highest dam in the world—and without question the most beautiful. Most dams are strictly utilitarian structures, and some are downright ugly plugs, but not this one. The Hoover Dam's dramatic modern styling was provided by architect Gordon Kaufman, who, incidentally, had never before worked on a major civil engineering project.

Arching gracefully across the canyon, the dam is several times stronger than it needs to be to hold back giant Lake Mead, which stretches fifty miles along the border of Arizona and Nevada. The lake impounds twelve trillion gallons of water—almost four million gallons for each of Los Angeles's 3.5 million residents. The dam's generators produce 1,376,250 kilowatts of electric power, enough to keep a lot of lights burning.

If you visit Las Vegas, Nevada, you are sure to notice the impressive new MGM Sphinx and Pyramid, but don't forget that only about thirty miles away is a much more authentic and functional monument—Hoover Dam. Its visitor center is located just off U.S. Highway 93, a few miles east of Boulder City, Nevada. For educational group tours and other information, call (702) 294-3517. For information on Lake Mead and other nearby attractions, write to Lake Mead National Recreation Area, 601 Nevada Highway, Boulder City, NV 89005, or call (702) 293-8920.

GO TO:

PAGE 61 FOR BROOKLYN BRIDGE
PAGE 120 FOR EMPIRE STATE BUILDING
PAGE 136 FOR GOLDEN GATE BRIDGE
PAGE 208 FOR NIAGARA FALLS

II

IDAHO POTATOES

Famous for Good Reason

 C HECK OUT the "Welcome to Idaho" signs as you cross the border from Montana or Washington State, and you'll see the words "Famous Potatoes." That is also what it says on Idaho automobile license plates, so you had better believe, those folks up in Idaho are serious about their potatoes.

The rest of us are serious about them, too, and for good reason. Potatoes are about the best thing that ever happened to a hot oven, a skillet, or a deep fryer. What is more, they are awfully good for you when you don't slather them with butter and sour cream of fry them in grease. Loaded with vitamins and minerals, they contain no fat or cholesterol whatsoever. Roughly equivalent to apples in calories, they provide an energy-rich shot of complex carbohydrates. And they are so delicious! Maybe that is why Americans eat more than 120 pounds of potatoes a year on average. Don't gasp—Germans eat almost twice that amount.

The tasty white-meat potatoes we love originated, not in Idaho or Ireland, but in the Andes Mountains of South America. The Inca Indians ate them so often that they measured their days in units equal to the cooking time of a potato. One might suppose that an Inca who wanted to count to ten would go "one potato, two potato, three potato, four," and so on.

In addition to the gold they had stolen from the Incas, the Spanish conquistadors took another sort of treasure back with them to Europe—the humble potato. From Spain its fame quickly spread to other countries, making history along the way. Germany and Austria fought a war over potatoes in 1751, and one century later, Ireland was nearly depopulated when a blight wiped out the potato crop.

Potatoes eventually circled back to this hemisphere, where Thomas Jefferson helped popularize them by serving America's first plate of French fries at a White House dinner.

Henry Spalding, a Presbyterian missionary, introduced potatoes to Idaho in 1836. He had hoped the Nez Perce Indians would take to growing them and become settled farmers. They did not (see "Chief Joseph's Last Stand" on page 169), but Mormons who moved into the area a few years later quickly discovered that potatoes thrived in Idaho soil. Other farmers soon learned the same thing, and the Idaho potato was on its way to becoming a legend.

Today, Idaho produces about a third of the thirty-five billion pounds of potatoes consumed by Americans each year. Washington grows almost as many potatoes as Idaho, but no other state even comes close. On the question of quality, there are those who will argue that Maine potatoes, grown mostly in a single county in the northern part of the state, compare very favorably to those grown in Idaho. Maybe, but you had better not mention that in Boise.

If you'd like to read more about Idaho's most famous export, send $1.25 to Idaho Potato Commission, P.O. Box 1068, Boise, ID 83701, to cover the shipping of an otherwise-free 203-page book called *Aristocrat in Burlap*. Of course, Idaho's aristocratic spuds can be found in the produce section of almost any grocery store. Those who would like their spuds straight from the field might consider ordering a twenty-pound premium gift box from the Sun Valley Potato Company; just call (208) 438-2605.

A tip on baking potatoes: Avoid microwaving them if at all possible. A tip on frying potatoes: As Thomas Jefferson—America's most famous Francophile—might have told you, a true French-fried potato must be fried twice. Cut the fries about one-quarter-inch thick, briefly blanch them in oil just above the boiling point to remove excess moisture, and then pull them out to cool. A few minutes later, place them in hot oil (about 325°) and cook until golden brown.

GO TO:

PAGE 146 FOR ALL-AMERICAN HAMBURGERS
PAGE 95 FOR COCA-COLA
PAGE 110 FOR DR PEPPER

IDITAROD

The Call of Alaska's Wildest Dogsled Race

ALASKA'S THIRTY thousand grizzly bears are asleep—most of them anyway—when the famed Iditarod dogsled race run each March. Otherwise, many of the dogs and sledders would likely end up as supper. Even without the bears to contend with, it is hard to see how the participants survive this grueling sporting event, which takes place near the crest of the Alaskan winter.

The Iditarod is an eleven-hundred-mile dash across some of Alaska's most rugged wilderness terrain. Held in March—not the time most of us would consider making a cross-country jaunt in Alaska—the race begins on the streets of downtown Anchorage and ends approximately two weeks later in Nome, on the shores of the far-off Bering Sea. Following the old Iditarod Trail, the course traverses several mountain ranges including the towering Alaska Range, runs along the banks of the frozen Yukon River, and then pushes several hundred miles to the sea at Nome. Along the way, mushers and their teams may encounter blizzards, flesh-and-bone-freezing temperatures, monumental snowdrifts, or dangerously thin ice, not to mention wolves, rampaging moose, and the occasional sleepless bear.

Completing this extraordinarily challenging course requires tireless dedication by the dogs, who run in teams of up to twenty and sometimes pay with their lives for the effort. The mushers themselves must have what is sometimes called "a brass anatomy."

Interestingly, this most demanding and dangerous of sporting competitions has been won several times by women. Libby Riddles became the first woman to win the race in 1985. Since that time, the amazing Susan Butcher has won it four times. Only Rick Swenson, with five victories, has won the race more often.

For successful teams and drivers, the margin of victory can be as much as a full day, but has been as little as one second. In 1978, forty-five-year-old Dick Mackey came into Nome neck and neck with perennial champion Rick Swenson. In a hard, driving finish, Mackey edged out Swenson by only a few feet—after more than eleven hundred miles of racing.

The Iditarod race has been held every year since 1973, but it honors a much earlier dash across the Alaskan wild. In 1925, Leonard Seppala made a heroic dogsled trek across nearly the full width of Alaska to deliver diphtheria serum to plague-stricken Nome.

If you have a dog team and want to race, or if you only want to watch the start of the race in Anchorage, contact the Alaska Convention and Visitors Bureau in Anchorage at (907) 276-4418. For the hale and hardy only, experienced guides offer sled trips on the Iditarod Trail; call (877) 923-2419.

GO TO:

PAGE 183 FOR JACK LONDON
PAGE 184 FOR LOON
PAGE 294 FOR GRAY WOLF
PAGE 143 FOR GRIZZLY BEAR

IVORY SOAP

Bathtub Battleship from Ivorydale

AMERICAN MOTHERS have long believed that when it comes to washing out the mouths of naughty children, nothing beats Ivory Soap (a registered trademark of the Procter & Gamble Company). This is because its reputation for being safe, mild, and pure is as solid and spotless as the marble of the Lincoln Memorial. It doesn't even taste all that bad. And should you drop it into a tubful of murky, child-colored water, not to worry—it floats!

Ivory Soap is an American institution, about as widely recognized as the Washington Monument and far better respected than Congress. It had already attained this lofty status when Theodore Roosevelt was still a rough-riding cowboy in North Dakota. Introduced in 1879 as an inexpensive white soap intended to rival the quality of imported Castiles, it was marketed to the masses by means of one of the first nationwide advertising campaigns. People were told that Ivory was "so pure that it floats," and the notion took hold. As a result, at least a half dozen generations of Americans have cleaned themselves with Ivory.

So many hands, faces, and baby bottoms have been washed with Ivory that the numbers defy the imagination. Not even Procter & Gamble knows how many billions of bars of Ivory have been sold. The company keeps a precise count, however, of the billions and billions of dollars it rakes in. The total annual sales of Ivory Soap, Ivory Snow, Crest toothpaste, Folger's coffee, and the hundreds of other products marketed under the Procter & Gamble umbrella now exceed the government revenues of entire nations.

The company has grown a bit since it was founded in 1837 in Cincinnati, Ohio, by a pair of immigrants named William Procter and James Gamble, each of whom pledged $3,596.47 to the enterprise. For decades, Procter & Gamble manufactured candles and soap in relatively modest quantities. It took more than twenty years for sales to top $1 million, which they did shortly before the Civil War. The company's big break came with the introduction of its floating soap and the realization that a concerted advertising campaign could turn a simple, though high-quality, product into a phenomenon. The soap's brand name was lifted from "out of ivory palaces," a phrase found in the Bible. So successful was this new product and the marketing effort that placed it in the hands of nearly every American that the company soon built an enormous new factory in a place called Ivorydale.

Procter & Gamble never forgot the advertising lessons it learned with Ivory. For instance, it was among the first manufacturers to use radio to reach consumers nationwide. In 1933, Procter & Gamble's Oxydol soap powder sponsored a radio serial called *Ma Perkins,* and daytime dramas were forever after known as "soap operas." Over the years, the company added dozens of new product lines such as Prell shampoo, Duncan Hines cake mixes, and the ubiquitous Tide, made "new and improved" many a time. To this day, however, Ivory Soap remains a Procter & Gamble mainstay.

Ivory remains a favorite among consumers, too, and no wonder. With a bar of Ivory Soap in your hand, you are holding a chunk of

American history. If you like, you can even wash your hands and face with it and be assured that it is "ninety-nine and forty-four-one-hundredths percent pure." And, yes, it still floats.

The latter quality of Ivory Soap is especially attractive to children. Generations of little boys armed with toothpicks, miniature flags, or leftover parts from model ships—there are always a few (see "Revell-Monogram Models" on page 242)—have converted bars of Ivory Soap into bathtub battleships. A note of warning for any small boys who may be reading this: Mothers tend to frown on the practice.

Ivory Soap can be found in grocery stores large and small. It is still less expensive than most soaps and still quite mild. For more information on Ivory Soap or other Procter & Gamble products, call (800) 765-5516. If you would like to try something different, you might give the Oregon Soap Company a call. A small, independent manufacturer not much bigger than Procter & Gamble was in 1837, it produces exceptional soap said to be even milder than Ivory. Oregon Soap has a pH level of about 7.9, while Ivory comes in at 10.1. There are several Oregon Soap "flavors," such as Country Lavender, Oregon Spice, and Morning Mist. For information or to place an order, write to Oregon Soap, P.O. Box 14464, Portland, OR 97293, or call (800) 549-0299.

GO TO:

PAGE 34 FOR APPALACHIAN COUNTRY STORES
PAGE 282 FOR VERMONT
PAGE 242 FOR REVELL-MONOGRAM MODELS

JJ

JACK DANIEL'S

Smooth-as-Silk Sipping Whiskey

I F YOU can't get airborne or in high spirits any other way, a shot of good old Tennessee whiskey is sure to do the trick. That is certainly the way a Tennessee fellow named Jasper Newton (Jack) Daniel saw it.

In 1866, just after the Civil War, Daniel bent over and took a sip from a mountain spring just outside the little town of Lynchburg, Tennessee. The water tasted pretty good to him, so he decided to put it in a bottle and sell it—that is, after he was finished cooking it a bit. Purified by limestone, the spring's iron-free water, flowing out of the ground at a constant 56 degrees, was to become a key ingredient in one of America's finest products and most genteel pleasures—Jack Daniel's Whiskey.

True Tennessee whiskey is distilled from a grain mash in much the same manner as bourbon. Unlike bourbon, however, it is "mellowed" by filtering it through charcoal. The Jack Daniel's Distillery uses the hardwood of mountain sugar maples for this purpose. Large stacks of this wood are burned out in the open. Afterward, the charcoal is crushed into pea-sized chunks and placed in large vats. Then the whiskey is allowed to filter down through the cleansing charcoal, one drip at a time. This removes any impurities in the whiskey, including its grain taste.

Whiskey making is a fine art, and few ever practiced it with more artistry than Daniel. His Tennessee Sour Mash Sipping Whiskey won him a gold medal at the 1904 St. Louis World's Fair. It has been winning the golden regards of whiskey sippers ever since.

You can find a fifth of Jack Daniel's Old No. 7 in any worthy store that sells spirituous liquors. Keep in mind that this is a

whiskey meant for sipping, not for guzzling. You must take the time
to savor it. A porch, a rocking chair, and a lazy, late spring morning
are helpful, though not necessary, to its appreciation.

If you happen to be in Tennessee hill country, you may want to
tour the Jack Daniel's Distillery. For information, write to Jack
Daniel's Distillery, Lynchburg, TN 37352, or call (931) 759-4715.

GO TO:
PAGE 26 FOR SAMUEL ADAMS BEER
PAGE 53 FOR BLUEGRASS
PAGE 34 FOR APPALACHIAN COUNTRY STORES
PAGE 265 FOR TEXAS CHILI
PAGE 264 FOR TABASCO

CHIEF JOSEPH'S
LAST STAND

I Will Fight No More Forever

AMONG THE last of the great western tribal chiefs to defy the
authority of the U.S. government was Chief Joseph of the Nez Perce.
At first, the Nez Perce had welcomed white settlers from the East,
but when the newcomers began to illegally move onto tribal lands,
conflict became inevitable. Realizing that his people would be hopelessly outnumbered and outgunned in a war with the whites, Joseph
spoke out against violence and did all he could to prevent blood-
shed. Despite his efforts, fighting broke out in June of 1877.

With the U.S. Army about to sweep down on the Nez Perce,
Joseph led approximately 150 braves and 550 women and children
into the trackless Bitterroot Mountains and the Yellowstone Country
beyond. The soldiers followed, but could never quite corner
Joseph's little band. The Nez Perce defeated army detachments in a
series of sharp engagements, invariably slipping away just before
the full, crushing might of the military could be brought to bear on

them. Retreating through canyons and over trails known only to them, the Nez Perce always kept one step ahead of capture. Their long trek took them through parts of Oregon, Idaho, Wyoming, and Montana—more than sixteen hundred miles in all.

The Nez Perce had come within a single day's journey of making good their escape when the army finally caught up with them at Bear Paw in northern Montana, about forty miles from the Canadian border. Joseph and his people had hoped to join Sitting Bull's Sioux on the Canadian plains to the north. But it was not to be.

On the morning of September 29, a large detachment of infantry and cavalry under Gen. Nelson Miles opened fire on the Nez Perce camp with rifles and artillery. Joseph's braves managed to hold the soldiers at bay for five long days. Then, during the evening of October 4, a warrior chief named White Bird and about 150 of the surviving Nez Perce managed to slip through army lines and reach Canada. Chief Joseph remained behind with those who were wounded, ill, or too exhausted and sick at heart to flee. On the following day, Joseph handed his rifle to General Miles. Here is a little of what the great chief said: "My people ask me for food, and I have none to give. It is cold, and we have no blankets, no wood. My people are starving. Where is my little daughter? I do not know. Perhaps even now, she is freezing to death. Hear me, my chiefs. I have fought. But from where the sun now stands, I will fight no more forever."

Although widely respected for his eloquence and valor, Chief Joseph was never allowed to return to the ancestral Nez Perce lands in Oregon and Idaho. He died on a reservation in Washington State in 1904.

Chief Joseph's magnificent surrender speech likely will live forever. An excellent way to honor him and to remember the valiant struggle of the Nez Perce would be to commit a few of his words to memory. Another would be to visit the rugged and extraordinarily beautiful region through which the Nez Perce passed during their historic retreat. The Bitterroot Mountains, accessible via Chief Joseph Pass from Missoula, Montana, remain wild and pristine.

The Nez Perce National Historical Park, established at Spalding, Idaho, in 1965, celebrates the saga of Joseph's people. Informative displays at the visitors center tell their story in considerable detail. For more information on the park and more than two dozen Nez Perce-related sites scattered throughout the Northwest, write to Superintendent, Nez Perce National Historical Park, P.O. Box 93, Spalding, ID 83551-0093, or call (208) 843-2261. Separate park sites at Big Hole off Montana Route 43 and Bear Paw off Route 240, about sixteen miles south of U.S. Highway 2 at Chinook, Montana, preserve key battlefields of the Nez Perce War.

GO TO:

PAGE 67 FOR BUFFALO-HEAD NICKEL
PAGE 223 FOR PENDLETON BLANKETS
PAGE 249 FOR CHIEF SEATTLE'S PLEA
PAGE 251 FOR SEQUOYAH

K

KANSAS

There's No Place Like Home

WHAT IS it that sets this country apart from all others? Our political system? There are a number of other democracies, probably more than you think. Wealth? Even little war-battered Kuwait is rich. Size? Canada, Brazil, and Australia are very nearly as big as the U.S., and, of course, there is that goliath, Russia, which stretches across two continents. No, what puts us in a category all our own is the fact that only here in the good old US of A can be found a place such as Kansas.

It's hard to think of an area anywhere in the world that can be compared to Kansas, but one that might compare is the Ukraine, breadbasket of the czars and the old Soviet Union. True enough, both Kansas and the Ukraine are sizable places, both consist largely of plains, and both grow an enormous amount of wheat, but there the comparison ends. Kansas is a much bolder place. While the Ukraine can boast its Cossacks, they are pussycats compared to Kansas State patrolmen. And, of course, only Kansas can claim a ruby-slippered girl named Dorothy.

A lot of people who have never spent much time there have the wrong idea about Kansas. For instance, they think it's flat. The truth is, Kansas is about as bumpy as any Midwestern state; there are just no Alps. There is, however, plenty of skiing if you don't mind the cross-country variety or a ten-hour drive to the Kansas mountains, all of which happen to be located in Colorado. Many skiers hereabouts refer to Colorado as West Kansas.

172

Okay, so it is pretty flat, but that doesn't keep it from being amazingly beautiful. It has been said that some east-west interstate travelers time their drives so they arrive at the Kansas border at sundown. That way, they'll hit the far end of the state at about dawn, just as the scenery is getting interesting again. Well, these folks have got it all wrong. If they'd just get off the four-lane and out into the country, they might never want to leave—and they wouldn't be the first to feel that way.

Kansas history reaches back as far as any other state. The Spanish adventurer Coronado came here in 1541 searching for gold, and he found it, too, in the form of giant sunflowers. Lewis and Clark, Zebulon Pike, and other American explorers took a loving look at Kansas, as did countless thousands of pioneers, many of whom were willing to live in sod houses in order to settle here. As if to do the old Union one better, the Territory of Kansas held a dress rehearsal of the Civil War before becoming a state in 1861, just as that fratricidal conflict was about to explode in the East. Since the war, Kansas has been a reasonably peaceful place, except for the occasional rampaging tornado, such as the one that carried Dorothy off on her search for the Wizard.

Here are some Kansas facts and figures you might find interesting. The state motto is *Ad Astra per Aspera.* It sounds as if the state officials who made that up were addicted to aspirin, but actually it's Latin, meaning "To the stars with difficulty." The state flower is the sunflower, of course, and the state tree is the cottonwood—well, there are not many Sequoias or Douglas firs in Kansas. The state animal is the buffalo, and the state song is "Home on the Range."

Spread out over approximately 82,000 square miles, Kansas is the fourteenth largest state, but only about 2.5 million people live there, giving the entire state a population roughly equal to that of Brooklyn, New York. A person could get lonely in Kansas, which has a population density of just over thirty people per square mile. By comparison, New Jersey has a density of more than a thousand people per square mile, and likely more than thirty of them would like to live in Kansas. And why not? Frank Baum's Dorothy had it right—there is no place like home—and to her, home was a humble farm right in the heart of America.

For a wealth of travel information on the Sunflower State, call (800) 2KA-NSAS ([800] 252-6727), or visit the official Kansas tourism website at www.travelks.com.

GO TO:

PAGE 64 FOR AMERICAN BUFFALO
PAGE 88 FOR CHICAGO, CHICAGO
PAGE 149 FOR HARLEY-DAVIDSON
PAGE 215 FOR OZ

KALAMAZOO

From Here To . . .

THIS CITY in southwestern Michigan is a long way from any other place, or at least, it is if you accept the popular adage "From here to Kalamazoo." Actually, Kalamazoo is close to just about everything. Located more or less smack in the middle of America, Kalamazoo is only 150 miles from Chicago and 140 miles from Detroit, and Battlecreek, the corn flake capital of the world, is just a hop and a skip down the interstate. Even New York City is only about a day's drive to the east. So why the adage? It can only be because the place has such a marvelous name, and, after all, Kalamazoo rhymes with "to."

This congenial city—thought to be one of the most livable in America—can thank the Potawatomi Indians for its name, which, as Shakespeare's Hamlet might have said, flows "trippingly on the tongue." Judging from what the tribe called themselves, the Potawatomi enjoyed words that were a lot of fun to say. When they said "kalamazoo," they meant "boiling water" or "river crossing."

Originally, the town that grew up around an old Potawatomi fur trading post was known as Bronson, after its founder, Titus Bronson. Unfortunately, Bronson turned out to be such a bad neighbor—the dastardly fellow was convicted of stealing a cherry tree—the villagers petitioned for a name change. By the time Michigan was admitted to the Union in 1837, the place was called Kalamazoo, and it's a good thing, too. Who would want to go "from here to Bronson."

On the other hand, Kalamazoo is a very nice place to go. Known to many as "the Bedding Plant Capital of the World," it just might be the quintessential American burg. There's a very nice downtown mall, a terrific museum, and lots of stately old homes, several of them designed by Frank Lloyd Wright. There is even a beautiful urban park named after—you guessed it—Titus Bronson. Settled comfortably into so fine a hometown, the citizens of Kalamazoo have never been able to hold a grudge.

For travel information, write to Kalamazoo County Convention and Visitors Bureau, 346 West Michigan Avenue, Kalamazoo, MI 49007, or call (800) 222-6363. You might also try www.kalamazoo.com, where you may find that "there is something for you in Kalamazoo."

GO TO:
PAGE 88 FOR CHICAGO, CHICAGO
PAGE 299 FOR FRANK LLOYD WRIGHT

KAZOO

Hummer's Delight

IT IS said that "if you can hum, you can play a kazoo." That's good news to those of us who gave up piano lessons at the age of ten. The kazoo has long been the best friend of music lovers with klutzy fingers and tin ears, and it allows us to believe, for a little while at least, that we are the equal of Benny Goodman.

Although in its current form the kazoo is more than 100 percent American, it is believed to have descended from the mirliton, an African instrument used to imitate human voices and animal sounds during sacred ceremonies. The first American kazoo was made during the 1840s in Macon, Georgia, which is also the birthplace of the highly musical nineteenth-century poet Sidney Lanier and of—

get this—*USA to Z* author Ray Jones. Considered a curiosity, that first kazoo was exhibited at the 1852 Georgia State Fair, right along with the oddly shaped peppers and overgrown pumpkins, by its creators, a black musician named Alabama Vest and German clockmaker Thaddeus Von Clegg. The rest, of course, is kazoo history.

Since 1852, the world population of kazoos has grown from one to a number so impossibly large that it is not worth counting. For more than a century now, kazoos have been a favorite Christmas gift to ten- and twelve-year-olds, and everyone has one or more of them in a drawer somewhere or packed away in a box of keepsakes. But there are also innumerable kazoo players. One kazoo band is said to have consisted of more than thirty thousand musicians.

To call a kazoo player a musician may be a bit of a stretch, but why not? With the marvelously adaptable kazoo, you can play "Row, Row, Row Your Boat" or, if you like, Beethoven's Fifth Symphony.

To learn more about kazoos and kazoo bands, contact Kazoobie Kazoos, the company founded by Kazoo King Rick Hubbard, at 6520 Industrial Avenue #4, Port Richy, FL 34668, or call (800) 326-0358. Another good source of kazoos and kazoo information is the Original American Kazoo Company at 8703 South Main Street, Eden, NY 14057; call (716) 992-3960.

GO TO:

PAGE 53 FOR BLUEGRASS
PAGE 100 FOR AARON COPLAND
PAGE 129 FOR FRISBEES
PAGE 138 FOR BENNY GOODMAN

L

LAKE SUPERIOR

Gitchee Gumee—The Lake That Swallowed a Thousand Ships

KNOWN TO Midwestern Native American tribes as Gitchee Gumee, or "Great Water," and to the rest of us as Superior, it is one big lake. More than 350 miles long, 160 miles wide, and a quarter of a mile deep, it covers 31,200 square miles of the continental heartland in a cold, dark blanket of blue water. A liquid highway for freighters carrying ore, grain, chemicals, and cargo of every description, it is one of the most heavily traveled bodies of water on the planet. Even so, its shores include some of the most isolated places in America.

Ten percent of the earth's fresh water is locked up in this one huge lake. Another 10 percent can be found in the other four Great Lakes: Michigan, Huron, Erie, and Ontario. Together, the five lakes impound approximately fifty-five hundred cubic miles of water. To get an idea of what that means, consider the following. If the lakes were empty and the entire flow of the Mississippi could be diverted into them, it would take the Big Muddy more than fifty years to fill them again. In reality, these truly Great Lakes are inland seas.

Located near the center of the continent, the lakes are raked by giant weather systems and as a consequence are stormier than most of the world's oceans and seas. For hundreds of years, sailors have battled the lakes' howling gales, and, like the twenty-nine crewmen who went down with the *Edmund Fitzgerald* (see page 125), more than a few have perished in the fight. A single storm in 1913 shattered the hulls of more than forty ships and drowned at least 230 sailors. In all, the lakes have gobbled up at least six thousand ships and drowned perhaps fifty thousand passengers and crewmen.

Many of these vessels disappeared without a trace. One such victim was the explorer La Salle's *Griffin*, the very first European-style vessel to sail on the Great Lakes. In 1679, the *Griffin* set out on her maiden voyage with a valuable cargo of beaver pelts and was never heard from again. As the *Fitzgerald* disaster illustrates, the losses have continued right down to our own times.

Fortunately, the dangers of navigating the lakes have not deterred seamen. Commerce on the Great Lakes has played an all-important role in the prosperous commercial development of the United States. We would be a much poorer nation without them. To understand why this is so, consider that a lake freighter of rather ordinary size can carry half a million bushels of wheat, enough for almost five million loaves of bread. It takes more than twenty thousand acres of farmland to grow that much wheat in a year, and at least twenty-five long railroad trains to haul it.

Longer, wider, and more northerly than its sisters, Superior is the stormiest and most dangerous of the lakes. Some would say it is also the most beautiful. Certainly its shores are more remote and pristine than those of the lower lakes. Like the other lakes, Superior is the child of glaciers that bulldozed great holes in the earth, and when the climate turned warmer, filled them with meltwater. When you stand on the shore at Whitefish Point or at Duluth, nearly 350 miles to the west, and gaze out across Superior's nearly endless crystal waters, it is impossible to fully grasp the immensity of the treasure the glaciers left behind—nothing less than the greatest lake in the world.

Travelers who love expanses of open water should not ignore the Great Lakes region, known to some nowadays as the nation's "Third Coast." Lapped by fresh azure waters that won't sting your eyes when you swim, the lakeshores are often cleaner and less crowded than ocean beaches. National lakeshores and lakeside state parks in New York, Ohio, Michigan, Indiana, Illinois, Wisconsin, and Minnesota offer an endless variety of recreational and educational vacation experiences.

Because of its distance from major metropolitan areas, less-adventurous vacationers all too often stop short of Lake Superior. Don't you be among the lazy ones. Miss the boat on Lake Superior, and you'll never see one of America's most spectacular scenic wonders. Smack in the middle of the lake is a seventy-mile-long rock with lots of trees and wildlife and almost no people. The biggest surprise is that you own the place. That's because it's all part of Isle Royale National Park, perhaps the least-well-known and most rarely visited of all the nation's major parks and monuments. Not surprisingly, it's hard to get there. You have to go by boat or floatplane, and, of course, the park is open only during the summer.

For information on transportation and reservations, write to Isle Royale National Park, 87 North Ripley Street, Houghton, MI 49931, or call (906) 482-0984. Slightly more accessible is the Apostle Islands National Lakeshore at the northern tip of Wisconsin. In addition to its extraordinary lake and island scenery, the lakeshore is notable for the half dozen or so historic lighthouses preserved within its boundaries. For information, write to National Lakeshore Headquarters, Route 1, Box 4, Bayfield, WI 54814.

GO TO:
PAGE 125 FOR EDMUND FITZGERALD
PAGE 208 FOR NIAGARA FALLS

LINDY HOP

It Don't Mean a Thing If It Ain't Got That Swing

ON MAY 21, 1927, Charles Lindbergh landed his *Spirit of St. Louis* on an airfield just outside Paris, becoming the first person to make a nonstop, solo flight across the Atlantic. The next morning, newspapers all across America were crowing about "Lindy's Hop." A few weeks later, at a dance marathon in New York City, one of the competitors broke away from his partner and took a solo flight of his own. The dancer's athletic moves were so eye-catching that a reporter later asked him what he was doing. His reply was "the lindy hop."

The dancer was a man named George Snowden, known to his friends as "Shorty" because he was barely five feet tall. Snowden was one of the first true "hop" or "swing" dancers who in the 1920s had started spinning across ballrooms, leaping and throwing their partners into the air in time with the era's new jazzy music. With an offhand remark to a New York reporter, Snowden had given swing dancing its permanent nickname, and it would forever after be known as "the lindy hop."

Moves like Snowden's were as much fun to watch as they were to dance. At a swing dance, everybody had fun, and the place where the most fun was had may very well have been the Savoy Ballroom in Harlem. The Savoy was the epicenter of the swing-dance earthquake that shook America during the late 1920s and 1930s. Talented dance wizards such as Shorty George, Leroy "Stretch" Jones, Willa Mae Ricker, Al Minns, and Frankie Manning were regulars at the Savoy. Young dancers all across the country began to copy styles pioneered by Savoy hoppers.

Some of the best Savoy hoppers became professional dancers. Rich New York City socialites often paid to have them dance at their parties. Many joined an internationally known dance troupe known as Whitey's Lindy Hoppers. The troupe was managed by Herbert "Whitey" White, a former boxer and Savoy ballroom bouncer who had an eye for dance talent. Whitey's Hoppers toured Australia and Europe and even danced for the British royal family. During the 1940s, Whitey's dancers were in such demand that at one time he had simultaneous engagements for them at the Moulin Rouge in Paris, Radio City Music Hall in New York, a Broadway production, and a Hollywood film. It is a good thing they were fast movers.

Swing dancing—in fact, dancing of all types—declined in popularity in the 1950s. It seemed that most people were too busy watching game shows on television to go out for a dance. In recent years, however, the lindy has made a comeback. People everywhere are trying it and liking it. The Savoy and many other fine old ballrooms fell to wrecking balls years ago, but all across the country municipal auditoriums and high schools are hopping to the sound of swing. Benny Goodman, George Snowden, and who knows, maybe even Charles Lindbergh, would just love it.

Lindy hop legends such as Frankie Manning can still be seen at their talented best in old dance movies dating to the 1930s and 1940s, or in documentaries about the golden age of swing dancing. Among the best are *Call of the Jitterbug*, with Norma Miller, Frankie Manning, George Lloyd, and Delilah Jackson; *Minnie the Moocher*, with scenes featuring Louis Armstrong, Fletcher Henderson, Doug Ellington, and many other jazz greats; *The Story of Jazz, Chicago and All That Jazz*, and *Swingin' the Blues*. For videotapes, write to Films Incorporated at 5547 North Ravenswood Avenue, Chicago, IL 60640-1199, or call (800) 323-4222; or Filmmaker's Library, Inc., 124 East Fortieth Street, New York, NY 10016, or call (212) 808-4980; or Movies Unlimited, 6736 Castor Avenue, Philadelphia, PA 19149, or call (800) 523-0823. If you don't know any lindy dance steps, but would like to, check the activity guide of your local newspaper for swing-dance organization listings. Every week or so, these groups host dances, more often than not featuring live jazz bands. They will be happy to hook you up with a dance instructor who will soon have you doing the hop like one of the Savoy's best.

GO TO:

PAGE 138 FOR BENNY GOODMAN
PAGE 141 FOR MARTHA GRAHAM

LIONEL MODEL RAILROAD

Last Train to Lilliput

At LEAST a half dozen generations of American boys have wanted to become railroad engineers. As a matter of fact, most adult males have always secretly harbored the same ambition. Luckily for both groups, this is an American dream that can easily be fulfilled.

Around the turn of the twentieth century, when major U.S. railroads stopped expanding, toy companies took over and launched an effort to lay miniature tracks in every home in the country. They darn near succeeded, and in little more than fifty years—about the same length of time it had taken the full-sized railroad industry to crisscross the nation with track. By 1950, practically every American home had its own railway, often complete with little stations, towns, mountains, forests, and tunnels. A model railroad had come to be seen as a necessary part of male childhood, second in importance to only a baseball glove. This may be due to the fact that fathers enjoyed the little trains as much or more than their sons.

During the 1940s and 1950s, most father-son model railroad teams wanted sets made by Lionel or American Flyer. These companies sold handsome freight and passenger trains that ran on tracks a little less than three inches wide. Their locomotives, boxcars, and gondolas ranged from eight to twelve inches long, and were so exquisitely detailed that except for their size, it would have been hard to tell them from the originals. The action was very lifelike as well. Tiny railroad men kicked off bags of mail at the station. Logs were loaded on and off at sawmills. Trains could be shunted onto spur tracks. By dropping a special pellet down the stack, you could get a Lionel steam engine to chug along in a cloud of smoke.

Founded in New York City in 1900 by J. Lionel Cowen, the Lionel Manufacturing Company got into the model train business by making electric models for store window displays. Soon the company was selling its trains to the public through toy stores and catalogs. Lionel pioneered the interlocking tracks, remote-control speed and coupling devices, and many other features that made model railroads much like the real thing. Despite competition from the Toy Company of America's equally innovative American Flyer trains, Lionel sales grew steadily over the years and then burgeoned after World War II. But like a landslide across a section of track, hard times lay just ahead.

As the century moved past its halfway point, the nation's railroads entered a long period of decline. Increasingly squeezed by aggressive airlines and trucking conglomerates, railway companies were often too big and cumbersome to withstand the competition. Ironically, at about this same time, the Lilliputian railroad companies Lionel and American Flyer began to have problems of their own—and for similar reasons. A plethora of new toys was pushing their trains out of the playroom. Other companies were producing the much smaller HO-gauge model trains, which were so compact that an entire set could be stored in a shoebox. These seemed a much better fit for the modern American family lifestyle.

Set in their ways and unable to adapt, the Lionel and American Flyer lines were doomed. Lionel eventually absorbed its old competitor, but even this did not halt the steady slide in the company's sales. Soon, Lionel itself was sold, and by the 1970s had all but stopped making trains.

Now here's the good news: Lionel trains are still being made and sold. In fact, there has been a resurgence of interest in them, and their beautiful, highly detailed locomotives and cars can be ordered or purchased at many toy stores and hobby shops. Catalogs are usually available at the dealer. For additional information, write to Lionel Trains, 26750 Twenty-three Mile Road, Mount Clemens, MI 48045, or call (586) 949-4100. Tours of the Lionel factory are available. Lionel maintains a special club for committed model railroaders. For information, write to Lionel Railroader Club at P.O. Box 748, New Baltimore, MI 48047-0748. Old Lionel and American Flyer trains are now hot items in the antique toy market. You can pay thousands for some engines or complete trains in good shape, but hey, they are worth every penny.

GO TO:
PAGE 151 FOR JOHN HENRY: STEEL-DRIVING MAN
PAGE 235 FOR RADIO FLYER
PAGE 236 FOR RAGGEDY ANN

JACK LONDON

The Call of the Wild

JACK LONDON wrote it, and if you haven't read it, you'd better take a look at your passport to make sure your nationality is listed correctly. *The Call of the Wild* is so quintessentially American, it should be required reading—right alongside the Constitution and the Declaration of Independence—for anyone seeking citizenship.

As you probably know, this short novel spirits readers away to the frigid Yukon country during the days of the Klondike gold strikes. Hurrying north with them is Buck, probably the most famous and likable nonhuman hero in literary history. Part St. Bernard and part shepherd dog, Buck is snatched from a comfortable existence on a ranch in sunny California and sold into the toiling servitude of pulling sledges across the blood-freezing tundra. In the course of the novel, Buck's gold-hungry masters learn that survival, not the pursuit of riches, is life's first and most important commandment. Buck himself discovers something even more fundamental: that in his soul is a wolf yearning for wilderness. This elemental sense of himself emerges in a pristine passage about midway through the novel. Buck's team, temporarily out of harness, flushes a rabbit and races after it in a howling pack. London describes the effect of the chase on Buck:

> There is an ecstasy that marks the summit of life, and beyond which life cannot rise. And such is the paradox of living, this ecstasy comes when one is most alive, and it comes as a complete forgetfulness that one is alive. This ecstasy, this forgetfulness of living, comes to the artist caught up and out of himself in a sheet of flame; it comes to the soldier, war-mad on a stricken field and refusing quarter; and it came to Buck, leading the pack, sounding the old wolf-cry, straining after the food that was alive and that fled swiftly before him through the moonlight. He was sounding the deeps of his nature, and of the parts of his nature that were deeper than he, going back to the womb of Time. He was mastered by the sheer surging of life, the tidal wave of being, the perfect joy of each separate muscle, joint, and sinew in that it was everything that was not death, that it was aglow and rampant, expressing itself in movement, flying exultantly under the stars and over the face of dead matter that did not move.

Here are words and a story that may live forever, and if they don't, they should. It has been said that William Faulkner wrote the ultimate hunting story with *The Bear* (1942), and that Ernest Hemingway wrote the ultimate fishing story with *The Old Man and the Sea* (1952). If so, then Jack London certainly wrote the greatest dog story of all time with *The Call of the Wild.*

In 1897, at the age of twenty-one, London himself had joined the rush to Klondike to hunt for gold. Not finding any, he returned to California and wrote, among other memorable stories, *The Call of the Wild.* London almost certainly realized his tale of gold fever, an icy and trackless wilderness, and a gentle California mongrel gone to the wolves was a classic. Unfortunately for him, he shared several unenviable traits with many of America's other great novelists: He was a brawler and an alcoholic, as unsuccessful in business as he was with women, and constantly in need of money. In 1903, London sold all his rights to *The Call of the Wild* to Macmillan Publishing Company for $2,000 and never received another dime in royalties for the book. Published later that year, the novel sold through its first printing in three weeks and has not been out of print since.

Those interested in Jack London and his life and times should consider a visit to the Jack London State Historic Park near Glen Ellen, California. The park encompasses eight hundred acres of the original fourteen-hundred-acre London estate and includes his house, a number of ranch buildings, and the cottage where London penned many of his later yarns at the unwavering pace of one thousand words a day. (It is said he would always stop when he reached one thousand words, even if he was in the middle of a sentence.) For more information on the park, call (707) 938-5216, or write to Jack London Historic Park, 2400 London Ranch Road, Glen Ellen, CA 95442. The park gift shop is loaded with London books and souvenirs.

If *The Call of the Wild* is not already on your bookshelf, you can find a copy in almost any library or bookstore. Some early editions contain delightful color illustrations, and you may come across one in some dusty used-book shop. If so, don't leave the store without it.

If you have not read *The Call of the Wild* or are in need of reading it again, you should turn to it as soon as you have finished *USA to Z.* Either you can spend the evening watching reruns on cable or reading Jack London. So, what's it going to be?

GO TO:
PAGE 164 FOR IDITAROD
PAGE 258 FOR JOHN STEINBECK
PAGE 294 FOR GRAY WOLF

LOON

An Uncommon American Species

LOONS ARE quiet most of the time, but when they do call, usually late at night, it sounds as if they are trying to reach someone or something in another universe. Campers who pitch tents beside remote northern lakes may feel a chill run up their spines when a loon call shatters the fragile silence. It may sound like insane laughter, or worse, as if someone out there in the lake is drowning and screaming for help. When you have heard a loon, you never forget it.

The otherworldly voices of loons are heard less and less often nowadays. Driven from the lakes by motorboats, highways, pollution, and development, the common loon is becoming quite uncommon, so much so that in many places they are considered an endangered species. Earlier in this century, however, these web-footed divers were plentiful throughout much of the northern U.S. and Canada.

Loons are members of the duck-like *Gaviidae* bird family. Because of their short legs, they can barely waddle along on land and spend most of their time in the water, where they are graceful masters of their environment. Able to dive to depths of up to two hundred feet, they can out-fish even the best human angler.

In summer breeding plumage, the loon has white neckbands and a black body with white spots. During the breeding season, they are especially vocal and fill the air with their amazing calls. They use their distinctive markings and calls to attract mates.

Ironically, loons mate on shore, where they are most awkward. Their nests are located on riverbanks, along the edges of lakes or, when possible, on small islands. Females usually lay two eggs, which hatch in about a month. Loon parents are very protective of their young and will sometimes carry them around on their backs. The chicks grow up quickly, however, and will learn to fly and be ready to go off on their own within twelve to fourteen weeks. Exasperated human parents may occasionally wish they were so lucky.

During the fall, loons migrate from the inland lake country to the seacoast, where they spend the winter. Theirs is rather the opposite of the schedule followed by people, who most often go to the shore in the summer and live upcountry during the winter.

In both inland and coastal areas, loons must now run a dangerous gauntlet. Conscientious hunters will not shoot them, but they are often caught in commercial fishing nets or die from lead poisoning after ingesting sinkers used by sport fishermen. They are extremely vulnerable to oil spills and other forms of pollution. But the greatest threat to loons may be the destruction of nesting areas by human activity and development.

For more information on loons and other wild birds, check your local bookstore for a guide. If you would like help with identifying birds, get a copy of the National Audubon Society *Field Guide to North American Birds* published by Knopf. If you are interested in preserving loons and their habitat, contact the North American Loon Fund, 6 Lily Pond Road, Gilford, NH 03246, or call (989) 772-9611. A nonprofit conservation organization, the Loon Fund offers a wealth of information on loons and other threatened bird species.

GO TO:

Page 102 for Coyote
Page 107 for Daffy Duck
Page 143 for Grizzly Bear
Page 294 for Gray Wolf

M

MAINE COON

The Cat with the Raccoon Eyes

SOME KNOW them as Yankee cats, while others mistakenly refer to them as raccoon cats. Occasionally, they are confused with the Norwegian forest cats of Scandinavia. Often, when they jump unbidden into their owners' unprotected laps with their long, sharp claws extended, they are called other things as well. But the only proper term for them is Maine coon.

Among the oldest natural breeds in America, the Maine coon is generally regarded as a native of the hardy state of Maine. With their long, heavy fur coats and enormous, snowshoe paws, it is easy to associate them with a place where winter is a serious matter. Indeed, today's Maine coons are thought to be descendants of Persian cats brought to America by Yankee sea captains who regularly wintered in the numerous coves and inlets along the Maine coast.

While this may be true, Maine coons are definitely not Persians. Their large paws, long, bushy tails, broad neck ruffs, huge furry ears, raccoon-like eyes, and overall large size (they can reach weights of twenty pounds or more) set them well apart from any other breed of cat. According to legend, they represent a cross between wild raccoons and domestic cats. Genetically speaking, this is impossible, but in the yard on a moonlit night, a tabby-stripped Maine coon could certainly be mistaken for a raccoon. A more likely though not widely accepted theory suggests that the Maine coon got its considerable size and other extraordinary features from interbreeding between Persian domestics and American wildcats. The wildcat theory makes perfectly good sense to anyone who has been raked—accidentally or otherwise—by a Maine coon's scimitar claws.

Luckily for their owners, Maine coons are good-natured animals. They are gentle, and even when provoked very rarely strike out at humans. They sleep a lot, eat a lot, and get into a lot of mostly harmless trouble. Seemingly, they never entirely quit being kittens and spend their lives playing the part of big, dumb goofs.

Well-bred Maine coons can be quite beautiful, and they regularly win prizes at cat shows. Since their coats display a variety of colors and markings, it is not always easy to recognize a Maine coon when you see one. Look for the big paws and dramatic, Elizabethan ruff. The Maine coon's most familiar and raccoon-like markings are those of the brown or mackerel tabbies. With their raccoon masks, these cats are very hard to miss and harder, if not impossible, to ignore.

If you would like to learn more about purebred Maine coon cats, contact the Native Maine Coon Cat Association at P.O. Box 1678, Windham, ME 04062, or call (207) 893-0499. If you would like to own one, you should consider working through a registered breeder. Otherwise, what you get may not be a true Maine coon. A list of recommended breeders is available from the Maine Coon Breeders and Fanciers Association, which can be reached on the Internet at www.fanciers.com/breedlist/.

GO TO:
PAGE 52 FOR BLUEBERRIES
PAGE 102 FOR COYOTE
PAGE 143 FOR GRIZZLY BEAR
PAGE 294 FOR GRAY WOLF
PAGE 231 FOR QUIET SIDE (MAINE)

MAMMOTH CAVE

Kentucky's Big Hole in the Ground

THE HEART of the Kentucky bluegrass region has many chambers. That's because it's a cave, in fact—the most extensive system of caverns in the world. Northeast of the town of Bowling Green, the lush Kentucky countryside begins to sag and give way like the roof of an old, abandoned tobacco shed. It's as if the supports that once held up the surface have rotted and fallen away. Sinkholes and caves perforate the area known to locals as the "Land of 10,000 Sinks." What has happened there is that a network of subsurface streams and rivers have dissolved and washed away the thick layers of limestone that once provided a solid foundation, leaving behind a winding labyrinth of interlocking underground passage-ways—at least three hundred miles of them. Filled with dazzling formations, these nearly endless halls and passages form a subter-ranean wonderland known to most nowadays as Mammoth Cave.

Native Americans first visited the caves thousands of years ago to hunt for crystals and other useful minerals or just to explore. The bones of some of the less fortunate of these prehistoric spelunkers have been found deep inside the cave, several miles from the nearest opening. It was, no doubt, easy to get lost in there, especially if your twig torch burned out.

Discovered by settlers as early as 1799, the caves have been put to an extraordinary variety of uses. They served as a strategic source of saltpeter for making gunpowder during the War of 1812, as a hideout for bandits, as a convenient hideaway for illegal stills, as a warehouse for perishables—the year-round temperature is 54 degrees—and even as a sanatorium for patients suffering from con-sumption (i.e., tuberculosis). Some of the larger halls have mar-velous acoustics, and during the nineteenth century were used as natural amphitheaters. The renowned Shakespearian actor Edwin Booth, brother of Lincoln assassin John Wilkes Booth, once recited Hamlet here. It is easy to imagine him holding a skull and calling out, "Alas, poor Yorick!" to the flickering shadows on the cave walls. World-famous performers such as the Norwegian violinist Ole Bull and the Swedish vocalist Jenny "the Nightingale" Lind appeared on stages inside the caves, and afterward could say with pride that their music had been heard deep inside the earth. Not surprisingly, blue-grass music has also been heard here. But the caverns themselves have always been Mammoth's primary attraction—the sparkling onyx and gypsum crystals, the waterfalls of stone, the underground rivers with their blind fish, the sheer unfathomable size of the place. Like Gotham City, this underground metropolis is much too big for people. Batman, however, would feel right at home here.

For more information, write to Superintendent, Mammoth Cave National Park, Mammoth Cave, KY 42259, or call (270) 758-2180.

GO TO:

PAGE 45 FOR BATMAN AND ROBIN
PAGE 53 FOR BLUEGRASS
PAGE 73 FOR CARLSBAD CAVERNS

M&M'S

Melt in Your Mouth, Not in Your Hand

M&M'S CAN be seen as a metaphor for Americans. They come in a variety of colors, but beneath their brittle armor, they are all pretty much the same at heart. These most democratic of candies are available to and enjoyed by members of every race, creed, and social class. No Godiva fussiness about the humble M&M.

If America had an official snack food, it certainly might be M&M's. We gobble them up in mind-boggling numbers. Approximately fifty billion are produced annually, and most are consumed right here in the U.S. On average, each of us eats about twenty thousand of them in a lifetime. Some of us, of course, will eat a lot more than that.

M&M's were the brainchild of master confectioners Forrest Mars and Bruce Murries, who began selling them in 1941 as an alternative to chocolate bars that got all gooey in the summer heat. Protected by a hard, sugary shell, M&M's milk chocolate melts—you guessed it— "in your mouth . . . not in your hand."

Despite the slogan, their resistance to heat never has been the chief attraction of M&M's. The key to their phenomenal success lies in the fact that eating them is a process. You can't just chow down on M&M's the way you would, say, a Baby Ruth bar. There are important decisions that must be made: Do you eat them one at a time or cram them into your mouth in great, heaping handfuls? Do you eat the red ones first? The yellow ones? The greens?

Our style of eating M&M's is very revealing. It has long been observed that some people immediately crush and chew their M&M's. Others slowly savor them, sucking off all the sugar coating before enjoying the chocolate, peanut, or almond centers. Psychologists might conclude that the former group lacks the ability to delay gratification, while the latter just doesn't know how to let go.

While they may or may not be much help to analysts, M&M's have a broad array of interpersonal uses. They are great at parties, since they can be served in bowls like bridge mix and don't interfere much with conversation. A wise, socially active young man will slip a package of M&M's into his jacket pocket before going out on a date. They take the awkwardness out of long waits in ticket lines and seating delays at restaurants. Savvy managers keep jars of M&M's on their desks, waiting to disarm any unruly employee or executive who might suddenly burst into their office.

M&M's have also found a home in the American kitchen. They make perfect substitutes for the chocolate bits in the Toll House cookies we pass around on special occasions. They are good in muffins and especially handy for decorating cakes, where they can be used to spell out names and messages and add a scatter of color. They can even be used as a tempting additive to homemade ice cream.

Although they originally came only in chocolate brown, colors were added to M&M's during the 1960s. To this day, brown remains the most common color, but of course we may also choose from red, yellow, green, and the rarely encountered orange. During the 1990s, the M&M/Mars Company created a stir by introducing a new color: blue. Newspapers nationwide reported on the decision to add blue to the mix. This may seem trivial as a news story, but consider: More people are likely to be eating blue M&M's than will ever vote in a presidential election.

For more information on M&M's, call (800) 627-7852, or, if you are a member of the plugged-in generation, visit the M&M's website on the Internet at www.mms.com. In addition to an online factory tour, the website offers recipes and a number of delightful features for children, as well as a shop where you can custom-order M&M's in a spray of twenty-four colors.

GO TO:

PAGE 95 FOR COCA-COLA
PAGE 110 FOR DR PEPPER
PAGE 270 FOR TOLL HOUSE COOKIES
PAGE 289 FOR WHITE MOUNTAIN ICE-CREAM FREEZERS

MODEL T FORD

Tin Lizzie Suited America to a T

YOU CAN paint it any color, so long as it's black," said Henry Ford. That is what he told his production managers shortly before the first Model T was assembled at the Ford plant on Piquette Avenue in Detroit on October 1, 1908. These were to be no-frills cars: tough, reliable, inexpensive, and all more or less the same.

There has never been an automobile like the Model T Ford and, doubtless, never will be again. The old "Tin Lizzies," as their owners were fond of calling them, coughed, sputtered, rumbled, and sometimes kicked like a mule, but they just kept going and going. At a time when many of the country's roads were nothing more than cleared paths through the woods, the Model T was ready for anything. No hill was too steep for it, no mud hole too deep. People drove their Lizzies not just for years but for decades. When the original black bodies finally rusted through and fell off, the owners rigged up wooden cabs, and the old cars kept on chugging.

Selling for as little as $300, Ford's Model Ts were so cheap that almost any family could afford one. It was the Model T that drew ordinary Americans onto the highways, that finally dragged American men down out of their saddles and ended their long love affair with the horse. They would have a new mistress now, the same one they still have today: the automobile.

Although it brought happiness to millions and an incredible energy to the American economy, the ubiquitous Model T was no happy accident. It was, in fact, a stroke of genius, the idea of a single man: Henry Ford.

When Ford was born in 1863, Abraham Lincoln was still president of the United States and the outcome of the Civil War still far from decided. Ford grew up in Michigan at a time when more than 80 percent of Americans made their livings on the family farm, and the most commonly known machine was the harvester. It was the horse and the mule that kept this America moving. Ford was destined to change all that.

At the age of sixteen, Ford migrated to Detroit to work in its burgeoning machine shops. It was here that he first came into contact with a revolutionary new device called the internal-combustion engine. But Ford did not make anything of it or with it right away. Ford was a slow starter—his Model Ts would later become famous for the same quality. Over the years he moved from job to job, tinkering constantly in a little shop near his home. He was well into his thirties by the time he built his first horseless carriage, a buggy frame mounted on bicycle wheels and powered by a deafening four-cylinder engine. Still more years would pass before he set up the Ford Motor Company, backed by a paltry $28,000 put up by a group of small investors. Established in 1903, the little company was a success from the start, producing more or less conventional models. But Henry Ford had an idea, and he could not let it idle.

Popular legend has it that Ford discussed his notion with the famous inventor Thomas Edison. "Young man," Edison is supposed to have said. "This concept will change the world."

Ford's plan was a simple one: to produce a car that anyone could afford. Up until that time, automobiles had been mostly a plaything of the rich. With the right design and production system, Ford was sure he could change that. "I will build a car for the multitude," Ford proclaimed in 1908 when the first Model T sputtered to life in Detroit.

Early touring-car versions sold for $550, but the assembly lines Ford set up became increasingly efficient, and within a few years the price had dropped to less than $300. This was well within the reach of anyone with a job, and soon people everywhere were puttering around the countryside in Model Ts. Ford had "democratized" the automobile.

During the nineteen years Model Ts rolled out of Ford's plants, more than 15,500,000 Tin Lizzies were sold. By the mid-1920s, almost half the automobiles in the world were Model T Fords. Ford switched to the larger and more comfortable Model A in 1927, but the old Ts were so sturdy, many of them outlived the newer models. Many are still running today, to the great delight of their owners and lovers of antique automobiles.

The Model T has become an indelible part of American folklore, and practically every family has a story about one. In most of these tales, the Tin Lizzie is not so much the subject as it is one of the characters, for while they all looked much the same, they each had their own personality.

For instance: One Texas panhandle farmer could start his Model T only if he kicked it—and in just the right place. After he died without revealing the magic spot, his family tried time and again to kick the car to life. But not knowing the magic spot, they could never again get it to start.

Model Ts had to be started with a crank at the front. They often started with such a jolt that they could be accidentally thrown into gear, with the result that many owners were actually run over by their own cars. One Georgia watermelon farmer was run over three times by his Lizzie. On a fourth occasion, he had a little warning and managed to run off down the road, the Model T puttering along after him. It finally ended up in a ditch.

A Connecticut doctor who had never driven a car went into town to pick up his new Model T and drove it back home where his large, extended family waited in the front yard to cheer his arrival. The family shouted and waved, but he drove right by the house without stopping. The good doctor had no idea how to use the brakes and had to keep driving until the car ran out of gas.

The best place to learn about Henry Ford, the Model T, and the Ford Motor Company is the Henry Ford Museum & Greenfield Village in Dearborn, Michigan. For information, write to Henry Ford Museum, 20900 Oakwood Boulevard, P.O. Box 1970, Dearborn, MI 48124-4088, or call (313) 271-1620.

Anyone interested in Model Ts or other old cars should consider joining the Model T Ford Club of America. Many members are Model T collectors, but you don't have to own one to join. Members get a bimonthly magazine called *The Vintage Ford*. Write to Model T Club of America, P.O. Box 126, 119 West Main Street, Centerville, IN 47330, or call (765) 855-5248.

GO TO:

PAGE 115 FOR THOMAS EDISON
PAGE 151 FOR JOHN HENRY: STEEL-DRIVING MAN
PAGE 202 FOR ALL-AMERICAN MULE

GRANDMA MOSES

Everybody's Granny

ANNA MARY Robertson Moses. What else could they have called her but Grandma? Art is not a field known for promoting longevity, and few of history's most famous painters ever reached the age of sixty, let alone eighty. Grandma Moses, on the other hand, was nearly an octogenarian by the time she started her painting career. What is more, she kept on painting and selling her pictures right on past the age of one hundred.

Born in 1860 in a small town in upstate New York, she married young and became, like most other women of that era, a hard-working farm wife. She handled chores around the family dairy, helped her husband, Tom Moses, with his milk route, and made hand-sliced potato chips for sale. Between 1888 and 1903, she gave birth to ten children, only five of them surviving into their teens.

As her children grew up and moved away to pursue their lives, she began to dabble with arts and crafts. What she loved best was making pictures with yarn, but in time arthritis made working with the yarn increasingly difficult. One day during her late seventies, she picked up a crude brush, dipped it into a can of house paint, and on a piece of canvas torn from a threshing machine cover, constructed a scene. What she painted was a vision of rural American life before the time of cars, trucks, telephone poles, and electric lights. That more tranquil age remembered from her childhood would continue to be her subject as she produced picture after picture over the next twenty-plus years.

Her first paintings, displayed at the W. D. Thomas Pharmacy near her home in Hoosick Falls, New York, sold for about $3 each. At some point in the late 1930s, however, her work came to the attention of New York City art dealers. In the fall of 1940, the Galerie St. Etienne on Fifty-seventh Street hosted a one-artist show titled "What a Farmwife Painted." A reviewer for the *New York Herald Tribune* referred to the newly discovered painter as "Grandma Moses"; the name stuck, and an art phenomenon was born.

Grandma Moses' "primitive" artwork would eventually draw crowds to exhibits throughout the United States as well as in Austria, Germany, Switzerland, Holland, and France. A Grandma Moses show in Moscow attracted more than one hundred thousand visitors. Her painting of President Eisenhower's home in Gettysburg, Pennsylvania, appeared on the covers of magazines and became one of the most widely reproduced pictures of the mid-twentieth century.

Like most of her other work, the Gettysburg scene was painted using photographs. Grandma Moses almost never left Hoosick Falls. Seldom working outdoors, she painted what she could see through the windows of her house or the wide-open door of her memory. Sometimes she used Currier & Ives prints for models.

During the last twenty-three years of her life, Grandma Moses turned out more than fifteen hundred paintings. She never had a studio and did her painting in her kitchen or on the front porch. Surprisingly, considering the prices some of her work fetches nowadays, she never sold a painting for more than $1,000. Always frugal, she mixed paint in old coffee cans, soaked worn brushes in empty cold-cream jars, and often painted on Masonite boards rather than stretched canvas.

Grandma Moses kept painting up until a few months before she died in 1961 at the age of 101. She spent her final weeks at the Hoosick Falls Health Center near her old home. Interviewed there, she said, "I look back on my life like a good day's work. It was done, and I feel satisfied with it."

The best place to see and enjoy Grandma Moses paintings is the Bennington Museum on West Main Street in Bennington, Vermont. On display are twenty-eight examples of the artist's work including a rustic, tilt-top table decorated with six old-time scenes. For information on the museum, call (802) 447-1571.

An added attraction of any trip to the Bennington Museum is the town itself. A college community where the making of holiday wrapping paper is a primary industry, Bennington is one of New England's most delightful small towns. Robert Frost is buried here in the cemetery of the Old First Church. For information on activities and lodging, write to the Bennington Chamber of Commerce, Veteran's Memorial Drive, Bennington, VT 05201, or call (802) 447-3311.

Don't you wish you had one of those $3 paintings sold at the old Thomas Pharmacy back in the 1930s? You could sell it and pay off the mortgage on your house, or you could just keep it and enjoy it. Grandma Moses' artwork is still occasionally available and still handled by her original dealer, the Galerie St. Etienne, which held a retrospective exhibit on the artist in 1996. Write to Galerie St. Etienne, 24 West Fifty-seventh Street, New York, NY 10019, or call (212) 245-6734.

GO TO:
PAGE 80 FOR GEORGE WASHINGTON CARVER
PAGE 282 FOR VERMONT

MOXIE

America's Hardest Soft Drink

THE TASTE is a little strange. Bitter, some people say. But Moxie was once the soft drink of choice for millions of Americans, and for a while it even outsold Coca-Cola. There are still plenty of people who

MOXIE   199

say that on a hot summer day nothing cuts thirst like an ice-cold bottle of Moxie. Most admit, however, that it is an acquired taste.

Originally sold as a dry powder to be taken for medicinal purposes, Moxie was the brainchild of one Dr. Augustin Thompson, a Massachusetts physician. Thompson combined sassafras with a little gentian root and a variety of herbs and gave the mixture a name: Moxie Nerve Food. That's right. It was supposed to be good for the nerves—nourishing, even—and who's to say it wasn't?

The good doctor prescribed his concoction for a long list of ailments—practically everything, really. For instance, he said it would help relieve paralysis, insanity, softening of the brain, and even "loss of manhood." Who wouldn't take it?

The trouble was that people found the stuff terribly difficult to swallow. To help them choke it down, Thompson started mixing Moxie with soda water. The soda was meant to hide the taste, certainly not to celebrate it. Even so, the taste of Moxie was destined to assault the tongues of millions of thirsty Americans. In a manner that could be described only as miraculous, Moxie quickly caught on with consumers, and bottles of the drink were soon rattling in crates and chilling in iceboxes everywhere.

Before long, Thompson's nerve food was fueling a big business. National advertising campaigns touted Moxie as the ideal "temperance beverage." Dressed in a spotless physician's smock, the "Moxie Man" appealed to readers from the pages of magazines and newspapers. "Learn to drink Moxie," he said. "It nourishes the nerves."

Millions of buyers armed with nickels responded. Among those who did was President Calvin Coolidge, a rock-ribbed Vermont Republican who enjoyed a cold bottle of Moxie whenever he felt he could spare a nickel, which may not have been often (see "Calvin Coolidge" on page 98).

By the early 1920s, up to twenty-five million cases of Moxie were being sold each year, and for a time it reigned as the nation's number one soft drink. Its ascendancy was short-lived, however. After the stock-market crash in 1929, Americans became more interested in their stomachs than their nerves. Sweeter, milder soft drinks—along with an endless array of harder beverages—took Moxie's place in the market.

For those with a taste for adventure, Moxie still can be bought at quaint corner markets and nostalgia-laced country stores. You can also find it sometime on the soft drink shelves in supermarkets. Occasionally, it is even available in the jumbo-sized two-liter bottles. Like so many other things nowadays, Moxie is bottled by Coca-Cola distributors.

If you're a really big fan of Moxie, seek out Joseph Veilleux's book *Moxie.* It's chock-full of old photographs and memorabilia. You also may want to attend the annual Moxie Festival in Lisbon Falls, Maine. For details, write to Moxie World, P.O. Box 444, Canton, CT 06019, or call (860) 693-8866.

GO TO:

PAGE 34 FOR APPALACHIAN COUNTRY STORES
PAGE 95 FOR COCA-COLA
PAGE 282 FOR VERMONT
PAGE 110 FOR DR PEPPER
PAGE 225 FOR LYDIA E. PINKHAM VEGETABLE COMPOUND

JOHN MUIR

Best Friend of Big Trees

THE SAVING of California's unique giant sequoias—and many other American wonders—can be credited largely to the efforts of one man. America's most influential naturalist, John Muir, was born in Dunbar, Scotland, in 1838. As a boy, he moved with his family to the Midwest where he attended the University of Wisconsin. He spent his twenties working on ingenious mechanical inventions, most of which proved commercially impractical. His life took a dramatic new direction after an industrial accident temporarily blinded him in 1867. Once he regained his sight, Muir resolved to "study the things of God rather than those of men."

With this new outlook, he set out on an epic, thousand-mile walk from Louisville, Kentucky, to the Gulf of Mexico, keeping a meticulously detailed journal as he went. One year later, he headed west on a trek across Nevada, Utah, Oregon, Washington, Alaska, and California. In the latter state, he visited Yosemite Valley and nearby encountered giant sequoias for the first time. The beauty of Yosemite and the magnificence of the sequoias had a profound effect on him, and he devoted much of the rest of his life to saving the trees for future generations. Muir wrote articles, lobbied Congress, and bent the ears of senators and presidents. By 1890, he was able to celebrate the establishment of Sequoia and Yosemite National Parks.

Muir understood, however, that conservation was a never-ending task. In 1890, he founded the Sierra Club to help him in his struggle and to carry on after he was gone. Muir had long urged the federal government to adopt a forest conservation policy, and in 1897, President Grover Cleveland designated thirteen national forests to be preserved from commercial exploitation.

Perhaps the most influential four days of John Muir's life were spent in the company of Theodore Roosevelt in 1903, when the two men went on a camping trip together in the Yosemite Valley. Moved by Muir's eloquence and sharing his love of nature, Roosevelt initiated the most comprehensive conservation program in American history. Thanks to the efforts of Muir and Roosevelt, we can still enjoy wide stretches of wilderness and at least a few fine groves of giant trees, some dating to the time of Moses.

On the Marin Peninsula, just north of San Francisco, are the Muir Woods, an especially lovely grove of coastal redwoods. The cathedral-like grove was set aside and protected in 1908 in honor of the famous naturalist. For information, write to Muir Woods National Monument, Mill Valley, CA 94941, or call (415) 388-2595.

Although quite beautiful, the Muir Woods are far from the only or most spectacular of the memorials to John Muir, who died in 1914. In a sense, the nation's entire national park and national forest systems are monuments to him. So, too, is the Sierra Club, which carries on his work today. For information or to join, write to Sierra Club, 85 Second Street, San Francisco, CA 94105-3441, or call (415) 977-5500. Members receive the monthly *Sierra* magazine and may take advantage of local club memberships as well as a national and international group outings program.

GO TO:

PAGE 136 FOR GOLDEN GATE BRIDGE

PAGE 294 FOR GRAY WOLF

PAGE 184 FOR LOON

PAGE 239 FOR REDWOOD TREES

PAGE 251 FOR SEQUOYAH

PAGE 268 FOR HENRY DAVID THOREAU

ALL-AMERICAN MULE

Get Up There, I Say

THOSE OF us whose memories stretch back far enough into the heart of the twentieth century may be lucky enough to have seen it—a pair of mules pulling a plow and a lone farmer stepping along behind, calling out "Gee!" and "Haw!" We may even be lucky enough to have seen a produce wagon rattling down a dirt road behind a mule whose enormous ears stuck out through holes in an old straw hat. Such scenes provided a better grasp of America's past than any history textbook. They offered a glimpse of our country's very soul.

America's soul is partly that of a mule. Without mules, there would have been no America, at least not the one we inherited. Traditionally, people made their living with mules. With a few fertile acres, a sturdy iron plow, and a mule, a farmer could feed a large family. With a mule, he could get his cash crops into town. With a mule, he had something to pull the family buggy. It was the mule that powered the nation's first industries, that pulled the wagons supplying the armies of Generals Lee and Grant, that plowed the Great Plains, transforming them into a planetary breadbasket.

Mules are more American than Model Ts. They were more crucial to the country's development than the discovery of oil in Texas. Yet, they are and always have been unassuming creatures. Perhaps that is because mules cannot reproduce and have no evolutionary history separate from their long association with humankind. A mule is a hybrid, the product of an unlikely tryst—arranged by a breeder, of course—between a male donkey and a female horse. If, on the other hand, the breeder sends a stallion and a female donkey off to the prom together, the resulting foal will be called a "hinny." Generally speaking, hinnies look and act exactly like mules, except that they are even more stubborn. People usually can't tell the difference, and for most of us, either a hinny or a mule is just a mule.

Like many of today's human offspring, mules and hinnies tend to grow larger than either of their parents. They are stronger and less high-strung than horses and not so prone to injury or fatigue. This accounts for their extraordinary usefulness as work animals.

Nothing accounts for their legendary stubbornness. If a mule thinks it is working too hard, it will stop, and no force on earth will get it moving again until it is ready. Farmers used to say, "It's a good thing mules like to work, or else we would have to pull these plows ourselves." And should its patience be tried beyond endurance, a mule can and will kick with devastating power and accuracy. It is said that unless it intends only a warning, a kicking mule never misses. More than one family farmer has been sent flying out of the field by "Max" or "Ol' Sadie." The stubborn willfulness of the mule is delightfully illustrated in the following lines from an old frontier hootenanny song:

> Whoa, mule, whoa!
> Whoa, mule, I say!
> I ain't got time to kiss you, Sal,
> 'Cause my mule has run away.

Mule breeding was more or less a British idea, but it was in America that the mule found its home and purpose. Where else could the tireless mule find a challenge equal to that of the western plains, where furrows stretched from horizon to horizon? Alas, mules are no longer needed to pull wagons or to break the rich loam of the prairies, but they are still widely appreciated for their strength and for the contributions they have made to the nation.

Mules continue to be bred in nearly every state in the union. On occasion, they are still hitched to plows or wagons, but you'll have to look far and wide to see such a sight. Your best chance to watch mules in action is at an old-fashion agricultural fair, where they often compete in "pull" competitions. To tell the mules from the draft horses, look for the ones with the flat, narrow heads and very long ears.

Believe it or not, some pari-mutuel tracks feature mule races. Usually, racing mules run standard quarter-horse distances of five hundred yards or less. They are not as slow as you might think, and they look quite sporty pounding down the track with their long ears flying out behind them. For racing dates or statistics, check the American Mule Racing Association website at www.muleracing.org, or write to the association at P.O. Box 660651, Sacramento, CA 95866.

If you have a back forty that needs plowing or you'd like a mule in your riding stable (they make excellent mounts), call the American Donkey & Mule Society at (972) 219-0781, or go to www.donkeys .com/ADMS.html on the Web. For a small fee, the society will provide you with a list of reputable breeders in your area. The society may also be able to direct you to a major mule show or auction. Some of the biggest and best of these are held in Tennessee and Texas.

GO TO:
PAGE 153 FOR JOHN HENRY: STRETCH-DRIVING RACEHORSE
PAGE 172 FOR KANSAS
PAGE 193 FOR MODEL T FORD

N

NAVAJO RUGS

On Spider Woman's Loom

To the Navajo, the earth is a textile, with every tree, branch, cloud, and grain of sand woven into its fabric. Navajo rugs represent this worldview, and as such are expressions of the history and mythology of an entire people. Made by hand with the skill that only ages of tradition can provide, they are also among the finest things produced by Americans.

According to tribal myth, it was Spider Woman who taught the Navajo women how to weave. Spider Woman's loom had cross poles made of earth and sky, healds of sheet lightning, and the sun's halo as a batten. The warp sticks were shafts of sunlight breaking through the clouds.

The Navajo artists who weave nowadays use wooden looms, but the designs they employ draw heavily on myth and nature. Navajo looms are upright, rather than horizontal like those of Mexican and Spanish-American weavers. The designs are rarely diagrammed. Instead, the weaver keeps a vision of the final rug in her head as she weaves.

Weaving is traditionally taught to daughters by mothers. Children are first given the task of cleaning the wool, nearly all of it sheared from sheep raised by the Navajos themselves. Later, young weavers learn to spin the wool and to work on a small hand loom.

Traditional patterns, known to the public by names such as Two Gray Hills, Crystal, and Teec Nos Pos, are still being woven, but weavers are exhibiting a more adventurous spirit nowadays. Many are creating their own designs, incorporating stylized animals and desert scenes, as well as whimsical elements such as trucks and school buses.

Since they are handmade works of art, Navajo rugs can be quite expensive. Most buyers view them as a long-term, if not lifetime investment. Obviously, considerable care should be taken in selecting and purchasing the rug that is right for you. It is best to buy from a reputable dealer who can certify the authenticity of the rug. Learn as much as you can from books and articles before you go shopping and make a selection.

For more information, write to the Indian Arts and Crafts Association at 4010 Carlisle NE #C, Albuquerque, NM 87107, or call (505) 265-9149.

GO TO:

PAGE 40 FOR ART DECO
PAGE 223 FOR PENDLETON BLANKETS
PAGE 228 FOR PUEBLO POTTERY
PAGE 249 FOR CHIEF SEATTLE'S PLEA

NEW YORK CITY BAGELS

A No-Holes-Barred Treat

SURE, YOU can find decent bagels other places, but usually that is all they are—decent. They are just not the same as the bagels you buy on the run at Grand Central Station or at the noshery over in Brooklyn.

Then, too, a lot of the bagels you get in places other than New York City—those remote outposts beyond the reach of the subway—are not even decent. In recent years, bakers everywhere have started making them (or trying to), but they just don't have the necessary generations of experience. It is similar to Russian athletes' trying to play baseball: The effort is commendable, but the result is far from major-league. And as we all know, New York is a major-league city.

It should be acknowledged that bagels are not a New York invention but rather a Polish one. According to legend, the first bagel was made in 1683 to honor Polish king Jan, whose horsemen had just helped the Austrians defeat a Turkish army. The bagel in question was meant to look like a stirrup. The Austrian word for stirrup is *beugel,* so that is how the bagel got its name. Centuries later, Yiddish folk took their stirrup roll with them to the boroughs of New York City, and there it has been ever since.

Essentially, a bagel is a round yeast bun with a hole in the middle. It is cooked first in boiling water and then baked. This makes the bagel crusty on the outside and tender inside. Nowadays, bagels come in a superabundance of flavors such as onion, Cheddar, poppy seed, sesame seed, cinnamon raisin, and blueberry, but older New Yorkers tend to prefer the plain or pumpernickel varieties.

A favorite way to enjoy bagels is to split them with a knife and smear the slices with cream cheese. They also go well with lox (thin slices of smoked salmon) and countless other fillings. Sometimes they are buttered and toasted as an accompaniment to a breakfast of eggs and sausage. But of course you can just chomp into one and enjoy its simple, unadulterated goodness. Just make sure it is a New York City bagel.

The superiority of bagels in the Big Apple is legendary. Perhaps there is something about the air in Manhattan, Brooklyn, Queens, and the Bronx (some say Staten Island bagels are questionable) that makes them taste better. You might think it was a cultural thing, but maybe not. Among the most frequently heard complaints of New Yorkers who visit Israel is that "you just can't get a good bagel in Tel Aviv."

So where do you get a good bagel? If you're in New York City, you don't have to go to a bagel shop. Just stop in at any deli or street-corner grocery. Big Apple bagels are so good that it is almost impossible to tell the difference between the great and the not-quite-so-great ones. However, if you are especially particular, you might try H&H Bagels at 2239 Broadway; Columbia Bagels at 2836 Broadway; Kossar's Bialys at 267 Grand Street; or Ess-a-Bagel at 831 Third Avenue, all in Manhattan. Even if you are not in the Big Apple, you don't have to settle for an imitation. You can order the real thing from the Bagel Oasis at 183-12 Horace Harding Expressway in Fresh Meadows, New York. Call them at (800) BAGEL61 ([800] 224-3561), or reach them by e-mail at bagel@bageloasis.com. They deliver anywhere in the United States.

GO TO:

PAGE 76 FOR CARNEGIE DELI

PAGE 120 FOR EMPIRE STATE BUILDING

PAGE 61 FOR BROOKLYN BRIDGE

NIAGARA FALLS

Marriage of Waters

EACH OF the earth's continents has at least one natural feature that stands out in our minds as a symbol for all its diverse lands and peoples. For Africa, that feature is probably the Nile; for Asia, Mount Everest; for Australia, Ayers Rock; for South America, the Amazon; for Europe, the Alps or perhaps the Greek Isles. Here in North America, however, the choice may seem a little more difficult. Depending on where you live and how much of this great land you've seen, you may at first favor the Mississippi River, the Colorado Rockies, Alaska's Mount McKinley, or perhaps the California Redwoods (see page 239). But if you give the question much consideration, the choices can easily be reduced to one.

A few miles from the city of Buffalo, New York, is a natural phenomenon so majestic and powerful that every year it strikes millions of people speechless with awe. Tourists flock to see it from every state in the Union, every Canadian province, and literally every nation on earth. Children the world over have heard of this place and no doubt have dreamed of traveling to America to see it and enjoy it for themselves. The phenomenon in question is, of course, Niagara Falls.

Actually a pair of falls, the American and the Horseshoe, one on each side of the U.S.-Canadian border, they form what is arguably the world's most popular natural wonder. And why shouldn't it be? Fed by the overflow from four of the earth's largest lakes, the Falls are very impressive indeed. More than forty million gallons of water plunge over them every minute, dropping almost 180 feet in a mighty white curtain. Every second, more than twenty-six thousand tons of water hit the rocks and the surface of the Niagara River below, throwing up thunder that can be heard for miles. This unforgettable display of nature's raw power has inspired poets, politicians, and countless ordinary people, not to mention generations of young couples who have flocked to the Falls to honeymoon.

The Falls have also attracted many daredevils. In 1859, the famed French tightrope artist Blondin defied clouds of mist and tricky air currents to walk over the very face of Horseshoe. Ignoring the roar of the water and the screams of a huge crowd of spectators who expected him to fall to his death at any moment, Blondin traversed a cable strung across the Niagara Gorge. Not satisfied with his feat, he then turned and walked back across the same cable. Over the years, he would safely complete the same incredible roundtrip on many occasions, the last time at age sixty-eight.

Many others who have tested the Falls have not been so lucky. During the late nineteenth century, it became something of a fad for young people to cram themselves into whiskey barrels—likely having helped empty them—and allow the river to sweep them over the Falls. None of these fools—there is no other word for them—survived until forty-three-year-old Annie Edson Taylor took the plunge in a heavily padded oak barrel in 1901. She escaped with only a few bruises, a queasy stomach, and a whale of a scare. To her credit, she never again attempted the feat.

Of course, the daredevils most commonly seen at Niagara Falls are the honeymooners who, having taken the plunge, so to speak, are testing the waters of matrimony. Napoleon's brother Jerome and his wife are said to have honeymooned there in 1803. They were not the first young marrieds to have their blood stirred by the thrill of the Falls and would certainly not be the last. More than fifty thousand honeymooning couples visit the Falls every year. Given the earthy power of the spectacle, it is not hard to understand why.

Geologically speaking, the Niagara Falls represent a marriage of waters on a leviathan scale. Millions of years ago, this region was covered by a warm, shallow sea where over the eons tiny shelled creatures built up an immense barrier reef. Several times during the last hundred thousand years or so, thick sheets of ice have covered much of the continent. With blades of ice a thousand miles long, these frozen bulldozers excavated the basins of the Great Lakes. When the ice melted and the lakes were filled, the old limestone reef became a natural dike, holding back the combined waters of Lakes Erie, Huron, Michigan, and Superior. Niagara Falls is the place where the lake waters finally push their way over the reef, and where the heart of the continent is married to the Atlantic.

Since Horseshoe is on the Canadian side of the river and is by far the largest of the Niagara cataracts, our northern neighbors may wish to claim that the best of the Falls is theirs and therefore not a proper subject for a book with a title such as *USA to Z*. It may be true that the Horseshoe, which carries almost 90 percent of Niagara's water, is more impressive, but since Americans and Canadians share so many things, such as our aversion to taxes and appreciation of pizza, why not the Falls? Canadians are more than welcome to include the American falls on the U.S. side of the border in any listing of Canadian attractions. Heck, if they like, they can even include the Grand Canyon.

The best time to see Niagara Falls is anytime you can see them. In winter or summer, during the day or at night, they offer a lifetime of awe and wonder in just a few seconds. In the evening, colored lights turn the falls into a huge postimpressionist canvas. On the Canadian side, tunnels carved out of the solid dolomite allow rain-coated visitors to get behind the falls and within a few feet of the water's vortex. The famous tour boat *Maid of the Mists* takes visitors close enough to the outer edge of the falls to get their clothes soaked.

For travel information, contact the Niagara Falls Visitors Bureau, 345 Third Street, Niagara Falls, NY 14303, or call (800) 338-7890. Canadian-side visitor's information can be obtained by calling (800) 263-2988.

GO TO:

PAGE 68 FOR BUFFALO, NEW YORK
PAGE 95 FOR COCA-COLA
PAGE 124 FOR FALLINGWATER

OLD HOLLYWOOD

Dreamland, USA

THE OLD Hollywood that produced the Victor Fleming and Judy Garland classic *The Wizard of Oz* and was itself an emerald city of the imagination has all but vanished. Hollywood was always more a dream than a place, and that is truer today than it was in 1939. The neighborhood in west-central Los Angeles known as Hollywood is now a run-down district filled with seedy dance clubs, T-shirt shops, and spare-changing teenagers. The place is badly in need of a little paint and a lot of renovation.

Of course, movies are still being made in Southern California—so many, in fact, that nobody knows exactly how many—but nowadays the studios are scattered all over the map. Paramount Pictures is the only remaining major film studio in Hollywood proper. Even so, the name Hollywood still evokes golden dreams of fame and fortune. Young actors and actresses the world over want to go to Hollywood and hit the "big time."

Early movie producers went to California for the same reason hordes of other folks have gone there over the years—to take advantage of the abundant sunshine. The film used during the early days of the movie industry was so slow (insensitive to light) that most pictures came out grainy and dark. At first, a majority of movie companies were located in New York City, New Jersey, and elsewhere in the East. Then in 1913, the young Cecil B. De Mille decided to shoot his feature *Squawman* in Los Angeles. There he found the sunlight so bright that he ended up with a much clearer, more watchable movie than he could have made in the East. Soon other filmmakers were loading up their cameras and heading west. Hollywood became the focus for most of their activities.

The large-scale movie production made possible by the California sunshine required enormous amounts of capital that could be raised only by big organizations. Small film companies were soon squeezed out of the business, and by 1930 most of the industry's best movies were being made by MGM, Warner Brothers, Universal, Paramount, and a few other mammoth studios. Actors, writers, directors, musicians, and practically everyone else in the business worked on contract for one or another of the big movie companies under an arrangement known as the "studio system." The studio moguls guided—and controlled—the careers of the artists who worked for them. No doubt this authoritarian and arbitrary system stifled the careers of many, but it greatly benefited others. It also allowed the studios to focus talent when and where it was needed to produce a higher-quality drama than we often see today.

By about 1960, however, competition from television and a new set of economic disciplines had destroyed the old studio system. When it was gone, so, too, was Hollywood's central position in the industry. The smaller and leaner film companies that survived moved away in search of less expensive offices and back lots, leaving the old Hollywood neighborhoods to slowly sink into ruin.

Today, a collection of entrepreneurs and civic groups are revitalizing Hollywood. It is hard to see how they could fail with all those dreams to work with, not to mention the most famous chunk of real estate on the planet.

There are many ways to see and enjoy old Hollywood, even without going to Los Angeles. A good way is to take in one of those classic movies made under the studio system during the 1930s and 1940s—for instance, *Casablanca* (see page 83). Revival movie houses sometimes feature them, and any good video rental agency will carry them. You may find bits and pieces of old Hollywood right in your own community, in the form of art deco and architecture made popular by the movies. Many old movie houses, and even some newer ones, sport spectacular decor in the flamboyant art deco style.

If you are determined to go to Hollywood itself, drive along Sunset and Hollywood Boulevards and enjoy the wonderful movieland architecture. You may see some of the best stuff in the residential neighborhoods. Of course Mann's (formerly Grauman's)

Chinese Theater, with all the footprints of movie stars set in concrete, is a must. Look for it at 6925 Hollywood Boulevard. For some late-night stargazing and a delicious snack, try Jerry's Famous Deli at 12655 Ventura Boulevard in Studio City ([818] 980-4245). Then, to work off the calories, drop into Gold's Gym at 358 Hampton Drive in Venice, where Arnold Schwarzenegger sweated while building up all those muscles ([310] 392-6004).

Film crews are constantly shooting scenes in and around Los Angeles. Lists of locations are published daily on a Shoot Sheet distributed in very limited quantities at 6922 Hollywood Boulevard, Suite 602, just across from Mann's Chinese Theater. To catch new releases before they are seen by folks in such provincial places as New York City, try the AMC Century Theater at 10250 Santa Monica Boulevard in Century City ([310] 289-4262). Finally, if you dream of going to Hollywood and seeing your name up in lights, consider that the odds are about 10,000 to 1 against that happening. In any case, go to acting school first. And keep your dreams alive.

GO TO:

PAGE 56 FOR HUMPHREY BOGART
PAGE 83 FOR CASABLANCA
PAGE 215 FOR OZ

OLD TOWN CANOES

From the Rivers of the Maine Backwoods

WHEN HENRY David Thoreau explored Maine's backwoods rivers during the mid-eighteenth century, he may have paddled right past Old Town, the site of a Penobscot Indian village. To the Penobscot, the river was a highway, and they built birch-bark canoes for travel and commerce. Their sturdy canoes were among the finest made by Native American tribes and attracted the admiration of boat builders all over New England. So it was highly appropriate that a generation after Thoreau passed this way, Old Town became the home of the nation's first major canoe company.

The Penobscot had long made a cottage industry of building canoes in their backyards and selling them to neighbors or woodsmen. By the turn of the twentieth century, established boat builders had begun to add canoes to their own lines of fishing boats, bateaux, and small sailing craft. In 1900, a young Bangor entrepreneur named George Gray jumped into the business. He saw potential in seeking a national market for the high-quality, handmade Maine canoes, and hired talented local craftsmen to build them in a lot behind Gray's Hardware Store in Old Town.

When these first elegant canoes sold instantly and orders poured in for more, Gray decided to move his business to an old, abandoned shoe factory and step up production. Quality lumber and other materials were readily at hand in the towering Maine woods, and plenty of highly skilled builders, many of them Penobscot, were available locally. Within six years, Gray's Old Town Canoe Company was producing as many as four hundred canoes a month. Today, almost a century later, Old Town Canoe is the largest and oldest canoe manufacturer in the world. Its elegant and durable crafts are sold internationally as well as by sports suppliers throughout America.

Most Old Town canoes now have fiberglass hulls, but the company still makes handcrafted models with ribs and hulls of natural wood. Referred to as the "Wood Classic" line, these elegant canoes are part of our national heritage. Paddling one along a woodland river makes you feel like an Indian warrior, a French fur trader voyaging to the Great Lakes, or Thoreau himself, seeking out the center of things.

For information on Old Town Canoes, write to Old Town Canoe Company, 58 Middle Street, Old Town, ME 04468, or call (207) 827-5514. Many boat or sporting goods suppliers handle Old Town Canoes and other Old Town products.

GO TO:

PAGE 125 FOR EDMUND FITZGERALD
PAGE 188 FOR MAINE COON
PAGE 268 FOR HENRY DAVID THOREAU
PAGE 231 FOR QUIET SIDE (MAINE)

OZ

Frank Baum's Wonderful Green Wizard

THEY CALLED it the "Emerald City" because its walls and streets—everything, in fact—were always bathed in a shimmering green light. Magic? Not exactly. The wizard who ruled the place had decreed that everyone wear special glasses. The trick being, of course, that the glasses were tinted green.

Oz can be seen as a metaphor for a wonderfully American way of looking at things. Here in this country, make-believe and real life get mixed up all the time, and occasionally the result is a better reality. Americans have vision—not infrequently tinted green—which draws us onward into tomorrow and makes possible things like skyscrapers, moon rockets, wondrous children's books, and blockbuster movies.

One of the most popular films of all time, *The Wizard of Oz* is a national icon. Generations of American children have danced down the Yellow Brick Road with Judy (Dorothy) Garland, the Tin Woodsman, the Scarecrow, and the Cowardly Lion toward the Land of Oz and its inscrutable wizard. In the movie, the wizard turns out to be a graying and befuddled old man who concocts the scheme of taking Dorothy back home to Kansas in a hot air balloon. She gets left behind, and for transportation has to rely on her magic slippers and the recollection that "there's no place like home." Dorothy and every eight-year-old who has ever enjoyed her story knows that the guy in the balloon is an impostor. There was a real wizard, but he was not it.

The real wizard of Oz was a journalist and dreamer by the name of L. Frank Baum. Born in Syracuse, New York, in 1856, Baum grew up in the East and showed an early interest in theater and literature. In 1882, he married fiery young Maude Gage, who had links to Susan B. Anthony, Elizabeth Cady Stanton, and other members of the Woman Suffrage Movement. When Baum's career in theater management fell on hard times, he moved to the Midwest, where the Gage family had business connections. In Aberdeen, South Dakota, he operated a modest store known as Baum's Bazaar and later ran a small newspaper called the *Saturday Pioneer*. These ventures failed, however, and in time Baum followed his own yellow brick road to the windy—and occasionally magical—city of Chicago to work as a journalist.

After years of struggle (to help make ends meet for his family, he labored part-time as a door-to-door china salesman), he had the good fortune to meet up with the spirited artist/illustrator Maxfield Parrish. Together, Baum and Parrish published a moderately successful *Mother Goose* children's book in 1897. Two years later, Baum teamed up with another illustrator, William Wallace Denslow, on *Father Goose*, which became the national best-selling children's book of the year. Baum was able to stop peddling plates and saucers and turn full-time to writing, a fortunate thing, since he had an entire Emerald City and a Kansas farm swirling around inside him.

By 1900, Baum had *The Wonderful Wizard of Oz* ready for publication. With illustrations by Denslow, it gave Baum another bestseller and established him as the nation's top children's book writer. Over the years, Baum took his orphaned farm girl Dorothy back to Oz a dozen more times. Readers were always happy to go along for the ride. Eventually, following the death of her aunt Em, Dorothy moved permanently to Oz. Apparently Baum himself took up residence there upon his death in 1919.

It was not until 1939, twenty years after Baum died, that MGM released the Victor Fleming and Judy Garland classic *The Wizard of Oz*. Featuring an array of musical hits such as "Over the Rainbow" and "We're Off to See the Wizard" and dozens of singing midgets as munchkins, the movie was a sure-fire hit. It won an Academy Award Oscar for best score, but lost out in the best-picture category to another Fleming masterpiece: *Gone with the Wind*. A great year for movies, no?

L. Frank Baum's children's books, especially those with the original illustrations, are very hard to come by nowadays. If you happen upon one and can afford the price, grab it. You'll have a wonderful keepsake and a highly valuable collector's item as well.

The Wizard of Oz movie is on television frequently and can be rented at any video store. Like most movies, it is best seen on the big screen, but unfortunately, theaters rarely show it.

Fans who just can't get enough of Oz may want to join one of the following organizations: The Royal Club of Oz offers a bimonthly magazine called *The Emerald City Mirror,* a Certificate of Ozzy Citizenship, and other green-tinted goodies. For information, call (800) 207-6968, or write to The Royal Club of Oz, P.O. Box 714, New York, NY 10011.

Founded in 1957, The International Wizard of Oz Club publishes *The Baum Bugle* three times a year and makes available a fascinating assortment of Oz-related books, pamphlets, and research materials. For information or to join, write to The International Wizard of Oz Club, P.O. Box 26249, San Francisco, CA 92146.

GO TO:

PAGE 29 FOR ALADDIN LAMPS
PAGE 88 FOR CHICAGO, CHICAGO
PAGE 115 FOR THOMAS EDISON
PAGE 138 FOR BENNY GOODMAN
PAGE 299 FOR FRANK LLOYD WRIGHT

P

PAPER-SHELL PECANS

They're Nuts About 'Em in Texas

THE PAPER-SHELL pecan is not the first thing that comes to mind when the subject of Texas arises in conversation. One is more likely to think of Sam Houston, the Alamo, cowboys, longhorns, the Chisholm Trail, Lyndon Johnson, or, of course, oil. If you have a taste for the South's favorite dessert, however, you might consider adding pecans to the list. If not for Texas, those sinfully delicious pecan pies—not to mention butter pecan ice cream and a hundred other wondrous concoctions—would be a lot harder to come by.

Pecan trees, close relatives of the hickory, thrive across the South, and annual U.S. production of the tasty nuts usually tops 250 million pounds. More than a third of that total is shaken from Texas trees. Texas orchards are marvelously productive. A single grower near Stephenville collects up to 3.7 million pounds of pecans—more than 1 percent of the national crop—from its 4,000 acres of trees. There are several other Texas pecan operations at least that large.

Even more important is the fact that nearly all of America's paper-shell pecans come from Texas. To grasp the significance of this, you need to understand that the pecan tree as we know it evolved in a constant state of war with squirrels and crows. The pecan developed its armor-like shell in order to frustrate these varmints and prevent them from nibbling the species into oblivion. Unfortunately, humans also love pecans and are equally frustrated by their tough, woody shells.

Around the turn of the twentieth century, a group of pecan growers near San Saba, Texas, successfully addressed this problem by somehow reversing evolution. The miracle they worked was the paper-shell pecan. You can crack open one of these beauties with your fingers. They are big, too, befitting the state that created them. The meat inside a paper-shell is often so substantial that it takes several bites to eat. Use paper-shells to bake a pecan pie, and you can count the nuts on top.

Of course, other pecan varieties are equally tasty. Stuarts, Wichitas, Cape Fears, and many other varieties are grown in Texas and throughout the South. You can't go wrong with any of them. Just keep on hand a sturdy nutcracker.

Excellent sources of paper-shells and other tempting pecans can be found in small east Texas towns such as San Saba, located right in the heart of pecan country. To order a bag of pecans, write to R. B. Bagley and Sons, 420 East Commerce, San Saba, TX 76877, or call (325) 372-5154. Another good source is the Oliver Pecan Company at 1402 West Wallace, San Saba, TX 76877; call (325) 372-5984. For additional information on gift boxes and, perhaps, a terrific pecan pie recipe, go online and check out the delightfully nutty website at www.pecans.com.

GO TO:

Page 31 for All-Day Preaching and Dinner on the Grounds
Page 52 for Blueberries
Page 132 for Georgia Peaches
Page 289 for White Mountain Ice-Cream Freezers

DOROTHY PARKER

Little Nell's Vicious Circle

Dorothy Parker has the reputation of being one of the sharpest-tongued people who lever lived. As a member of the legendary Algonquin Round Table, the Promethean literary circle that met for lunch at New York City's Algonquin Hotel during the 1920s and 1930s, she skewered books, plays, politicians, society at large, and occasionally even herself. Of the Broadway play *The House Beautiful*, Parker said, "*The House Beautiful* is The Play Lousy." Concerning the book *House at Pooh Corner,* she commented, "This weader fwowed up." On learning that former President Calvin Coolidge was dead, she remarked, "How could they tell?"

Born in 1893, Parker became a member of New York's literary set at an early age. At twenty-two, she published a poem in *Vanity Fair* and soon after was hired by the magazine as a critic. Parker's reviews were acerbic, even by the highly urbane standards of *Vanity Fair.* For instance, she described an early Katharine Hepburn theater performance as running "the gamut of emotions from A to B." Her razor-sharp wit eventually got her fired, and she turned to freelancing poetry, reviews, and short essays, mostly for the *New Yorker.*

In 1919, Parker helped found the Algonquin Round Table, which became a forum for her increasingly famous wit. Other Round Table regulars, such as Alexander Woollcott, George Kaufmann, and Harpo Marx, considered her the "queen" of their almost daily lunchtime gatherings. So, too, did newspaper and magazine writers, who listened in to see what she would say next and then hurried off to print her comments in their publications.

Readers reveled in barbed Parker remarks. Concerning literary style: "Brevity is the soul of Lingerie." About a female acquaintance: "You know, that woman speaks eighteen different languages, and she can't say no in any one of them." About a male acquaintance: "His body has gone to his head." When a pretentiously dressed young man walked into the room: "Look at him, a rhinestone in the rough." And concerning her own lack of success with the opposite sex: "Men seldom make passes at girls who wear glasses."

Woollcott described Parker as "an odd blend of Little Nell and Lady Macbeth" who wore "a lacy sleeve with a bottle of vitriol concealed in its folds." But Woollcott and most of Parker's other acquaintances—she had few close friends—understood that her verbal slashes were never intended solely to wound. They were her own personalized form of literary expression and the vehicle for wide-ranging social commentary. "Wit has truth in it," said Parker. "Wisecracking is merely calisthenics with words."

During the 1930s, Parker abandoned the Round Table and left New York to work as a screenwriter in Los Angeles. Although she published several books and one of her short stories, "Big Blonde," won an O'Henry Prize, she was destined never to achieve the financial success or literary status achieved by many of her former Roundtable colleagues. Eventually returning to New York, she lived more or less in anonymity, which was probably what she wanted. "Are you Dorothy Parker?" a stranger asked her at a party. "Yes," Parker answered. "Do you mind?"

Parker was plagued by alcoholism and depression all of her adult life. She died in 1967.

The 1994 Robert Altman movie *Mrs. Parker and the Vicious Circle* offers viewers a seat at the old Algonquin Roundtable, plus a poignant look at the life of Dorothy Parker. The movie is well worth seeing and can be found in most video stores.

To sample Parker's writing, try *Not Much Fun: The Lost Poems of Dorothy Parker*, published during the 1990s by Scribner. Some consider her poetry to be an acquired taste, but you may find these gems to be more than a little fun. Included, for instance, is "The Passionate Freudian to His Love," which ends:

> So come dwell a while on that distant isle
> In brilliant tropical weather;
> Where a Freud in need is a Freud indeed,
> We'll all be Jung together.

For a more personal sense of what the Round Table and Dorothy Parker were all about, consider a stay at the Algonquin Hotel, now part of the Westin chain. The dining room still looks much the way it did when Parker, Woollcott, Noel Coward, and other literary figures lunched there during the 1920s. For information. write to The Algonquin Hotel, 59 West Forty-fourth Street, New York, NY 10036. For reservations, call (800) WESTIN-1 ([800] 937-8461). You are unlikely to find any more romantic accommodations than those offered by the Algonquin. Dorothy Parker herself likely appreciated the hotel's romantic feeling. Despite her public cynicism and the fact that her own love life was mostly unhappy, she apparently placed great importance on authentic romance. As she approached a taxi at a New York street corner, the driver said, "Sorry, lady, I'm engaged," to which she replied "Then, be happy."

GO TO:
PAGE 98 FOR CALVIN COOLIDGE
PAGE 183 FOR JACK LONDON
PAGE 258 FOR JOHN STEINBECK

PARKER HOUSE ROLLS

A Baker's Dozen, Please

FOLDED TO make them softer, moister, and easier to pull apart, Parker House rolls are an institution in New England and throughout much of the rest of the country as well. They are also about the best thing ever to come out of a baker's oven. Each tender, crustless roll is an open invitation to butter, jam, or honey.

First baked during the 1850s at—an easy one—the Parker House in Boston, they remain to this day a mainstay in the dining rooms of this elegant old hotel (it's now known as the Omni Parker House). It is said that Oliver Wendell Holmes adored the rolls at the Parker, as did Ralph Waldo Emerson. And people still love them; the hotel's kitchens bake as many as fifteen thousand of them every week.

Among the famous names associated with Parker House rolls is that of Ho Chi Minh. As a young student in Boston, long before he became leader of communist Vietnam, Ho earned pocket money by working in the Parker House kitchen, where, among other things, he turned out countless thousands of rolls.

For those who would like to serve their own Parker House rolls, recipes can be found in a variety of cookbooks. The recipe on the next page is a home-kitchen version of the original.

The Omni Parker House at 60 School Street in Boston still sells its delicious rolls to the public. Reservations can be made at (800) 843-6664. For dining reservations or information, call (617) 227-8600.

GO TO:
PAGE 48 FOR BEAN SUPPERS
PAGE 270 FOR TOLL HOUSE COOKIES

PARKER HOUSE ROLLS

1 package dry yeast
3 teaspoons salt
¼ cup lukewarm water
3 tablespoons butter
2 cups milk
6 cups flour, divided
2 tablespoons sugar
1 cup melted butter

Grease a large bowl and set aside. Butter a cooking sheet and set aside. In a large bowl combine the yeast and water. In a saucepan combine the milk, sugar, salt, and butter. Scald and cool until lukewarm. Stir the mixture into the water and yeast, add three cups of the flour, and beat with a spoon until smooth. Cover the bowl with a damp cloth, put in a warm place, and let the mixture rise for about an hour. Add enough of the remaining flour to make soft dough, knead it for about 5 minutes, and then place in the prepared bowl to rise until doubled. On a floured board or waxed paper roll out the dough until ⅓ inch thick. Cut into squares and brush with the melted butter. Stretch the squares and fold them over so the end is under the roll. Place on the prepared cooking sheet and let rise for about 45 minutes. Bake at 400° for 10 to 12 minutes. Remove from the oven and brush again with butter. Makes 2 to 3 dozen.

PENDLETON BLANKETS

Warm Tributes to Native America

ONLY A few years after Chief Joseph died in 1904, the Pendleton Woolen Mills in Oregon honored the great Nez Perce leader with a specially designed blanket. The Chief Joseph blanket and other finely crafted Pendleton wool products soon became very popular among Native Americans, especially those in the West. The jacquard-loomed Pendleton blankets were of the highest quality, and their bright colors and fine detailing enhanced their appeal. Tribal motifs often were included in their design.

For many years, Pendleton robes and blankets played a key role in what was known as the "Indian trade." They were bartered for silver jewelry, pottery, and other art and craft items, which were then resold at a profit. Even fine Navajo rugs were sometimes traded for Pendleton blankets.

To this day, Pendleton blankets are considered status symbols and treasured as heirlooms by Native American families. It is said that young Indian couples felt secure once the man owned a Bulova watch and the woman had a Pendleton blanket. If hard times made such a thing necessary, either or both of these prized possessions could be sold.

Pendleton still sells about half its blankets to Native Americans. However, sales to the general public in the U.S. and abroad are steadily increasing. Especially popular are Pendleton's "Legendary Series" blankets. Among the finest and most sought after of these are the Circle of Life blanket, which honors tribal elders; the Turtle blanket, a tribute to the old Iroquois Confederacy; the Sioux Star blanket, inspired by a tribal quilt pattern; and the Coyote, which celebrates the important place of this sly desert animal in Native American legend and mythology.

For additional information on Pendleton Woolen Mills or their products, call (800) 760-4844. Pendleton's well-crafted blankets are expensive, but can be expected to last a lifetime.

GO TO:

PAGE 23 FOR ACOMA, NEW MEXICO
PAGE 169 FOR CHIEF JOSEPH'S LAST STAND
PAGE 205 FOR NAVAJO RUGS
PAGE 228 FOR PUEBLO POTTERY
PAGE 249 FOR CHIEF SEATTLE'S PLEA
PAGE 251 FOR SEQUOYAH

LYDIA E. PINKHAM VEGETABLE COMPOUND

Gentlemen, Please Avert Your Eyes from the Following

IT IS the oldest malady known to woman. It is even mentioned in the Bible, where a certain set of symptoms that bedevil women—and only women—approximately once in every cycle of the moon are described as being "in the way of a woman." These very well-known symptoms, often including weakness and an endless variety of aches and pains, are actually too numerous to list here—or anywhere. And for as long as women have suffered in these ways, they have longed for a remedy. Okay, so here it is:

THE FORMULA

6 parts Fenugreek Seed
4 parts True Unicorn Root
4 parts False Unicorn Root
3 parts Life Root
3 parts Pleurisy Root
3 parts Black Cohosh

Mix or blend the ingredients, add licorice for flavoring if you wish, and take as needed (and at your own risk).

This, ladies—but not you, gentlemen—is the unpatented formula for the famous Lydia E. Pinkham Vegetable Compound. A white-haired Massachusetts grandmother, Ms. Pinkham brewed and bottled dozens of different home remedies on the stove of her kitchen in Lynn, northeast of Boston. Most she gave away to ailing friends and neighbors. But around 1885, she started selling her Vegetable Compound for women to the general public. The compound came in liquid, pill, or lozenge form and sold for $1. It was accompanied by a four-page brochure with gently worded advice on some of the more intimate concerns of women.

"Do you suffer from 'periodic' female weakness?" inquired a Pinkham advertisement. "Are you troubled by distress of female functional monthly disturbances?"

The solution to these problems, of course, was the Pinkham compound, which offered safe, effective relief. It said so right on the bottle: "Will at all times and under all circumstances act in harmony with the laws that govern the female system. It is invaluable for Young Girls. Pleasant to the taste, efficacious, immediate, and lasting in its effect."

The Lydia E. Pinkham Vegetable Compound or similar preparations can be found in health food stores and some pharmacies. Or you can make it yourself as described above.

GO TO:

PAGE 34 FOR APPALACHIAN COUNTRY STORES
PAGE 282 FOR VERMONT
PAGE 198 FOR MOXIE

POTBELLY STOVES

Dippers, Chewers, and Whittlers with Potbellies

IT'S FASHIONABLE today, and in some cases economical as well, to heat homes with woodstoves. This is especially true in New England, where winter means business and husbands like to prove their manhood by swinging axes and carrying hefty loads of kindling in subzero temperatures. This allows them to think of themselves as the equal of Abe Lincoln, Nanook of the North, Paul Bunyan, or perhaps Babe the Blue Ox. The use of woodstoves is considered by many an environmentally sound heating option, and it appeals to the frugal instincts of New Englanders by keeping down oil, gas, and electric bills. Also, wood is unusually efficient as a fuel in that it warms you twice, once when you chop it and a second time when you burn it.

Unfortunately, missed by many nowadays are the social benefits of heating with wood. The woodstove was once a natural family gathering place, where cold fingers and toes were toasted and mostly true stories told. That function has now been usurped by the television, at the expense of warm fingers and conversation. Woodstoves once served as social magnets for communities as well. Indeed, they may be counted among the reasons small-town Americans have managed to live together in relative harmony.

Traditionally the wood-burning stoves of country stores served as the warm social heart of small communities or, to put it in other terms, as gathering places for the idle. The honor fell to them because dipping, chewing, and whittling were generally frowned upon at churches and town halls. Also, the stores were convenient locations for these activities since they had an inexhaustible supply of chewing tobacco, snuff, and wood from pine boxes waiting to be cut down to nothing, one shaving at a time, with razor-sharp pocketknives.

During the winter, dippers, chewers, and whittlers laid siege to the stove, usually located in the rear of the store. Perched on cane-backed chairs, benches, barrels, and packing crates, they used the stove for target practice, striking it repeatedly with wood chips and tobacco wads. Since very few storekeepers could be described as fastidious, they seldom complained about the abuse of their stoves, often joining in the fun themselves. A stream of spent snuff, however, might draw a sizzling protest from a red-hot stove grate.

It is only fair to note that these daily gatherings around potbellies had a serious purpose: that of constructive political, scientific, and philosophical debate. A single afternoon was often enough to resolve most national and international problems, while also settling several of the more vexing questions concerning the nature of the cosmos.

The whittlers were, perhaps, the most successful woodstove debaters. Shaving curls and angles into a length of pine required close concentration, so it was possible to cut an opponent's argument to pieces without ever looking him in the eye. Of course, talented whittlers could carve unflattering likenesses of anyone unable to recognize the truth when it hit him in the face, and it was always possible for the knife blade to slip and send a chip of wood hurtling toward the nose of a particularly tiresome speaker. Generally, dippers and chewers could not match the firepower of whittlers, since it was considered ill-mannered to spit tobacco juice on another person except, of course, during a presidential election year.

Unfortunately, gatherings of dippers, chewers, and whittlers are a rare sight nowadays, and their rip-roaring debates are seldom heard. In rural communities throughout America, however, there are still a few old-timers who can rightly claim to be experts in the fine art of wasting time beside a woodstove. You may find them occasionally at country stores in the Appalachians, the Midwest, or New England. And if the store's wood-burner isn't putting out enough heat, they may very well decide to warm things up a bit with a tall tale, a snatch of history, or an opinion or two.

A good place to look for chewers, dippers, and whittlers might be the Mast General Store or Todd General Store in North Carolina (see "Appalachian Country Stores," page 34). But your best bet may be to start your own time-wasting tradition by installing a wood-stove. Check with your local hardware store for details and a list of models that might serve well in your home or workshop. More or less an American invention, woodstoves are a joy unto themselves, and it would be a shame to go through life without ever having known the pleasure of stoking one. They are just as much fun as a fireplace, and they provide a lot more heat. If you are really adventurous, you can also install a woodstove, just the thing for baking New England-style beans.

GO TO:
Page 34 for Appalachian Country Stores
Page 44 for Baked Beans
Page 282 for Vermont

PUEBLO POTTERY

Cookware with a Two-Thousand-Year Guarantee

ONE OF the astounding things about the American Southwest is that no matter where you go, someone has likely lived there before. The evidence of human habitation is all around. You see it in the incredibly old walls and buildings scattered here and there in the desert, in artwork scratched into cliff faces, in roads that seem to lead nowhere, in the arrowheads, piles of chipped rock, and bits and pieces of broken pottery that can be found almost everywhere.

The pottery shards are particularly interesting. Even the tiniest shattered pieces offer clues to the worth and beauty of the original. Their smooth, gently curving surfaces are covered with colorful geometric shapes and patterns, loops and swirls, even fanciful little animals and animated human figures. Before they were crushed by time, these ancient pots had been carefully made, artistically decorated, and no doubt lovingly used.

Hordes of amateur archaeologists have scratched their heads in wonder at the walls, the art, and the shards. Who made them? And why did the makers vanish, leaving behind all these marvelous artifacts? Such questions have led to wild stories about alien visitations or powerful desert kingdoms long ago destroyed by calamity. Even some professional archaeologists still say the answers remain shrouded in mystery. But there were no alien spaceships or mighty kingdoms here. As it turns out, there's not even much of a mystery.

The Anasazi, or "ancient ones," who left behind the ruins that intrigue us, were merely the ancestors of today's Hopi and Pueblo tribes. You are likely to meet their descendants walking down the street in Albuquerque, Gallup, or Taos. If you visit the old town square in Santa Fe, you will almost certainly meet them, since every day of the week Pueblo artists spread out offerings there on the bricks in front of the governor's palace. Carefully examine the pottery, and you are likely to find some of the same designs that appear on ancient shards lifted from the dust far out in the desert.

Traditional southwestern pottery should be counted among the wonders of the world. The Pueblo, Hopi, and their ancestors have been making it in more or less the same way for almost two thousand years. They do not use wheels, but rather construct their pottery using coiled ropes of clay. The designs, often applied in earth-tone colors using brushes made from yucca leaves, draw on an artistic heritage as ancient as Imperial Rome or the Athens of Pericles.

Every tribe or village has a style of its own. The pottery of Santa Clara Pueblo is famous for its highly polished black finishes; that of

Acoma, Laguna, and Santa Domingo for its black, brown, red, and orange designs; that of Taos and Picuris for sparkling flecks of mica. At the same time, each potter's work is unique, reflecting an individual as well as a tribal view of life and nature.

Pueblo pottery is art in it purest and truest form. With every lump of clay the potters shape, every bowl they fire in their beehive kilns, every seed jar they decorate with ancient designs, they forge a link with spiritual and cultural traditions that reach back to a time beyond memory. This puts Pueblo potters in close touch with the origins of their civilization—and origin is the wellspring of art.

Collectors have begun to recognize authentic Native American pottery as high art. Nowadays, very fine pots may go for staggering sums (although nothing like what some foolish people are willing to pay for bronzed vacuum cleaners or framed celebrity signatures). If you are looking for "art" that looks as if it may indeed be the work of space aliens, you can find it in big-city "art" shops. On the other hand, if you want something real, earthy, and exquisitely beautiful, try collecting Pueblo pottery. It can be an affordable and deeply satisfying investment. As with all art collecting, you want to make sure that what you are getting is the real thing. For helpful advice, write to Indian Pueblo Cultural Center, 2401 Twelfth Street NW, Albuquerque, NM 87104, or call (505) 843-7270. For general travel information, write to New Mexico Department of Tourism, 491 Old Santa Fe Trail, Santa Fe, NM 87503, or call (505) 827-7400.

GO TO:

PAGE 23 FOR ACOMA, NEW MEXICO
PAGE 169 FOR CHIEF JOSEPH'S LAST STAND
PAGE 205 FOR NAVAJO RUGS
PAGE 223 FOR PENDLETON BLANKETS
PAGE 249 FOR CHIEF SEATTLE'S PLEA
PAGE 251 FOR SEQUOYAH

Q

QUIET SIDE

To the East of Down East

THIS BRIEF geographic aside is not so much about quiet as it is about extremely beautiful scenery and the tastiest lobster on this or any other planet. Mostly it's about the lobster.

A substantial portion of Maine's Mount Desert Island is given over to the wilds and beauties of Acadia National Park, with its red-rock mountains, lakes, and fjords, but there are also towns, business, and houses there. During the summer, when tourists and fair-weather residents march on the coast of Maine, parts of the island begin to resemble midday Manhattan—well there's the suggestion of that, anyway. Despite the crowds and bustle in Bar Harbor, Acadia's gateway city, however, people on the other side of the island always manage to keep their cool. They like to call their corner of the island "the Quiet Side." And so it is.

The Quiet Side consists of a scatter of tiny communities that are not exactly bucolic, but certainly not twenty-first-century or even twentieth-century. For instance, there is Northeast Harbor, where upper-class Brahmin spent summers at the turn of the previous century and their children's children's children now do the same.

Just across Somes Sound from Northeast Harbor is the aptly named Southwest Harbor, home of the Claremont Hotel. The latter clapboard establishment still hosts croquet tournaments and dishes up the sort of elegant getaway that might have charmed the Great Gatsby and his Daisy.

Still more to the southwest, Bass Harbor nestles against a blue-water anchorage bobbing with dozens of workboats painted in a crayon-box array of colors. If quiet is the soul of this place, these vessels are its heart. They are lobster boats.

Now, you can get great lobster in Bar Harbor. You can get it up and down the New England coast. You can order it in New York City or even, if you dare, in San Diego. But you cannot—cannot—find more delicious crustaceans than the ones they pull from the seas off the Quiet Side. The waters here are clear and cold and just right for raising big, happy lobsters. And so, so tasty. With all due respect to a well-meaning culinary and political movement, it is impossible to eat a Quiet Side lobster and remain sympathetically vegan.

You know the best thing about Maine? The Quiet Side on Mount Desert Island is not the only quiet area. All along the coast—it runs mostly east to west, not north to south—are other quiet, out-of-the-way corners where, as they say in Maine, "life is, as it should be." Visit one of these locales sometime and enjoy some of the world's best seafood.

You will find a plethora of information sources on travel in Maine, but here are two you might find especially helpful in your search for a quiet corner. Write to the Bar Harbor Chamber of Commerce, 93 Cottage Street, Box 158, Bar Harbor, ME 04609, or call (207) 288-5103. Write the Camden, Rockport, and Lincolnville Chamber of Commerce, Public Landing, Camden, ME 04843, or call (207) 236-4404.

GO TO:

Page 48 for Bean Suppers
Page 52 for Blueberries
Page 282 for Vermont

AMERICAN QUILTS

The Fabric of Time

QUILTING HAD a long history before it arrived on these shores with the first European immigrants, but in America, quilts and the painstaking process of making them have become a high art. Despite popular myths about quilting during the colonial era, quilts were rare in early America, mostly because homemakers lacked the necessary time and materials. Most early quilts were made by cutting flowers or other motifs from fine printed cloths and then stitching them onto a larger solid fabric or by layering together a solid top and adding a filling and backing. Only a few such fine Colonial quilts have survived.

During the 1840s, American textile plants began to produce large quantities of quality cloth. Meanwhile, the nation's increasing prosperity had begun to spare women from at least some of their daily drudgery, leaving them with the hours and hours needed for quilting. As a result, quilts became the leisure activity of choice for women in small towns and farm communities all across the country. After all, quilting served the practical purpose of helping the family keep warm, but it also served as a creative outlet. Quilts became the canvases on which women stitched their own unique visions, whether bold or subtle, pictorial or geometric, folksy or urbane.

Nowadays, quilting has lost most of its practical purpose, but its artistic appeal remains irresistible. One may find quilts, not just in antique stores and folk art galleries, but in fine art museums. There is no shortage of quilters, either, as quilting clubs and other such organizations have cropped up all over America. These allow aspiring quilters to learn and practice their art as well as to enjoy the social benefits of working together on a quilt.

There are actually two arts associated with quilts: the art of creating them and the art of shopping for them. The latter form allows the less-gifted among us—especially ham-handed males—to get into the act, while providing quilters with a welcome source of income. Be forewarned, however, that it is unwise to indulge in quilt shopping without a healthy balance in your bank account.

Many would agree that the best quilts are still to be found in the small towns and villages of the southern Appalachians, New England, and the Midwest. An expedition to the rugged mountain counties of Georgia, Tennessee, Kentucky, Virginia, or the Carolinas may yield unforgettable experiences, and, if one is very lucky, the quilt of a lifetime. This extraordinarily beautiful and soulful region is replete with quilters who learned their art from their mothers or their mothers' mothers' mothers. You may very well see examples of their work hanging from ordinary clotheslines or even draped across some bushes. But when you ask the price, do not expect to hear some discount house figure like $49.95. Even—perhaps especially—in rural America, you get what you pay for.

An excellent source of additional information is the National Quilters Association, P.O. Box 393, Ellicott City, MD 21041-0393; call (410) 461-5733.

GO TO:

PAGE 34 FOR APPALACHIAN COUNTRY STORES
PAGE 205 FOR NAVAJO RUGS
PAGE 228 FOR PUEBLO POTTERY
PAGE 282 FOR VERMONT

R

RADIO FLYER

Your Little Red Wagon

MOST SMALL children feel their lives are incomplete without a wagon. Kids want wagons for the very sensible reason that they are so practical. They can be used to pull cats, dogs, little sisters, little brothers, bats, balls, baby dolls, and many other worthwhile things. In a pinch, as when parents make a fuss about the chores, they can be pressed into service hauling scattered toys to the closet or broken stuff to collection bins. They are also quite versatile and can be transformed easily into racecars, doll carts, covered wagons, picnic baskets, spaceships, battle tanks, or delivery trucks. In other words, wagons play about the same role for very short people that bicycles will when they grow tall or that cars will when they grow even taller. For a tyke, a wagon puts things in focus.

Since they are much more than mere toys, wagons should be made of durable materials such as solid wood or steel. And, if at all possible, they should be red. Unless you work for Mary Kay Cosmetics, you wouldn't want to drive a pink Cadillac, right? Well, not many kids would want to pull a pink wagon, either, let alone a turquoise one.

No doubt, you had a little red wagon when you were kid. It was probably sitting out under a tree gathering rust the last time you saw it. Don't you wish you had it now? If you did, you could fix it up and give it to one of your own children. That is probably not possible, but the alternative is even better. You can give them a spanking new wagon almost exactly like the one you used to own!

The Radio Flyer Company is still in business, and still makes those practically indestructible red steel wagons we all remember.

Antonio Pasin started the company in 1917 using a one-room work-shop as a factory. Pasin's tiny company grew up quickly and in 1927 introduced its all-steel wagons. Within three years, it had become the world's largest producer of children's coaster wagons. The company celebrated by building a forty-five-foot-tall "Coaster Boy" wagon for the 1934 Chicago World's Fair. Soon kids everywhere wanted a bright red Radio Flyer, and even during the Great Depression, their parents usually found a way to buy one for them.

Today, the company is owned and operated by a third generation of Pasins. Perhaps that's one reason Radio Flyers still show traces of the streamlined deco styling they picked up during the 1930s. And with their seamless bodies, rolled edges, and molded wheels, the steel wagons are just as tough as ever. You can count on one to last indefinitely and produce memories that last forever.

For more information on Radio Flyer wagons and other products made by the Radio Flyer Company, call (800) 621-7613.

GO TO:
PAGE 181 FOR LIONEL MODEL RAILROAD
PAGE 236 FOR RAGGEDY ANN
PAGE 247 FOR CHARLES M. SCHULZ

RAGGEDY ANN

Marcella's Floppy Girl

NOTHING MADE of plastic will ever beat an old-fashioned Raggedy Ann. You can drag her around by the leg, the arm, or the hair; you can whack her against bedposts; you can cram her down into drawers or toy boxes, and she just pops right back for more. You can sit on her, with very little harm done to either the doll or you. Even the family dog is unlikely to do much irreparable damage to a Raggedy Ann. And, best of all, she can stand up—or flop down—to the overwhelming love of a three-year-old.

Raggedy Anns and Andys have been around since World War I, bringing happiness to countless little girls and no few little boys. Ironically, the story of these dolls has a tragic beginning. In 1915, young Marcella Gruella lay dying at her home in Chicago, apparently from the effects of a poorly administered smallpox vaccination. To comfort her, her family gave her an old rag doll they had found in the attic. Her father, political cartoonist John Gruella, told Marcella all sorts of stories about the adventures the old doll had lived through.

A few years after his daughter died, Gruella wrote a collection of his Raggedy Ann stories as a memorial to Marcella. Many of those who read the stories wanted a doll to accompany them, so Gruella designed one. The Marshall Field's department store in Chicago was the first to sell Gruella's dolls. Eventually, Ann's companion, Andy, joined her at Field's and on toy store shelves around the country.

Over the years, several different manufacturers have produced Raggedy Anns and Andys, and they are still being made and sold today. Of course, there are hundreds of imitations and variations on the Raggedy Ann theme. Probably parents are the only ones who care whether the dolls are authentic Raggedies. The little folks who love them only want a doll likely to love them back.

Many of the Raggedy Anns today's adults remember were produced by the L. L. Knickerbocker Company during the 1960s, and classic Raggedies patterned after dolls of this period are once again available. For information, write to L. L. Knickerbocker, 30055 Comercio, Rancho Santa Margarita, CA 92688, or call (800) 779-5335.

Not surprisingly, antique Anns and Andys, some of which date all the way back to the time of Gruella's original designs, are hot items among doll collectors. Some are worth thousands. As with other types of collecting, do not venture into the doll market unless you are well informed. A number of guides available in bookstores or libraries offer valuable advice on doll collecting.

GO TO:

PAGE 181 FOR LIONEL MODEL RAILROAD

PAGE 235 FOR RADIO FLYER

PAGE 247 FOR CHARLES M. SCHULZ

RAINBOW TROUT

The Flavor of Freedom

HOW LUCKY we are that America is a land of so many rainbows. All are beautiful, and some are very good to eat. Of course, you've got to catch them first, and that is not always so easy.

Our country is very fortunate, indeed, to be the one and only home of the rainbow trout. Marked by a subtle rainbow stripe from head to tail, these prized sport fish are easy to identify, but anglers know them by the forceful way they take the line. Solid strikers who dazzle fishermen with breathtaking leaps and fight like the very dickens, rainbows are more fun to catch than, well, anything but another and bigger rainbow. And after you have caught them, you get to eat them for breakfast, lunch, or dinner—it doesn't matter. Mark Twain said the rainbow trout he had eaten were "more delicious than the less illegal forms of sin."

Known to those who dare to attempt the pronunciation as the *Oncorhynchus mykiss*, rainbow trout are related to salmon. Some rainbows live in landlocked lakes and streams; others run to the sea like their salmon cousins. The latter are sometimes called steelheads. Landlocked rainbows average one to three pounds, although patient anglers have pulled in specimens weighing ten or more pounds. No fisherman is ever ashamed of a one-pound rainbow trout, however. It will still make a heavenly meal. Steelheads grow much larger, of course, and the record catch for one of these is a whopping forty-two pounds. How would you like to eat one like that for breakfast?

Originally, rainbows were found only on the west side of the Continental Divide, but they are now pulled from rivers, streams, and lakes throughout the U.S. and Canada. To the delight of anglers and all others who dream of baked fresh trout and potatoes, there has been a rainbow revolution. State hatcheries started seeding rainbows far and wide about a half century ago, and nowadays you can catch them almost anywhere—if you are good enough. Arkansas operates one of the nation's most successful hatchery programs, allowing the state to boast some of the best trout-fishing waters on the planet.

West Virginia, Colorado, Idaho, Montana, and other mountainous states also have excellent hatchery programs and offer fine fishing.

According to the legend, rainbows lead to gold. Many of the prospectors who poured into California during the gold rush never found any glittering metal in the clear, rushing streams of the Sierra. What they saw instead were rainbows. So, if they didn't strike it rich, at least they had some good eating—that is, if they knew a little of the art and science of angling. Fishing has nearly always been more rewarding than prospecting. That is especially true in the Sierras now that most of the gold is gone. Happily, the rainbows are still there.

For information on guides and lodges that cater to fishermen, call Kaufmann's Fly Fishing Expeditions at (800) 442-4359. If you are conservation-minded and would like to help keep America's streams clear-running and filled with rainbow trout, contact the Izaak Walton League at 707 Conservation Lane, Gaithersburg, MD 20878, or call (301) 548-0150. Named for the seventeenth-century English sportsman/conservationist who wrote the literary classic *The Compleat Angler,* the league fights to protect our country's soil, air, woods, waters, and wildlife. Not long after it was founded during the 1920s, President Calvin Coolidge named the Izaak Walton League to lead the nation's first water pollution inventory.

GO TO:
PAGE 294 FOR GRAY WOLF
PAGE 143 FOR GRIZZLY BEAR
PAGE 200 FOR JOHN MUIR
PAGE 213 FOR OLD TOWN CANOES
PAGE 311 FOR YELLOWSTONE PARK

REDWOOD TREES

As Old as the Pyramids and Almost as Tall

THE OLDEST of them were tiny sprigs pushing up through a mat of needles on the forest floor about the time Ramses II was building all those monuments in Egypt—more than three thousand years ago. They are among the most ancient living things on this earth—and also among the biggest. Many tower three hundred feet or more into the western sky. A 250-foot-tall specimen is considered to be of modest stature.

The California redwoods, also known as sequoias, are an American treasure. Given their age and magnificence, however, they belong not just to us, but to the entire world. People travel from all over the planet just to see them, and it is easy to see why.

A walk through a grove of sequoias is an experience like no other. It places us—and life itself—in proper scale, both in terms of size and time. It takes us back to a primordial age, to the era of the dinosaurs and even before. The two sequoia species date back more than one hundred million years, and they did in fact once tower over the tyrannosaurus and triceratops. While we may think that distant time to have been violent and threatening, the sequoia forests of today suggest that it was surprisingly gentle. Covered with a thick carpet of needles, the land is lush with ferns and small shrubs. The forest floor is a patchwork of deep shade and luminous sunlight, and it is so quiet that you can almost hear the trees growing and the time passing. There is peace to be found here, an ageless sense of being. Standing beside these grand (a better word for them is *sacred*) trees has the inevitable effect of shrinking the ego, not so much because they make us feel small as because they help us see we are a part of something bigger than ourselves.

There are two very different species of California sequoias: the coastal redwoods (*Sequoia sempervirens*) and the giant sequoias (*Sequoiadendron giganteum*) of the Sierra Nevada Mountains. A third species, the dawn redwoods (*Metasequoia glyptostroboides*) is found in small numbers in central China. The coastal redwoods are taller and are found within a few miles of the Pacific—only as far inland as the fog is likely to reach. Although not quite as tall as their coastal cousins, the mountain sequoias have much bigger trunks and grow only in the Sierra foothills, hundreds of miles from the ocean.

Giant sequoias are unbelievably big. They can grow to more than three hundred feet tall, and their trunks may reach a diameter of more than forty feet—wider than many roads. Even the reddish bark may be almost three feet thick. The largest is estimated to weigh more than 2.5 million pounds. Coastal redwoods, on the other hand, top out at better than 360 feet, with trunk diameters of more than twenty feet. The biggest may weigh more than 1.6 million pounds.

The trees are covered with a shaggy bark that is soft and yielding to the touch, like an old, familiar coat. The bark does not burn easily. This, in part, may account for the sequoia's extraordinary ability to survive the raging forest fires that sometimes sweep the California hills. Some trees show the black scars of fires that burned hundreds of years ago. Chemicals in the bark and the wood make them inhospitable to most insects.

While sequoias may live three thousand or more years, they, like all other living things, do eventually die. Sequoias usually meet their end in one of only two ways. Incredibly, these huge trees have very shallow roots, and their long lives are spent in a precarious balancing act involving thousands of tons of sap and wood. As a result, they are vulnerable to high winds that, blowing off the Pacific, may send them thundering down. It would never do to be standing on the wrong side of them when this happens.

The other, more likely way for a redwood to perish is to be cut down by loggers. Of the approximately two million acres of virgin redwood groves that once covered the California coast, less than 5 percent, or about eighty-six thousand acres, remain. Of that, about eighty thousand acres of the old trees are now protected on state and national parklands. The other six thousand acres—about ten square miles now in private hands—are threatened. Unless something is done to save them, the old trees will be cut and hauled away on trucks to become planters and siding for hot tubs.

The giant sequoias in the mountains have been more lucky. They were never numerous, and more than a third of them were felled before action was taken to stop the cutting. The other two-thirds remain, however, in about seventy-five separate groves.

Because of their size, sequoias do not photograph well, and while they are celebrated by some fine documentaries and photo books, the only way to fully appreciate them is to visit redwood country. Isolated redwood groves can be found along the California coast from Big Sur north to the Oregon border. The most extensive and beautiful of these trees are located in Redwood National Park, Prairie Creek Redwoods State Park, Del Norte Coast Redwoods State Park, and Jedediah Smith State Park, all in Del Norte and Humbolt Counties, California. For information, write to Redwood National and State Parks, 1111 Second Street, Crescent City, CA 95531, or call (707) 464-6101. When you go, be prepared to walk— there is simply no other way to enjoy them—and please, please leave the land as you found it.

Some eight miles up Redwood Creek, in Redwood National Park near Eureka and Orick, stands the tallest tree in the world. Discovered and measured by the National Geographic Society, it soars 367 feet. The name given it by the awed National Geographic naturalists is simply "The Tall Tree."

Giant sequoia groves are located in Sequoia and Kings Canyon National Parks in the Sierras. Follow Highway 180 into Sequoia, or Highway 198 into Kings Canyon. For information, write to Superintendent, Sequoia and Kings Canyon National Parks, Three Rivers, CA 93271, or call (559) 565-3341. For twenty-four-hour road and weather information—essential in the Sierras—call (559) 565-3351.

GO TO:
PAGE 294 FOR GRAY WOLF
PAGE 143 FOR GRIZZLY BEAR
PAGE 200 FOR JOHN MUIR
PAGE 251 FOR SEQUOYAH

REVELL-MONOGRAM MODELS

More Authentic than the Original

GENERATIONS OF American children have grown up with the notion that the true essence of almost any object can be captured successfully in plastic or balsa wood. All it takes is a little patience and a dab or two of glue.

Since the mid- to late 1940s, when the originally separate Revell and Monogram companies started selling model kits, American homes have undergone a startling transformation. Entire fleets of ships, perfectly reproduced in nearly every visual detail, have replaced the dishes in china cabinets. Saturn-5 booster rockets, lunar landers, and Mars probes have taken up residence on bedside tables, and flashy red Corvettes and Indy racecars have edged out the books and bowling trophies on library shelves.

It all began in 1945, when Monogram's founders marketed their first balsa-wood models of World War II ships. A few years later, a small California company called Revell introduced its meticulously detailed all-plastic model kits. With an hour or two of snapping and gluing, you could create an exactingly detailed scale model of the Maxwell car made famous by comedian Jack Benny, the War of 1812 frigate USS *Constitution,* or a battle-ready aircraft carrier, complete with a squadron of jet fighters.

Monogram soon followed Revell's lead into plastics, and before long, model spaceships, tanks, destroyers, jet bombers, German V-1 rockets, battleships, and sports cars were filling mantlepieces and garage shelves not just in every neighborhood in America but all over the world. These miniatures even found their way into the movies, often as stand-ins for the real thing. One rather obscure Japanese science-fiction movie (sorry, but we must omit the title) featured a Revell rocket. Someone forgot to remove the Revell ensign, and the words "Revell Authentic Kit" could be clearly seen on one of its fins.

Since 1950, very few American males have grown to adulthood without building at least one plastic-model ship, airplane, rocket, or automobile. Most have put together dozens, and some have cluttered their rooms and distressed their mothers with hundreds of models. Little girls and their fathers also have been known to take up model building. In fact, when a father buys a model for his kid, it's hard to say who is happier.

After decades of competing with each another, the Revell and Monogram companies merged in 1986. Today, they turn out more ships, planes, and cars than all the shipyards, aircraft factories, and auto manufacturers on the planet. Of course there are other companies selling fine kits nowadays, but the Revell-Monogram models remain among the best. Theirs are the names and the models we grew up with.

Revell-Monogram models can be found in almost any toy store or hobby shop. For more information, call the Revell-Monogram office of consumer affairs at (800) 833-3570, or see new models online at www.revell-monogram.com.

GO TO:

PAGE 50 FOR JACK BENNY

PAGE 129 FOR FRISBEES

PAGE 181 FOR LIONEL MODEL RAILROAD

PAGE 193 FOR MODEL T FORD

PAGE 235 FOR RADIO FLYER

S

SANTA FE, NEW MEXICO

City of Fire and Mud

EARLY IN the evening on the Friday after every Labor Day, throngs gather in Santa Fe's Fort Marcy Park. Blankets are spread on the grass, fruit and slices of cheese and nachos are passed from hand to hand, and you can hear wine corks popping like firecrackers at a Fourth of July fireworks display. In fact, there will be fireworks later, but first come the anticipation and the good cheer. This is an especially congenial crowd, as well it might be, since these people have come to see their cares and sorrows go up in flames.

About the time darkness sets in over the high desert, someone—nobody ever knows who—shouts, "Burn him!" Others are of the same opinion. "Burn him!" they say. "Burn him!" Slowly but surely, the crowd picks up the chant: "Burn him! Burn him! Burn him!"

Throughout the evening, the complaints and moans of the intended victim can be heard pouring through speakers strategically positioned around the park. You might imagine people would feel sorry for him, but no one ever does. "Burn him!" is all anyone has to say on the matter.

Eventually, a dancer in a flaming-red costume appears bearing a flaming torch. At this, the victim's cries grow even louder and more plaintive. His concern is understandable, since he is made entirely of paper. A forty-foot-tall papier-mâché puppet named Zozobra is the victim, and he represents the spirit of doom and gloom. Before the evening is over, he will be reduced to a pile of ashes, and all his gloominess vanquished to make way for the joy of the annual La Fiesta de Santa Fe.

The oldest continually observed festival in the United States, La Fiesta has been celebrated since 1712. It commemorates the reconquest of New Mexico by Don Diego De Vargas in 1692 (the Indians had driven the Spanish out of the colony twelve years earlier in the great Pueblo Revolt of 1680). However, today's Fiesta-goers are much more interested in food, wine, and dance than in conquistadors. Theirs is a celebration of life and of things Santa Fe.

After all, Santa Fe is a city worth celebrating. There is not another place like it on the planet. Where else could you sleep in an adobe (mud brick) hotel? Fill up at an adobe gas station? Eat a double-cheese pepperoni in an adobe pizzeria? Shop for computer software in an adobe electronics store? The entire city apparently is made of mud, or at least made to look that way. One has to wonder what would happen if they ever had several days of northwestern-style rains around here. Would the whole magical town just melt away? Of course not, and anyway, Santa Fe gets only about fourteen inches of rain a year. Zozobra has little or no hope that a freak cloudburst will put him out once he has caught fire.

New Mexicans and Santa Feans have made do with a smattering of rainfall for a long time. Despite the desert conditions, Pueblo farmers have survived in the region for thousands of years. Although not nearly as old as some of the nearby Pueblo Indian villages, Santa Fe is, nonetheless, older than any other American city. Founded in 1607, thirteen years before the Pilgrims landed at Plymouth, Santa Fe was capital of Spanish New Mexico for more than two centuries and remains the capital of the state to this day.

Built in 1610, the Palace of the Governors served as the administrative center of New Mexico until the 1860s. The oldest public building in the United States, it still stands on the old plaza downtown. Zebulon Pike was interrogated as a spy at the palace after his capture by the Spaniards in 1807. Territorial governor Lew Wallace wrote the novel *Ben Hur* while serving his term at the palace from 1878 to 1881. The covered walkway in front of the palace is an excellent place to shop for pottery, jewelry, and other Native American wares. Almost every day, artisans spread out their offerings on blankets along the front of the palace.

Several excellent restaurants are located on or near the plaza. You may find the Mexican food here the most delicious you have ever tasted—also the hottest. Hot enough, in fact, to drive away the gloom.

For travel information, contact the Santa Fe Convention and Visitors Bureau at P.O. Box 909, Santa Fe, NM 87504, or call (800) 777-2489. The bureau is located at 201 Marcy Street, one block north of the plaza.

GO TO:

PAGE 23 FOR ACOMA, NEW MEXICO
PAGE 102 FOR COYOTE
PAGE 205 FOR NAVAJO RUGS
PAGE 228 FOR PUEBLO POTTERY

CHARLES M. SCHULZ

Charlie Brown's Peanuts Gallery

THEY ARE the kids we used to play with in the sandy back lot, and we know every one of them. First there is Snoopy, notable because it is not every neighborhood dog that can walk, think out loud, write terrible novels, and fly biplanes. An extroverted beagle with a Walter Mitty complex, he is totally fearless except when confronted by the cat next door. Then there is Lucy, the bossy fussbudget who wins her arguments with overwhelming displays of illogic. And Woodstock, who speaks in a language made up entirely of exclamation points. And Linus with his security blanket. And Schroeder with his fascination for Beethoven. And Peppermint Patty with her freckles. And Marcie, Patty's constant and obedient companion. And finally, of course, there is Charlie Brown, the round-faced kid destined to go through life pulling a little red wagon, never having won a baseball game or successfully kicked a football (Lucy will see to that).

Then there is that other Charlie, the guy with the pen and ink. We never see his face in the comics, but his innocent view of childhood and of life in America is always there. Born Charles M. Schulz on November 26, 1922, he wanted to become a cartoonist from the day he first read a newspaper comic strip. Some of his earliest and best memories were of sitting with his father, a St. Paul, Minnesota,

barber, and leafing through the Sunday comics. His first art education came from a correspondence course he took during his teens.

After he got out of the army following World War II, Schulz held
a variety of jobs. One of them was as a teacher in an art school, where
he worked with one man named Charlie Brown and another named
Linus. These friends, along with the Lucys, Pattys, and Marcies the
artist met here and there, would eventually have their names immor-
talized in color Sunday supplements published all across America.

Schulz's big break as a cartoonist came in 1947, when he sold a
daily feature called *Li'l Folks* to the St. Paul Press. Three years later,
he landed a United Feature Syndicate contract for a daily strip with
characters similar to those in *Li'l Folks*. The syndicate named the
strip *Peanuts* and as a test placed it in seven dailies, where it proved
an immediate hit. The syndicate knew they had a winner on their
hands, and so did Schulz. "I'll be drawing this for the rest of my
life," he told himself, a prophecy he was destined to fulfill.

Schulz penned his last *Peanuts* cartoon just a few weeks before
he died in February 2000. By that time, he had drawn more than sixteen thousand separate *Peanuts* strips. "Good grief, Charlie Brown!"

Reprints of *Peanuts* strips can still be read and enjoyed in most
newspapers. Also available is a wide assortment of books, video, and
software adaptations, as well as a never-ending supply of cards,
dolls, toys, and other merchandise. Animated television specials such
as *A Charlie Brown Christmas* have been shown on television since the
1960s. Although Schulz never did the animating himself, he did produce stories and storyboards to guide the studio animators.

Those interested in learning more about Charlie Brown and
Charles Schulz or *Peanuts* collectibles should contact the Peanuts Collector Club online at www.peanutscollectorclub.com. The club publishes a quarterly newsletter and makes available an array of *Peanuts*
products and merchandise. Annual membership dues are $20.

GO TO:
PAGE 21 FOR HANK AARON
PAGE 45 FOR BATMAN AND ROBIN
PAGE 134 FOR RUBE GOLDBERG
PAGE 235 FOR RADIO FLYER

CHIEF SEATTLE'S PLEA

How Can You Sell the Sky?

IN 1854, the U.S. government asked the Suquamish tribe to sell its ancestral lands in what is now Washington State. As with most such dealings between Native American peoples and federal authorities, this request was actually a demand, likely to be backed up by well-armed troops. Speaking for himself, his people, and for all who regard the earth as sacred, Seattle, the famed chief of the Suquamish, replied as follows.

The president in Washington sends word that he wishes to buy our land. But how can you buy or sell the sky? the land? If we do not own the freshness of the air and the sparkle of the water, how can you buy them?

Every part of the earth is sacred to my people. Every shining pine needle, every sandy shore, every mist in the dark woods, every meadow, every humming insect. All are holy in the memory and experience of my people.

We know the sap which courses through the trees as we know the blood that courses through our veins. We are part of the earth and it is part of us. The perfumed flowers are our sisters. The bear, the deer, the great eagle, these are our brothers. The rocky crests, the dew in the meadow, the body heat of the pony, and man all belong to the same family.

The shining water that moves in the streams and rivers is not just water, but the blood of our ancestors. If we sell you our land, you must remember that it is sacred. Each glossy reflection in the clear waters of the lakes tells of events and memories in the life of my people. The water's murmur is the voice of my father's father.

The rivers are our brothers. They quench our thirst. They carry our canoes and feed our children. So you must give the rivers the kindness that you would give any brother.

If we sell you our land, remember that the air is precious to us, that the air shares its spirit with all the life that it supports. The wind that gave our grandfather his first breath also received his last sigh. The wind also gives our children the spirit of life. So if we sell our land, you must keep it apart and sacred, as a place where man can go to taste the wind that is sweetened by the meadow flowers.

Will you teach your children what we have taught our children? That the earth is our mother? What befalls the earth befalls all the sons of the earth.

This we know: The earth does not belong to man, man belongs to the earth. All things are connected like the blood that unites us all. Man did not weave the web of life, he is merely a strand in it. Whatever he does to the web, he does to himself.

One thing we know: Our God is also your God. The earth is precious to him and to harm the earth is to heap contempt on its creator.

Your destiny is a mystery to us. What will happen when the buffalo are all slaughtered? The wild horses tamed? What will happen when the secret corners of the forest are heavy with the scent of many men and the view of the ripe hills is blotted with talking wires? Where will the thicket be? Gone! Where will the eagle be. Gone! And what is it to say good-bye to the swift pony and the hunt? The end of living and the beginning of survival.

When the last red man has vanished with this wilderness, and his memory is only the shadow of a cloud moving across the prairie, will these shores and forests still be here? Will there be any of the spirit of my people left?

We love this earth as a newborn loves its mother's heartbeat. So, if we sell you our land, love it as we have loved it. Care for it as we have cared for it. Hold in your mind the memory of the land as it was when you receive it. Preserve the land for all children, and love it, as God loves us.

As we are part of the land, you too are part of the land. This earth is precious to us. It is also precious to you.

One thing we know—there is only one God. No man, be he Red man or White man, can be apart. We are brothers after all.

Chief Seattle's letter, as you see it above, was probably pieced together by others from a number of things the Suquamish leader said. He was known for his eloquent oratory. Likely, it has been edited and rewritten so often over the years that it bears only a vague resemblance to the chief's original words. Even so, it beautifully expresses a reverence for land and nature commonly held by Native American peoples. When confronted by miners, settlers, or government officials wanting to acquire land, eighteenth- and nineteenth-century tribal leaders often replied, as Chief Seattle did, that the earth was sacred and the notion of buying or selling it was completely alien to them. This attitude, if not the letter itself, is an indelible part of our national heritage.

Increasingly, Americans are learning to put our country's vast natural resources to profitable use while preserving the natural beauty and integrity of the land. Every day, conservationists are finding new ways to work with business and vice versa. Particularly adept at bringing the interests of business and nature together is a national organization called The Nature Conservancy. For information, write to TNC, 1815 North Lynn Street, Arlington, VA 22209, or call (703) 841-5300.

GO TO:

PAGE 64 FOR AMERICAN BUFFALO
PAGE 169 FOR CHIEF JOSEPH'S LAST STAND
PAGE 200 FOR JOHN MUIR
PAGE 239 FOR REDWOOD TREES
PAGE 251 SEQUOYAH (BELOW)

SEQUOYAH

The Man Who Made Leaves Talk

IN ALL of known history, no one has ever done it. None, that is, except for the Cherokee warrior Sequoyah. He invented a written language entirely by himself.

Born in the 1770s, Sequoyah was the son of a white frontiersman and a Cherokee woman of the Paint Clan. Although raised a Cherokee, he was occasionally known by the English name George Gist, given him by his father. Steeped in the traditions of his tribe, Sequoyah was fascinated by the ways of his father's people.

Early in his life, Sequoyah demonstrated an ability with words and language. While he had little or no formal education, he could speak several languages fluently. His grasp of English made him a consummate negotiator in the fur trade.

Having fought alongside Andrew Jackson in the Creek War of 1813–14, Sequoyah became convinced that in order to survive, his tribe must adopt the ways of the whites. In fact, this process was already well under way. The Cherokees were not nomads, but rather settled farmers who lived in villages and towns. They had begun to dress and do business in ways not unlike those of their white neighbors. On tribal lands in the southern Appalachians, they established a government with its own constitution and legislature. Their capital was the well-planned city of New Echota in north Georgia. Its carefully surveyed streets were dominated by government buildings and lined with Cherokee-run businesses.

Sequoyah decided that his contribution to this developing Cherokee society would be a written form of the tribal language. Even though Sequoyah could not read or write English, he understood the importance and power of the written word. He somehow possessed the genius to grasp the phonetic principles on which most written languages are based. Borrowing symbols from an English grammar book and making up others as he needed them, Sequoyah devised a syllabary of eighty-five characters representing all the combinations of vowel and consonant sounds in the Cherokee language.

Creation of the syllabary took many years. Some of Sequoyah's friends and family said he was crazy and accused him of practicing witchcraft. Sequoyah tried, often in vain, to explain what he was doing. "It is said that in ancient times, when writing first began, a man named Moses made marks on stone," he told them, pointing to his own symbols. "That will be writing and can be understood."

Sequoyah continued his work. When it was completed in 1821, he demonstrated it for astonished tribal leaders, who referred to his pages as "talking leaves." News of Sequoyah's accomplishment quickly spread throughout the tribe, and within months, people in every Cherokee town and village were learning to read and write.

By 1828, the Cherokees were publishing their own newspaper, the *Phoenix*, on a hand press in New Echota. Printed and distributed weekly, it was the first newspaper ever published by a Native American people.

Ironically, it was also in 1828 that gold was discovered in the north Georgia mountains. This set off a mad rush similar in intensity, if not in size, to the one that would occur twenty years later in California. An army of prospectors poured onto Cherokee lands, and miners began to demand that the tribe be relocated to the Indian Territories in the West. In the midst of this crisis, Sequoyah was sent to Washington to argue the case for his people involving the Cherokee rights to their ancestral lands guaranteed to them by treaty. Why shouldn't they be allowed to stay? Sequoyah and other tribal leaders were respectfully received but ultimately ignored. Finally, in 1835, President Andrew Jackson ordered the removal of the Cherokees, and the tribe set out for Oklahoma on a long march that would come to be known as "The Trail of Tears." More than four thousand Cherokees died along the way.

Sequoyah survived the march and lived in Oklahoma until his death in 1843. He is remembered to this day by his own people and others as history's greatest Cherokee. With such a hero to admire, it is not surprising that today the Cherokees have the highest literacy rate in America. Nor is it surprising that they enjoy the highest standard of living of any Native American people.

The Cherokees have not been the only ones to honor Sequoyah. In one of the most astounding tributes ever paid to an individual, the great redwood trees in California were named after him. Both the tall coastal redwoods and the giant mountain species are called Sequoia (see page 239). The name is appropriate. Written language resembles a tree in that it has roots, branches, and a solid trunk of grammatical structure. And like the ancient redwoods, it can live almost forever.

The New Echota Historic Site, near Calhoun in north Georgia, is a state park dedicated to the memory of Sequoyah and the old Cherokee capital. The site includes a replica of the original Cherokee Supreme Court Building and print shop, where *The Phoenix* was once published. For information, write to New Echota Historic Site, 1211 Chatsworth Highway, Calhoun, GA 30701, or call (706) 624-1321.

The heart of the Cherokee's original eastern homeland is now protected by the Smoky Mountain National Park. Visitors to this land of tall, misty peaks and lush forests have no trouble seeing what the Cherokees loved about it. Embracing some of the oldest mountains on the planet, the park stretches over 517,000 acres of North Carolina and Tennessee and offers some of the best hiking and stream fishing to be found in the East. For information, write to Great Smoky Mountains National Park, 107 Park Headquarters Road, Gatlinburg, TN 37738, or call (865) 436-1200.

Along the southern border of the Great Smoky Mountain Park is a small reservation, established during the nineteenth century for a scattering of Cherokees who remained behind after the infamous "removal." During the summer, vacationers throng to the reservation, which has become something of a tourists' mecca. Shops in the reservation town of Cherokee offer beautiful Native American craft items as well as made-in-Asia tomahawks, headdresses, and arrowheads. The most valuable thing you'll find, however, can be seen in the faces of the Cherokees who still live and work on the reservation—a distant glimpse of the warrior/linguist Sequoyah.

GO TO:

PAGE 169 FOR CHIEF JOSEPH'S LAST STAND
PAGE 200 FOR JOHN MUIR
PAGE 223 FOR PENDLETON BLANKETS
PAGE 249 FOR CHIEF SEATTLE'S PLEA

STATUE OF LIBERTY

Mother of Exiles

FOR THE French, it's the Eiffel Tower; for the British, Buckingham Palace; for the Chinese, the Forbidden City; for the Russians, Red Square; for the Egyptians, the Pyramids; for the Greeks, the Acropolis. Every nation has a symbol, a place, or a structure that seems to sum up things, that says to one and all, "This is who we are." So what is that symbol for Americans? The White House? The Capitol dome? Pikes Peak? The bald eagle? No way. For us, it is a lighthouse.

The Statue of Liberty has been holding her torch high in the air for more than 110 years. Yes, she is a lighthouse, and from the beginning was intended to serve as one; to this day ships follow her beacon into the port of New York. But her light is and has always been far more than a convenience for harbor pilots. Her lamp is meant as an invitation and a proclamation that this nation is different from any other on the planet—precisely because we so openly welcome others.

Let there be no doubt about what this means, about what the Statue of Liberty represents. Anyone who has doubts should visit the statue—an outing every American should take at least once—and read the Emma Lazarus poem engraved on the pedestal. Here is what it says:

The New Colossus

Not like the brazen giant of Greek fame,
With conquering limbs astride from land to land;
Here at our sea-washed, sunset gates shall stand
A mighty woman with a torch, whose flame
Is the imprisoned lightning, and her name
Mother of Exiles. From her beacon-hand
Glows world-wide welcome; her mild eyes command
The air-bridged harbor that twin cities frame.
"Keep ancient lands, your storied pomp!" cries she
With silent lips. "Give me your tired, your poor,
Your huddled masses yearning to breathe free,
The wretched refuse of your teeming shore.
Send these, the homeless, tempest-tossed to me.
I lift my lamp beside the golden door!"

Fittingly, the Statue of Liberty was a gift from the French, who were so helpful back during the Revolution when we drove off the redcoats and set about deciding what sort of nation this was to be. Lady Liberty's light first switched on in the imagination of Edouard de Laboulaye, a nineteenth-century French historian who admired the U.S. and its political institutions. Laboulaye suggested the French give the Americans a monument to commemorate the 1876 centennial of the signing of the Declaration of Independence and in recognition of the long friendship between the two peoples. The idea caught on, and the project was placed in the hands of Frederic Auguste Bartholdi, a renowned Parisian sculptor. Bartholdi envisioned a colossal statue at the entrance of New York harbor welcoming the people of the world with the torch of liberty.

Originally, the statue was to have been in place by the end of 1876. However, the privately raised funds for its construction were slow in coming. What is more, the 150-foot-tall, 450,000-pound statue confronted Bartholdi with technical obstacles he had not anticipated. How could he get his enormous lady to stand upright and not topple over in a high wind? He eventually would be forced to call on Alexandre Gustave Eiffel, the engineer who would later build the Eiffel Tower, for structural advice. To solve Bartholdi's problems, Eiffel designed a massive iron pylon and secondary skeletal framework to keep the lady permanently on her feet.

The project was delayed even further by a lack of funds in the U.S., which was responsible for preparing the statue's pedestal on Bedloe Island. A newspaper editorial campaign pushed by publisher Joseph Pulitzer, for whom journalism's Pulitzer Prizes are named, finally shamed the public into contributing the necessary money. With the pedestal complete, the French frigate *Isere* arrived in New York with the statue, which had been separated into 350 pieces and packed in crates. By October of 1886, the big lady was back together again and ready for her dedication. The ceremony took place on Bedloe Island—eventually renamed Liberty Island—on October 28, 1886, with President Grover Cleveland officially accepting the statue on behalf of the United States. "We will not forget that Liberty has made her home here," he said.

With a 150-foot-tall, green-tinted giant of a woman to remind us, how could we forget? Incidentally, her official name is the Statue of Liberty Enlightening the World. Perhaps it is not too much to think that is exactly what she does, sometimes at least. She can certainly enlighten us Americans, if we let her, by reminding us of who we really are. And as for the rest of you folks huddled somewhere out there on the planet, are there any among you who long for liberty? If so, then we welcome you to join our nation of open-spirited and independent-minded people. There are no racial or religious requirements. All you have to do is want to be an American and to unite with us in our quest to build a better world free of superstition and the chains of the past. We'll leave the light on for you.

Here are some fun facts about the Statue of Liberty:

Height from the base to the torch: 151 feet
Height above the ground: 305 feet
Length of the hand: 16 feet
Length of the index finger: 8 feet
Thickness of the head: 10 feet
Length of the right arm: 42 feet
Width of the mouth: 3 feet
Length of the tablet: 23 feet

To reach the crown, you have to climb 354 steps, about enough to get you to the top of a twenty-story building. It can be a queasy climb, since in a high wind the statue may sway from side to side as much as three inches. The crown has twenty-five windows, which symbolize the twenty-five gemstones found in the earth, and affords a spectacular view of New York Harbor. The seven rays in the crown represent the earth's seven oceans. The statue's green hue is due to oxidation of its copper skin.

The Statue of Liberty is a well-known feature of the New York skyline and can be seen from many points in Lower Manhattan. It can also be seen from the Staten Island Ferry and from the windows of passenger jets landing at La Guardia Airport.

Unfortunately, due to post-9/11 security concerns, the interior of the Statue of Liberty is closed to the public. Even so, the thrill of seeing Lady Liberty up close makes the $7 roundtrip ferry ride from Manhattan's Battery Park to Liberty Island well worthwhile. For visitor information, write to Statue of Liberty National Monument & Ellis Island, Liberty Island, New York, NY 10004, or call (212) 363-3200. For information on ferry schedules, call (212) 269-5755.

Ellis Island, where countless thousands of immigrants were once held before being allowed to enter the U.S., is now part of the Statue of Liberty National Monument. The Ellis Island Immigration

Museum offers exhibits and programs detailing the island's history and providing insight into the immigrant experience. The moving documentary *Island of Hope, Island of Tears* is shown continuously. For information or special group reservations, call (212) 363-7620.

GO TO:

PAGE 274 FOR U.S. CONSTITUTION (BILL OF RIGHTS)

PAGE 115 FOR THOMAS EDISON

PAGE 206 FOR NEW YORK CITY BAGELS

PAGE 239 FOR REDWOOD TREES

PAGE 287 FOR WASHINGTON MEMORIAL

JOHN STEINBECK

Of Mice and Great Men

EVERY AMERICAN harbors a secret ambition to write the "Great American Novel." We are an immodest crowd, all budding novelists. The thought that perhaps we are not good enough never crosses our minds. We are, every one of us, convinced that if we only had the time, we would do it. We would write *the* novel that everyone would read and say, "This is it. This is the story of America." And who is to say we would not? If we only had the time. The fact that we never seem to find the time does not discourage us.

On the other hand, we are haunted by the possibility that maybe, just maybe, the Great American Novel has already been written. That is why we habitually avoid the "S" shelves of libraries and bookstores and why we will shield our eyes if we accidentally stumble across books with titles the likes of *The Grapes of Wrath* or *Of Mice and Men*. That is why we feel a chill, as if someone has left a window open in February, whenever we hear or read the name John Steinbeck.

Apparently Steinbeck made it his mission to shrink us all down to life-size or, in a few extreme cases, mouse-size. Steinbeck started out the way most writers do—scruffy and poor. Born in 1902, he was raised in the farm country of the Salinas Valley, which later would be the setting for so many of his stories. As a young man, he drifted from job to job, working on farms and ranches and doing factory and construction labor. At some point in his twenties, he began to write fiction and in 1929 published *Cup of Gold,* his first novel. Several other books followed, but none of them attracted much attention from critics or the public. He was already well into his thirties by 1935, when his novel *Tortilla Flat* hit reviewers and the market with both fists. Suddenly John Steinbeck was a writer of national renown.

It was at this point that Steinbeck's life and career entered the period so troubling to other writers who would like to think of themselves as his equal. He plunged into the agriculturally rich California heartland where he had grown up. There he mingled not with wealthy landowners, but with migrant laborers, union organizers, and hoboes. This was the height of the Great Depression. Many of the people Steinbeck met had lost jobs, homes, and farms, but while their lives and families may have been all but destroyed, they themselves refused to be defeated. From the stories these unfortunates told, Steinbeck began to distill the essence of the American spirit.

In 1936, he wrote *Something That Happened,* a short novel of the sort that used to be called a novella. Before the manuscript could be packaged and sent off to the publishers, Steinbeck's literarily omnivorous setter, Toby, ate the whole thing—digesting it, so to speak, in a single sitting. The writer was forced to reconstruct the novel from memory and from the shredded scraps Toby had found unappetizing. The rewrite may have been a worthwhile exercise, however, because the book Steinbeck dropped in the mail about two months later was, even for him, a rare creation. Retitled *Of Mice and Men,* it was published in February 1937 by the New York firm of Covici-Friede, and it immediately created a stir.

Steinbeck himself had not expected much from the novel. "I guess we'll have to pull in our horns financially," he told his agent. "I don't expect the little book *Of Mice and Men* to make any money." He was wrong. Within two weeks, the novel had sold 117,000 copies. "That's a hell of a lot of books," said Steinbeck.

It was selling because it was a hell of a lot of book. *Of Mice and Men* is the story of George and his simple-minded friend, Lennie, a pair of drifters who possess a powerful attachment to one another and little else. Signing on as harvest laborers at a ranch in the Salinas Valley, they go to work on their dream of having a place of their own. But as even our "best-laid schemes" often do, their plans go awry. Lennie's physical strength is such that he invariably destroys the things he loves, and this leads to tragedy.

The key to understanding the book and the extraordinary impact it has on readers can be found in the seemingly mysterious link between George and Lennie. The two are not blood relatives. "If I thought I was related to you, I'd shoot myself," George tells his companion. But in Lennie and the vision they shared, he had found a different sort of family.

In 1939, only two years after *Of Mice and Men* appeared, *The Grapes of Wrath* landed with a heavy thump on the desk of Steinbeck's publisher. Although a much longer novel than the former (Toby had played no role in its creation), its setting and theme were similar. This time the central figures were dispossessed farmers, "Okies" who had been wiped out by the Great Depression and the Dust Bowl drought of the 1930s. *The Grapes of Wrath* attracted not only critical and popular acclaim, but condemnation for its strong language and frank treatment of the plight of migrant farm workers. Even so, it firmly established Steinbeck as a tower in American literature.

It also left Steinbeck in a quandary no other writer had ever faced—what to do with himself after writing *Of Mice and Men* and *The Grapes of Wrath*. What he did was to go on writing. Before dying of heart disease in 1968, Steinbeck produced dozens more books and novels, including *Sea of Cortez, Cannery Row, East of Eden, Winter of Our Discontent, Travels with Charley,* and *America and Americans.*

In 1962, Steinbeck won the Nobel Prize for Literature. In accepting he said: "Literature is as old as speech. It grew out of human need for it and has not changed except to become more needed. . . . The writer is delegated to declare and celebrate man's capacity for greatness of heart and spirit—for gallantry in defeat, for courage, compassion and love."

An excellent way to learn about the life and work of John Steinbeck is to visit the Steinbeck Center, a nonprofit museum in Salinas, California. For more information, write to the Steinbeck Center and

Foundation at 371 Main Street, Salinas, CA 93901, or call (831) 775-4721. Those who want a better feeling for Steinbeck the man should take time to tour the central California region where he lived and worked. Monterey, Pacific Grove, and, of course, Salinas are rich in Steinbeck homes and haunts. There one also finds the settings for many of his books. Bus excursions and self-guided driving tours are available. The Monterey Visitors Information Center can be reached at (831) 647-6400 or (831) 648-5350. Every summer, Salinas hosts a highly literary Steinbeck Festival. Finally, if your ambition is to write the great American novel, don't give up. John Steinbeck would not have wanted you to give up, and besides, there is always room in the world for more great writing. The advice most published writers offer their less-experienced friends is to "read, read, read" and then "write, write, write." For more specific, although not necessarily better advice, you might consider attending one of the many writers' workshops held each year around the country. Among the best is the Iowa Summer Writing Festival. Send mail inquiries to Writing Festival, University of Iowa, 100 Oakdale Campus, Iowa City, IA 52242, or call (319) 335-4160. Young writers seeking to sell their work should get a copy of *The Writer's Market*, published annually by *Writer's Digest* and available at most bookstores.

GO TO:

PAGE 136 FOR GOLDEN GATE BRIDGE
PAGE 183 FOR JACK LONDON
PAGE 219 FOR DOROTHY PARKER

STETSON HATS

Boss of the Plains

ALL THOSE white hats you've seen cowboys wear in the movies were Stetsons. So were most of the black hats. That's because we invariably identify the Stetson with the old west and, too, because they look darned good. If a man doesn't look good in a western hat, then maybe he should wear a sack over his head.

Since the first wagon trains headed westward beyond the Mississippi, cowboys, sheriffs, bad guys, and rough riders of every variety—not to mention the greatest rough rider of all, Teddy Roosevelt—have worn wide-brimmed hats. In addition to keeping the harsh desert sun out of a man's face, the big hats are useful for all sorts of other things. You can store stuff in them, use them to lift water out of a stream, or put them on top of something you would just as soon nobody else notice—like a hand of aces and eights. But their most important attraction is that they look just fine, especially on a man riding a horse.

The best-known form of western headgear is the broad-brimmed, high-peaked affair commonly referred to as the Stetson (after the famous trademark). These are the hats traditionally worn by nineteenth-century cattle barons, trail bosses, and ordinary cowboys—when they could afford them. For much of this century, it has mostly been the actors in western movies who wore Stetsons. The high-peaked hats serve as the movie cowboy's identifying symbol, much the way feathers are the mark of Hollywood Indians. But nowadays you don't have to be a cowboy or an actor to wear a Stetson. The rise in popularity of western-style music and dance has made western clothing fashionable again, and men are often seen sporting Stetsons along Fifth Avenue in New York.

John B. Stetson may not have known what he started, but then again, he probably did. Stetson was not a westerner himself, but rather a Philadelphia hat maker. As a young man in the 1860s, Stetson went west, hoping the dry air would help him recover from tuberculosis. While traveling in snowy Colorado one winter, Stetson made himself a protective hat using felted rabbit fur. A wealthy cattleman noticed Stetson's hat and offered him $5 for it. Being short on cash, Stetson gladly accepted the money.

Once he had recovered his health and returned to Philadelphia, Stetson remembered the broad-brimmed style the cattleman had found so attractive. Starting out in a thirty-by-hundred-foot factory, he began to manufacture a hat he called "Boss of the Plains." After sending his first samples to dealers in the West, he was inundated with orders. Even the Texas Rangers adopted the "Boss" as their official headgear. By 1906, when Stetson died at the age of seventy-six, his company was producing hundreds of thousands of "Stetsons" each year.

Stetson-brand hats are still being made. You can buy them or order them at most western wear stores.

GO TO:

PAGE 64 FOR AMERICAN BUFFALO

PAGE 136 FOR GOLDEN GATE BRIDGE

PAGE 223 FOR PENDLETON BLANKETS

PAGE 265 FOR TEXAS CHILI

T

TABASCO

Hot as Hell Pepper Sauce

MADE OF Vinegar, Red Pepper, and Salt." It says so right there on the diamond-shaped, red and green label they paste onto every bottle of Tabasco Pepper Sauce. It's hard to imagine that anything with such a short list of ingredients could pack so much flavor punch. But you had better believe it does. This is the original hot, hot stuff—not for the faint of heart or anyone with a wimpy tongue.

Available nowadays in practically any grocery, this blazing red liquid is a real old-fashioned Louisiana treat. It's made down on Avery Island in much the same way it has been made ever since Edmund McIlhenny, a farmer with a fireproof tongue, started selling his special pepper sauce just after the Civil War. Fresh peppers are mashed and seasoned with a measure of salt mined right there on the island. The salted pepper mash is aged for up to three years in handmade white-oak barrels and then blended with a premium vinegar before bottling. A comparison to a fine California wine or a great old Tennessee whiskey is inescapable.

A little Tabasco goes a long way, and for this reason, the McIlhenny Company packagers keep quantities small. Usually their red sauce is sold in a two-ounce bottle about the size and shape of a .50-caliber machine-gun cartridge. The bottles are designed so the sauce won't pour. Instead, it leaks out in judicious drips from the bottle's skinny business end, and that is a good thing. You get carried away with this stuff, and you can blast the hell out of a pot of stew or a bowl of chili. But just the right amount and—ah-h-h!—savory perfection.

One of the most adaptable culinary aids known to civilized man or woman, Tabasco may be used to improve the flavor of almost any dish. It won't do much for ice cream, but a dash or two will add some real *zip-a-dee-doo-dah* to an otherwise lifeless sandwich or bowl of soup. Say the kids have let out a monstrous yawn at the suggestion of dinner at home and started to put on the heat for a trip to McDonald's. Just add a few drops of magic hot sauce to some ground beef and—*Shazam!*—you've got brontosaurus burgers. A few drops more, and you've got tyrannosaur tacos. Any more than that and you'll probably end up at McDonald's anyway.

So who says you can't buy heaven in a bottle? For 120 years, the McIlhenny Company has been squeezing heaven and hell into the same bottle, and a small one at that. Not surprisingly, the makers emphasize the heavenly qualities of their product while trying to downplay its blowtorch reputation. But even *they* suggest their sauce be used "a drop or two" at a time. Who's afraid of a little fire, anyway? Bring on the brisket.

For more information and who knows what else, write to McIlhenny Company, Avery Island, LA 70513, or try out their website at www.tabasco.com. For a free Tabasco gift catalog, call (800) 634-9599.

GO TO:
PAGE 32 FOR ALLIGATORS
PAGE 109 FOR DAGWOOD SANDWICH
PAGE 146 FOR ALL-AMERICAN HAMBURGERS
PAGE 265 FOR TEXAS CHILI (BELOW)

TEXAS CHILI

Today, Hot Tamale

THAT'S THE weather report every day in Texas where hot food is even more prevalent than warm sunshine. Chili, that often-fiery combination of chili peppers and/or chili powder, beef, and sometimes beans, is nowadays a universal phenomenon. In roadside diners—and classy restaurants—from Boston to San Diego, Kansas

City to Kabul, Peoria to Paris, they serve up one or another version of the stuff. If there were cooks on Mars, you can bet they'd be stewing up a mess of chili to brace them against the -200-degree Martian subzero afternoon temperatures. There are good reasons for all this interest in chili. It is filling, delicious, inexpensive, and, if you make it right, it will wake up your taste buds.

Anybody who makes chili, and that includes just about everybody on the planet, believes that their own variety of the tasty brown brew is the very best. We can't all be right, can we? Almost, maybe, but the fact is that the best chili in the world is made in the American Southwest and more specifically in Texas. Folks down there take their chili very seriously and with lots of jalapeños.

As anyone in the Lone Star State will happily inform you, chili is "the national cuisine of Texas." The delicacy enjoyed today both in and out of Texas got its start on cattle drives back in the 1840s. Cowboy chow was said to be "hot, brown, and plentiful," and chili filled the bill on all three counts. To help the wranglers taste the stuff through all the trail dust coating their tongues—or on occasion to teach them a lesson—chuck-wagon cooks made their chili fiery hot. The rule of thumb (or, if you prefer, rule of tongue) was about the same then as it is today: If it doesn't make the eyes water, it's not real chili.

In Texas and elsewhere, chili cooking has become a major competitive sport. Every September, thousands of cooks gather in San Marcos and hang their cast-iron kettles over campfires for the annual Republic of Texas Chilympiad. An event like none other on this planet, it features nonstop, Texas-style country and western music, a Miss Chilympiad beauty pageant, jalapeño-eating contests, and bowl after bowl of the hottest stuff this side of the Kilauea volcano. Some very unusual ingredients have found their way into Chilympiad chili—alligator meat, for instance, and all sorts of other things that won't be mentioned here. It's all good, though. And that is exactly what you tell the chili cook who offers you a sample. Otherwise, you may have to fight your way out of the place.

If you're looking for a hot-hot chili recipe, you might want to try (at your own risk) my own recipe:

WORLD'S ALMOST VERY BEST RATTLESNAKE RED

2 large white onions
2 garlic cloves
1 pound hot sausage (German is best)
2 pounds extra-lean ground beef
1 16-ounce can of green chili peppers
2 large cans of stewed tomatoes
Cumin, paprika, and oregano
Chili powder (the hottest variety available)
1 12-ounce can of beer
Tabasco Pepper Sauce

Dice the onions and garlic. Cut the sausage into thin slices or small chunks and sauté it in a skillet with the onions and garlic over low heat until the onions are cooked. Drain all the sausage grease you can from the pan. Add the ground beef and brown. Dice the chilies and add them along with the tomatoes and about 1 teaspoon each of cumin, paprika, and oregano. Pour in the beer and add about 2 tablespoons of chili powder. Cover and simmer for as many hours as you have available, tasting occasionally to see how it's turning out. Very carefully add more spices and chili powder as needed to bring out the flavor you want. If it's not hot enough for you, add a few dashes of Tabasco, but for crying out loud, go easy.

If you don't have time for the above, just go to the nearest diner, order, and listen to the waitress call out, "Coffee light, chili dark." Make sure the diner stocks plenty of Tabasco.

For information on the annual Republic of Texas Chilympiad, or to order tickets, write to Chilympiad, P.O. Box 188, San Marcos, TX 78667, or call (512) 396-5400. For information on other chili cook-off celebrations, contact the International Chili Society at P.O. Box 1027, San Juan Capistrano, CA 92693, or call (949) 496-2651.

GO TO:
PAGE 38 FOR ARMADILLO
PAGE 157 FOR HOMINY GRITS
PAGE 264 FOR TABASCO

HENRY DAVID THOREAU

Walden's Lonely Drummer

IN 1839, at the age of twenty-one, Henry David Thoreau joined his older brother John for a canoe trip down the scenic Concord and Merrimac Rivers in New Hampshire. The adventure deeply impressed young Henry and helped form his belief that the truth about life could be found only in the out-of-doors.

Less than three years after the brothers returned from their river journey, John Thoreau nicked his finger while shaving and died of lockjaw. The loss saddened Thoreau to the point that he withdrew from friends and acquaintances in his hometown of Concord, Massachusetts, and lived in a small hermitage on nearby Walden Pond. There, as a tribute to his brother, he wrote a book called *A Week on the Concord and Merrimac Rivers* and spent the rest of his time "sauntering" through the forests. Free of distractions, he had plenty of time to think, and he kept a meticulous record of his ponderings in a journal. The journal later would grow into *Walden,* one of the best-known books of the nineteenth century. *Walden* and many of Thoreau's famous essays, such as "Civil Disobedience," are filled with ideas that occurred to him while he lived beside Walden Pond. Here are a few of the things he pondered while walking in the woods:

- "I never found the companion that was so companionable as solitude."

- "I went to the woods because I wished to live deliberately, to front only the essential facts of life, and see if I could not learn what it had to teach, and not, when I came to die, discover that I had not lived."

- "Most of the luxuries, and many of the so-called comforts, of life are not only not indispensable, but positive hindrances to the elevation of mankind."

- "I heartily accept the motto, 'That government is best which governs least.'"

- "A man is rich in proportion to the number of things which he can afford to let alone."
- "What the first philosopher taught, the last will have to repeat."
- "It is never too late to give up our prejudices."
- "It is only when we forget our learning, do we begin to know."
- "What does education do? It makes a straight-cut ditch of a free, meandering stream."

Thoreau often returned to the New England backwoods rivers that he and his brother had so enjoyed. Two of his journeys took him into the wilds of Maine, where he paddled down the Allegash and Penobscot Rivers and climbed the mile-high Mount Katahdin. In Maine, Thoreau found a much bolder variety of wildness than he had known in the more genteel countryside around Concord. This raw land he described as made out of "Chaos and Old Night" . . . "no man's garden" . . . "not lawn, nor pasture" . . . "the fresh and natural surface of the planet earth." It is into this latter variety of wilderness that lovers of nature frequently follow Thoreau today. They no doubt agree with him that "in wildness is the preservation of the world."

Those interested in learning more about Henry David Thoreau, his ideas, or an appreciation of wilderness, should contact the Thoreau Society at 44 Baker Farm, Lincoln, MA 01773, or call (781) 259-4750. The society operates a delightful shop at Walden Pond near Concord, where you can buy books and gifts related to Thoreau. Write to Shop at Walden Pond, 915 Walden Street, Concord, MA 01742, or call Walden Pond State Park at (978) 369-3254. A nonprofit preservationist group known as the Thoreau Institute publishes *Different Drummer,* a magazine focusing on outdoor and conservation issues. Write the Thoreau Institute, P.O. Box 1590, Bandon, OR 97411, or call (541) 347-1517. Perhaps the best way to remember Thoreau is to take to the wilds yourself. As you do, keep in mind one of Thoreau's most famous insights: *If a man does not keep pace with his companions, perhaps it is because he hears a different drummer.*

GO TO:

PAGE 200 FOR JOHN MUIR
PAGE 219 FOR DOROTHY PARKER

TOLL HOUSE COOKIES

The Cookie Monster's Favorite

THE IDEA of baking cookies with chocolate chips in them is such a natural, you may think the ubiquitous Toll House cookie had no single originator. If so, you are wrong. Massachusetts innkeeper and master baker Ruth Wakefield invented them in 1933—more or less by accident. Working with a cookie recipe that called for melted chocolate, she decided to save time by stirring in broken bits of the candy. The rest is sinfully delicious history.

Alas, the old New England Toll House, the famed inn run for many years by Kenneth and Ruth Wakefield, burned down in 1984. But the cookies that made Toll House a household term throughout America continue to be just about everybody's favorite temptation. They are, in fact, part of the social goo that holds the country together. Heaping platefuls of chocolate chip cookies are carried to church socials, given away at Christmas, dropped off as house-warming gifts for new neighbors, and mailed by parents to college students as a bracer for exams. The behavior of children improves dramatically when a couple of dozen Toll House cookies are in the oven. They also improve the behavior, and the mood, of adults.

Toll House cookies are great for special occasions. Or for no occasion. People have even been known to celebrate the conclusion of a successful stretch of dieting with several dozen of these choco-late-laden delights. Makes plenty of sense, huh?

Toll House cookies come in all shapes and sizes. Some like them bite-sized, while others prefer them about the size of a wagon wheel. With M&M's substituted for the chocolate chips, they take on color and can even be decorated like a cake.

There are about as many recipes for Toll House cookies as there are ovens in America. Here is one:

TOLL HOUSE COOKIES

⅔ cup soft shortening
1½ cups sifted flour
½ cup granulated sugar
½ teaspoon soda
½ cup brown sugar
½ teaspoon salt
1 large egg
½ cup chopped nuts
1½ teaspoons vanilla extract
6 ounces semisweet chocolate

In a bowl mix thoroughly the shortening, sugars, egg, and vanilla extract. Stir in the flour, soda, salt, nuts, and chocolate morsels. Drop rounded inch-thick balls of cookie dough about 2 inches apart on an ungreased baking sheet. Bake at 375° for 8 to 10 minutes or until light brown. Makes 3 to 4 dozen cookies.

Toll House cookie recipes are very adaptable, and nowadays people jazz up their cookies with all sorts of additives. A delicious shot of tartness can be added to the above recipe by throwing a handful or two of ripe cranberries into the mix.

Want to order some amazing home-style Toll House cookies? Try www.worldsgreatestcookies.com, which can be reached either online or at (703) 314-5218. Yummers!

GO TO:
PAGE 52 FOR BLUEBERRIES
PAGE 104 FOR CRANBERRIES
PAGE 191 FOR M&M'S
PAGE 222 FOR PARKER HOUSE ROLLS

U

JOHNNY UNITAS

All-American Times 47

EVERY AMERICAN male, and perhaps female as well, has their own favorite, all-time great football hero. There's Joe Montana. There's Knute Rockne. There's a bunch of them, hundreds, maybe even thousands. Not all of them were professionals, not by a long shot, and not all them even played the game—for instance, Rockne is best known as a coach (Notre Dame). But they all stood for the same things: strength, speed, agility, and, most of all, an overwhelming will to succeed, to gain that last three yards, that last inch, to put that ball over the goal line. We'll let Johnny Unitas stand for all of them.

Usually, when Unitas needed three more yards, or for that matter, thirty, he passed for them. During his eighteen seasons as a National Football League quarterback, all but one of them with the Baltimore Colts, Unitas threw for 290 touchdowns and 40,239 yards—that's almost twenty-five miles' worth of passing yardage. You bet, Unitas was the greatest, but you might never have guessed he had that sort of potential had you followed his early career in the sport.

Unitas got to play quarterback at high school in Pittsburgh only because the team's regular quarterback broke an ankle. When it came time for college, Notre Dame turned Unitas down flat, and he ended up calling signals for the Louisville—you've heard of them, haven't you?—Cardinals. Still, he played well enough on the college gridiron to be drafted ninth by the NFL's Pittsburgh Steelers. Unfortunately, as it turned out for both Unitas and the Steelers, he didn't make the team. Afterward, his star sank so low that he was forced to do construction work to make ends meet. Meanwhile, he kept playing football—for a semiprofessional team that played games on a grassless field that had to be sprayed with oil to keep down the dust. But his luck was about to change.

Early in 1956, Unitas got a call from the lowly Baltimore Colts, a hapless NFL franchise that had never won the league championship, and in fact, had never even played in a championship game. The Colts offered Unitas a contract for $7,000—NFL quarterbacks get about a thousand times that much nowadays—and he signed without a moment's hesitation. Hey, he wanted to play football, and play he did.

In 1958, just two years after he was signed, Unitas led Baltimore to its first NFL championship, and he did it again the following year. In all, Unitas quarterbacked the Colts to three league titles, two Super Bowls, and one World Championship. Along the way, he established a host of professional records, including one that may never be broken: a mind-boggling streak of 47 consecutive games with at least one touchdown pass.

Unitas developed heart problems during the 1990s, and he died in 2002 from a heart attack suffered while working out at a physical therapy center in Baltimore. No one will ever know what, if anything, flashed through his mind at the end. However, it is tempting to think he may have remembered the 1958 NFL Championship he had played in more than forty years earlier—some say it was the greatest game ever played. Down by three to the New York Giants, the Colts were pressed against their own goal line with only ninety seconds to play. Unitas completed a pass, then another, another, and another, moving his offense within reach of a game-tying field goal. Then, in overtime, he marched the Colts eighty yards down the field. Touchdown!

If you are a big fan of Johnny U or any other football pro, you'll certainly want to visit the Pro Football Hall of Fame in Canton, Ohio. It's located about two hours south of where the Cleveland Browns play home games. For information, write to Professional Football Hall of Fame, 2121 George Halas Drive NW, Canton, OH 44708, or call (330) 456-8207.

GO TO:
PAGE 21 FOR HANK AARON
PAGE 93 FOR TY COBB
PAGE 313 FOR YOGI [BERRA]

U.S. CONSTITUTION
(BILL OF RIGHTS)

Mr. Mason's List

THE DECLARATION of Independence proclaims our inalienable rights to "life, liberty, and the pursuit of happiness." To secure those rights, we all have agreed to a contract called the U.S. Constitution. While the latter document was written more than two hundred years ago by people who knew nothing whatsoever of computers, supersonic aircraft, or nuclear power—and likely could never have imagined such things—it has proved phenomenally durable and adaptable. Its formulas have enabled American government to proceed in a more or less orderly fashion for more than two centuries.

Were the framers of the Constitution extraordinarily wise or pre-scient? Perhaps, but they were also ordinary people with ordinary concerns much the same as ours, and they did not always agree or even get along with one another. Meeting in Philadelphia in 1787, they hammered (*hammered* is the right word) together the Constitution in the time-honored political way, by shouting, pounding the table, and eventually reaching a compromise.

Not all the convention delegates were interested in compromise, however. Least of all George Mason, a Virginia delegate with inflexible opinions on the subject of human liberty. A genteel farmer and neighbor of George Washington, Mason was less concerned with the building blocks of the new constitutional government than he was with protecting people from it once it was established.

Mason's wife had died years before, leaving him with nine children to raise and a plantation to run. Not surprisingly, he was often ill-tempered. Mason had no time for fools and suffered them badly. After serving in the state legislature, he described the experience in a letter to Washington: "I was never in so disagreeable a situation, and almost despaired of a cause which I saw so ill conducted. Mere vexation and disgust threw me into such an ill state of health that before the convention rose, I was sometimes near fainting in the house."

Despite Mason's low opinion of political processes in general and of the Virginia legislature in particular, he pitched in to help write a new constitution for the state. His most important contribution was a "Bill of Rights," which limited the authority of the state and strengthened the rights of individuals. In time, one or another version of his bill of rights became part of nearly every state constitution. This accomplished, Mason retired to his home and let it be known that he would consider any effort to bring him back into government "an oppressive and unjust invasion of my individual liberty."

Years later, however, Mason was called on to help write a constitution—this time for the nation. He reluctantly agreed and threw himself into the task, although he was very uncomfortable in Philadelphia and grew "heartily tired of the etiquette and nonsense so fashionable in this city." The political maneuvering at the constitutional convention was even less to his liking, especially after it became clear that a strong, centralized federal government was to be the result. Mason particularly disliked the idea of a ten-mile-square federal district, likely in his opinion to become a haunt for the "creatures of government." Ironically, the very federal city he had hoped to never see would in time come to be located almost on his doorstep.

Mason hoped to convince the convention to take a stand against the continuing slave trade. Although a slaveholder himself, he abhorred the institution, as it ran directly counter to his strongly held belief that all men ought to be free. In his view, every slave master inevitably became "a petty tyrant." When he could find no majority for his antislavery stand, Mason threatened to quit the convention and go back home.

Alarmed at the prospect of losing the support of so prominent a man, Mason's friends and even his opponents clambered for him to stay. What could they do, they asked, to keep him involved in the convention? Mason knew precisely what they could do. He had a list for them, a few items he wanted to see included in the nation's new constitution. The following version of his list would later become quite familiar to American civics students:

Item One: Congress shall make no law respecting an establishment of religion, or prohibiting the free exercise thereof; or abridging the freedom of speech, or of the press; or the right of the people peaceably to assemble, and to petition the Government for a redress of grievances.

Item Two: A well-regulated militia being necessary to the security of a free state, the right of the people to keep and bear arms, shall not be infringed.

Item Three: No soldier shall, in time of peace be quartered in any house, without the consent of the owner, nor in time of war, but in a manner prescribed by law.

Item Four: The right of the people to be secure in their persons, houses, papers, and effects, against unreasonable searches and seizures, shall not be violated, and no warrants shall issue, but upon probable cause, supported by oath or affirmation, and particularly describing the place to be searched, and the persons or things to be seized.

Item Five: No person shall be held to answer for a capital, or otherwise infamous crime, unless on a presentment or indictment of a Grand Jury, except in cases arising in the land or naval forces, or in the militia, when in actual service in time of war or public danger; nor shall any person be subject for the same offense to be twice put in jeopardy of life or limb; nor shall be compelled in any criminal case to be a witness against himself, nor be deprived of life, liberty or property, without due process of law; nor shall private property be taken for public use without just compensation.

Item Six: In all criminal prosecutions, the accused shall enjoy the right to a speedy and public trial, by an impartial jury of the State and district wherein the crime shall have been committed, which district shall have been previously ascertained by law, and to be informed of the nature and cause of the accusation; to be confronted with the witnesses against him; to have compulsory process for obtaining witnesses in his favor; and to have the assistance of counsel for his defense.

Item Seven: In suits at the common law, where the value in controversy shall exceed twenty dollars, the right of trial by jury shall be preserved, and no fact tried by a jury shall be otherwise re-examined in any court of the United States, than according to the rules of common law.

Item Eight: Excessive bail shall not be required, nor excessive fines imposed, nor cruel or unusual punishments inflicted.

Item Nine: The enumeration in the Constitution, of certain rights, shall not be construed to deny or disparage others retained by the people.

Item Ten: The powers not delegated to the United States by the Constitution, nor prohibited by it to the States, are reserved to the States respectively, or to the people.

Although efforts were made to include some or all of the above provisions in the final draft of the Constitution, the political tide ran against them, and they were left out. Mason was so incensed that he packed up and went home in a huff.

"Colonel Mason left Philadelphia in an exceeding ill humor indeed," James Madison wrote to his friend Thomas Jefferson. As it turned out, Madison shared Mason's liberty-minded sympathies, and when the first U.S. Congress met in Philadelphia in 1789, he proposed the ten items listed above as a series of amendments to the Constitution. Jefferson strongly supported this move, and by 1792, the amendments had been ratified by the states. You may recognize them as the first ten amendments to the U.S. Constitution, known as the American Bill of Rights.

In 1989, the National Archives in Washington, D.C., celebrated the Constitution's bicentennial with a major exhibit. In one of the display cases was a page from the ledger used to note the various votes taken on a particular day. Judging from this page, the delegates could barely agree on anything. There were eleven state delegations present that day, and the number of 6–5, 5–6, and 7–4 votes taken shows how torn the delegates were over issues such as the composition of the executive branch or the powers of Congress. The delegates could not even agree to stop for lunch; a motion to adjourn failed on a split vote of 5–5 with one abstention. But on one key point, the convention was unanimous. A resolution calling for the various states to compensate delegates and pay their expenses passed by a vote of 11–0. Apparently, Americans haven't changed much in more than two centuries.

The National Archives Exhibit Hall is located on Constitution Avenue between Seventh and Ninth Streets. For general information on National Archives holdings, exhibits, and programs, write to National Archives and Records Administration, Seventh Street and Pennsylvania Avenue, Washington, DC 20408, or call (202) 501-5000. One of the nation's finest educational institutions now honors the name of the man who helped protect our liberties. George Mason University, located near the old Gunston Hall Plantation, offers programs in a wide variety of liberal arts and technical fields. Write to GMU, Fairfax, VA 22030-4444, or call (703) 993-1000. Of course, we can best honor Mason by respecting the principles for which he fought. This means recognizing each and every liberty granted under the Bill of Rights and being willing to extend these rights to all. Freedom of speech means freedom of speech. Let's not forget it.

GO TO:

PAGE 31 FOR ALL-DAY PREACHING AND DINNER ON THE GROUNDS
PAGE 278 FOR USS CONSTITUTION
PAGE 149 FOR HARLEY-DAVIDSON
PAGE 287 FOR WASHINGTON MEMORIAL

USS CONSTITUTION

Wooden Ship with an Iron Will

IT'S A grand old ship and in near mint condition, its oaken hull as iron-hard and impervious to broadsides of cannon as it was when it first sailed into battle almost two hundred years ago. Launched in 1797 at the Edmund Hart shipyard in Boston, the forty-four-gun USS *Constitution* was one of several frigates authorized by Congress to protect American merchant vessels from the depredations of pirates and hostile foreign navies.

Not nearly as powerful as some of the big ships-of-the-line that the British and other European navies could boast, the *Constitution* was built for speed. With an overall length of 204 feet and relatively narrow beam of 43 feet 6 inches, it could outmaneuver enemy ships or, if necessary, outrun them. When its 42,720 square feet of sail were filled with wind, the ship could do more than thirteen knots. That made the *Constitution* faster than most warships of the day, faster even than many of the steam-powered vessels that began to ply the ocean during the nineteenth century.

Nonetheless, the *Constitution*'s builders knew it would have some hard fighting to do. To armor the frigate for battle, they brought in special lumber from an island off the coast of Georgia, where a legendary grove of live oak was known to produce wood so rock-hard that it repelled axes. Powerful cannons were cast in Rhode Island, and copper fittings were made locally in Boston by Paul Revere himself. On the stern, an American eagle emblazoned a flag-like shield. This was truly an all-American ship—and still is. The USS *Constitution* remains afloat today, still very much a part of the U.S. Navy. It is, in fact, the oldest commissioned warship the world.

It has been a long time since the *Constitution* did any fighting, but during its active years as the pride of the navy's high-seas battle fleet, it was a tiger. The Barbary pirates found this out the hard way in 1803 when the *Constitution* bombarded Tripoli, pulverizing fortress walls and toppling minarets.

During the War of 1812, which was largely fought at sea, the *Constitution* ceaselessly harried British shipping from Brazil to the far North Atlantic. Whenever larger, more powerful Royal Navy warships thought they had it cornered, the *Constitution* would fill its sails and outrun them. If there was any chance of victory, however, it would stand and fight. The British frigate *Java* felt its claws in December 1812 off the coast of Brazil. The *Constitution* shot away all the *Java*'s spares and rigging, leaving the enemy vessel a riddled hulk too badly damaged to salvage. Later in the war, off the west coast of Africa, the *Constitution* was caught in crossfire between a pair of British warships, the *Cyane* and the *Levant*. The ship received their broadsides and roared back with its own. Before the afternoon's fighting had ended, both British ships had struck their colors and surrendered.

In perhaps the most famous shootout of its career, the *Constitution* squared off with the British frigate *Guerriere* some six hundred miles east of Boston. In a classic tall-ship duel, the two pounded away at each other with broadside after broadside. More often than not, the amazed British gunners saw their cannonballs harmlessly bounce off the *Constitution*'s oak planking. "Huzzah!" they cried. "She has sides of iron." But the *Constitution*'s shots had much greater effect, splintering the *Guerriere*'s hull, knocking down masts, and forcing the ship to strike its colors. After its battle with the *Guerriere,* the *Constitution* would always be known as "Ironsides."

Following the War of 1812, the *Constitution* retired from combat duty. Over the years since, it has served as a diplomatic ship, naval academy training ship, and even a floating office building. In 1905, it became a national monument. While the ship remains to this day a part of the U.S. Navy, it serves primarily as a museum. Appropriately, its permanent berth is in Boston, right across the harbor from where it was launched in 1797.

Although it looks the part, even down to the smallest detail, the ship we see today is not actually the ship that blasted the Barbary pirates in 1803 or vanquished the *Guerriere* during the War of 1812. What British cannonballs could not do, time eventually accomplished. Salt water and rot have eaten away at the ship for two centuries, and the *Constitution* has been repaired, restored, and refitted so many times that only about 15 percent of its 1797 planking and other materials remain. Even so, when you step aboard "Old Ironsides" today, you'll find its original fighting spirit completely intact.

Located in Building 22 of the Charlestown Navy Yard, the USS *Constitution* Museum is open to the public seven days a week. The museum offers an abundance of information on the history of "Old Ironsides" and other U.S. Navy fighting ships. The *Constitution* itself is berthed nearby. For information, write to USS Constitution, P.O. Box 1812, Boston, MA 02129, or call (617) 242-0543.

GO TO:
PAGE 26 FOR SAMUEL ADAMS
PAGE 60 FOR BOSTON TEA PARTY
PAGE 274 FOR U.S. CONSTITUTION (BILL OF RIGHTS)
PAGE 287 FOR WASHINGTON MEMORIAL

V

RUDY VALLEE

Your Time Is My Time

WE'LL ALWAYS think of him as Rudy, the college boy crooner, and likely as not, that would be okay with him. His name wasn't Rudy, but he did spend quite a bit of time knocking about New England Universities. Born Hubert Prior Vallee in 1901, he became an early fan of the saxophone. While attending the University of Maine, he earned the nickname Rudy by driving his classmates crazy with records by saxophonist Rudy Wiedoft.

Perhaps because his friends in Maine had about all of Wiedoft they could take, Vallee transferred to Yale, where he formed a band called the Yale Collegians. The band debuted at the Heigh Ho Club in New York City, the sort of place where young ladies wore sparkling outfits and people said things like "Poopoopeedoo" and "Hiya, old sport." The Heigh Ho was just right for Vallee, and his distinctive, slightly nasal voice proved so captivating that his performances were soon being broadcast by ABC Radio.

Everyone wanted to hear the college crooner, and Vallee's early recordings such as "A Dream" and "Nola" were smash hits. Vallee's stage performances were set apart by his use of a megaphone, which considerably amplified his naturally mellow voice and made him look like he was leading cheers for the college team.

Vallee became a superstar of the 1920s flapper set. When radio moguls gave him his own talk show in 1928—the *Rudy Vallee Hour*—he reached an international audience of more than two hundred million listeners, nearly twice the population of the U.S. at the time.

Vallee is probably best remembered for his 1930s megahits, including "Life Is Just a Bowl of Cherries" and "As Time Goes By," which he sang more than a dozen years before it became central to the plot and spirit of the movie *Casablanca*. However, most have forgotten that he was also a movie star. He appeared in no fewer than thirty-three films, the first of them *Vagabond Lover* and the last *How to Succeed in Business Without Even Trying*. That was the thing about Vallee; everything came easy, and he never seemed to be trying at all. As with the Ivy League collegians he represented, trying hard was not only unnecessary, it was downright plebeian.

Not surprisingly, Rudy Vallee's voice sounds best when pouring from the horn of a gramophone or Victrola. So, if you can find a few old 78's and an antique machine, give a listen. Otherwise, try your local CD outlet, as there are sure to be some Vallee titles on display. Heigh-ho, everybody!

GO TO:

PAGE 91 FOR PATSY CLINE
PAGE 117 FOR ELVIS PRESLEY
PAGE 291 FOR HANK WILLIAMS
PAGE 179 FOR LINDY HOP
PAGE 231 FOR QUIET SIDE (MAINE)

VERMONT

Sharp Cheddar and Bitter Moxie

ON AN unusually hot day during the summer of 1777 a few hundred stouthearted Vermonters turned back an army of redcoats at Bennington. The beating administered by Vermont's Green Mountain Boys so weakened the British under Gen. John Burgoyne that they were later defeated and captured at Saratoga, New York. Otherwise, Burgoyne might have succeeded in his plan to march down the Hudson, split the colonies in two, and put an end to the American Revolution, with the likely result that, nowadays, we'd all be eating fish and chips instead of hamburgers and, who knows, perhaps even speaking the English language. So it is to Vermont that we Americans owe not just razor-sharp Cheddar cheese or the sour-faced President Calvin Coolidge, but independence itself.

Vermont should also be credited with the preservation of that most American of institutions, the country store. Nearly every hill-and-dale village in the Green Mountain State can boast at least one clapboard general store. Many are properly fitted out with wood-stoves, bronze cash registers, cracker barrels, and hoops of hard cheese. These places are filled with the aroma of home-baked bread, freshly ground coffee, spices, and aging wood, with brightly colored cans and cartons reaching all the way to the ceiling, with crackers, cashews, penny candy, popcorn, and pickles, with refreshing soft drinks and spring water, with personality, and with memories.

In establishments of this sort, the man or woman behind the cash register or out in the aisles stocking shelves or in the back grinding meat is almost certainly the owner. And customers are likely to know the owner as well as a member of their own family. If they don't, they will before they are finished shopping.

Everyone in Dorset, Vermont, knew Perry Peltier, who owned the town's market from 1913 to 1977. Older Dorset townsfolk still wince at the thought of Peltier's cigar ashes, which sometimes peppered his otherwise high-quality ground beef. It is said he ripped his bibbed aprons up the middle so he could pull them on and off without taking his cigar out of his mouth. The story is still told of a dissatisfied customer who approached Peltier one day with a complaint.

"Perry," she said, "the cream I bought yesterday was sour."

"Don't worry," replied the storekeeper, "so was mine."

To get an idea of what stores like Peltier's Market are all about, consider this: The place opened its doors for business in 1816 when James Madison was president of the United States, almost a full century before Perry Peltier first pulled on an apron and stepped up to its register—and that was before World War I. Another century has more or less evaporated since Peltier took over, and the market is still in business.

Peltier's Market is operated as a traditional Vermont country store by its current owners, who have resisted the temptation to turn it into an antique shop or some sort of museum. Instead, Peltier's continues to sell hamburger buns, salad dressing, canned tomatoes, fresh celery, self-rising flour, measuring cups, whiskbrooms, and birthday candles to the neighborly folks of Dorset. That is the test of an authentic country store: If you can't buy hamburger buns, pickle relish, or a can of beans there, it's not the real thing.

Vermont is a treasure trove of fine old country stores like the one in Dorset, and these are among the many good reasons for visiting this skinny little state. Other reasons to visit are the gorgeous mountain scenery, the pristine villages, and the friendliest people on this, or perhaps any, planet. Vermont is so pleasant that some have suggested the whole state be declared a national park. Vermonters would never stand for this, however. They would gather with their flintlocks and muskets and block the way to Bennington.

The following are a few Vermont country stores you might want to visit. Keep in mind that this is a mere sampling; there are many other great old stores in the state. To find them, just get in your car and drive Vermont's back roads. The F. H. Gillingham Store, established in 1886 on Elm Street in Woodstock, sells groceries, hardware, gardening supplies, and gifts. Write to the store in Woodstock, VT 05091, or call (800) 344-6668. The J. J. Hapgood Store, established in 1827 just off Route 30 in Peru, sells groceries, candy, and gifts. Write to the store at P.O. Box 117, Peru, VT 05152, or call (802) 824-5911. Peltier's Market, established in 1816 just off Route 30 on Dorset Common, sells groceries, gourmet foods, and excellent wines. Write to the store in Dorset, VT 05251, or call (802) 867-4400.

GO TO:

PAGE 34 FOR APPALACHIAN COUNTRY STORES
PAGE 98 FOR CALVIN COOLIDGE
PAGE 95 FOR COCA-COLA
PAGE 110 FOR DR PEPPER
PAGE 166 FOR IVORY SOAP
PAGE 225 FOR LYDIA E. PINKHAM VEGETABLE COMPOUND

VICTROLA

His Master's Voice

WHEN YOU'D like to crank up a little music, say a touch of ragtime or Rudy Vallee, nothing beats a Victrola. Capitalizing on technology developed by Thomas Edison, a number of manufacturers turned huge profits on record-playing machines during the early twentieth century. Among the most successful of these firms was the Victor Talking Machine Company, the one with the dog and "His Master's Voice" logo.

Founded by Eldridge Johnson in 1901, the Victor Company sold a machine much like those of its competitors. The turntable and cranking device were fitted into a wooden box with a large horn attached to amplify the sound. The big horn proved a nuisance for Victor's customers. The trouble was, it got in the way of the flying elbows of dancers, the broomsticks of housemaids, even the wagging tails of large dogs. By 1905, John had solved this problem by stuffing the horn into a wooden cabinet along with the other components.

Christened the Victrola, this cabinet-style machine was intended for a decidedly upscale market. Various models sold for prices ranging from $200 to as much as $1,000, which would be a lot even by today's standards. The Victor Company had manufactured and sold about fifteen thousand Victrolas by 1909, the year it introduced a lower-cost tabletop model priced at about $100. With music machines now within the reach of nearly every family's budget, the Victor Company's sales exploded, and by 1913, it was selling Victrolas at an annual rate of more than 250,000.

Shortly before World War I, electric motors began to be added to Victrolas, which eliminated the need for cranking. Called Electrolas, these new "electrified" phonographs didn't catch on with the public until the flapper era of the 1920s. Unfortunately for the Victor Company, something called radio also caught on during the 1920s. Offering better sound quality and nearly endless variety, radios began to replace phonographs as the entertainment of choice in most homes.

In 1929, RCA bought out Victor, forming a new company known as RCA Victor. By that time, electronic sound amplification had made acoustic phonographs obsolete, and old family Victrolas began to be shoved into attics or shadowy corners, where they were used as display tables for clocks or vases. Decades would pass before Victrolas began to emerge from their hiding places for sale as valuable antiques. You would be happy to have one nowadays, as mint-condition models may bring thousands at auction.

If you'd like to buy a Victrola, keep an eye on the antique column in the classified section of your local newspaper. If you are really lucky, you might find one in an antique shop or at an auction. You may also want to try www.victrolas.com, either online or at (610) 409-8742.

GO TO:

PAGE 115 FOR THOMAS EDISON
PAGE 281 FOR RUDY VALLEE

WASHINGTON MEMORIAL

Don't Miss the Point in D.C.

WHEN PEOPLE in other countries hear the words "United States of America," many different things may come to mind. For instance, they may be reminded of the Coca-Cola logo, the Olympic basketball Dream Team, or the Statue of Liberty. But among our enduring national symbols, few stand out more prominently than the Washington Monument. The 555-foot-tall marble obelisk at the center of the National Mall is to Washington, D.C., and America what the Arc de Triomphe is to Paris and France.

The grand monument, intended to honor the man who more or less invented our nation, was almost never built. The idea for such a memorial had circulated around the capital for decades before Congress finally approved a plan for the structure in 1833. Engaged by the Washington National Monument Society, architect Robert Mills designed a substantial column with a large colonnade at its base, where statues of Washington and other founding fathers were to be displayed. Since funds were raised privately and, as it turned out, slowly, there was not enough money available for construction until 1848.

Only part of Mills's original vision had been realized by 1854, when work on the project came to a dead stop. In that year, members of the controversial American—or "Know-Nothing"—Party gained control of the Monument Society. In addition to their strident opposition to immigration, the Know-Nothings were against public expenditures or large-scale projects of any sort, and they effectively shut down construction.

It was not until 1876, more than a decade after the Civil War, that interest in the monument was revived. Patriotism and a sense of national purpose ran high during that national centennial year, and Congress finally appropriated funds to finish building the monument. The U.S. Army Corps of Engineers began work on the obelisk in 1878, and by 1884 had completed it. President Chester A. Arthur dedicated the monument in 1885.

The Washington Monument is made of two different shades of marble. This is because the stone used in the first phase of construction during the late 1840s came from a different quarry than that used later by the Corps of Engineers. A winding staircase of 897 steps leads to a landing at the five-hundred-foot level. However, the stairs are now closed to the public, except for tours led by National Park Service rangers. Others may reach the landing via a seventy-second elevator ride from the base.

The popular landing near the top has windows offering extraordinary views of the city of Washington and the surrounding countryside. Looking to the east, you can see straight down the grassy National Mall, flanked by Smithsonian buildings, to the Capitol at the far end. Looking to the south down the Potomac, one can see Mount Vernon in the distance.

The Washington Monument is open until near midnight every day from April through September, and from 9:00 a.m. until 4:45 p.m. the rest of the year. Tickets are required for the elevator, but they can be obtained free of charge at a kiosk on Fifteenth Street near the base of the monument.

For more information on the Washington Monument, write to National Capital Parks, The National Mall, 900 Ohio Drive SW, Washington, DC 20242, or call (202) 426-6841. Advance monument tickets are available for a service charge through Ticketmaster at (800) 551-7328.

Every year on the evening of July 4, Independence Day, Washington puts on an enormous fireworks display. The monument is used as a centerpiece for the display, creating a spectacular effect heavy with patriotic feeling. If you would like to see the display, be sure to arrive early, as every square inch of grass and concrete will be covered with spectators long before the first rockets are airborne.

GO TO:
PAGE 120 FOR EMPIRE STATE BUILDING
PAGE 71 FOR CAPE HATTERAS LIGHTHOUSE
PAGE 254 FOR STATUE OF LIBERTY
PAGE 274 FOR U.S. CONSTITUTION (BILL OF RIGHTS)

WHITE MOUNTAIN ICE-CREAM FREEZERS

If You Want the Best, Churn It Yourself

LIFE OFFERS many pleasures, but few more satisfying than a bowl of homemade ice cream. Sure, there are some delicious commercial varieties of the icy dessert: sorbet, frozen yogurt, premium ice cream (and the less-than-premium sort). The commercial brands may taste terrific, but they cannot give you the authentic ice-cream experience. For that you need the following elements: a warm summer afternoon, a back porch, a hefty wooden tub, a sizable stainless-steel can with a rotating dasher, a father or grandfather to help with spreading newspaper and adding crushed ice and salt to the container, a mother or grandmother to pour several quarts of sweet, fruity cream into the tub, a crank to turn about two thousand times—sorry, but electric ice-cream makers are just not as much fun—an hour or two to spend in mouthwatering anticipation, and, finally, a hefty crockery bowl and a big spoon. Oh yes, there is one other thing. You need to be about eight years old.

Some of the items on the list may be hard to come by, but you still can find wooden-tub, hand-cranked ice-cream freezers if you walk through the door of the right hardware store. Among the best are the four-quart capacity white-pine and steel models made by the White Mountain Freezer Company. These handsome freezers are more or less the same as those White Mountain has been making since it was founded in 1853. The hand-coopered tubs are made of three-quarter-inch, tongue-and-groove pine staves. The heavy-duty stainless-steel cream cans will last a lifetime if you keep them clean. Scraper blades are made from hardened Norwegian beech wood.

For more than a century, the company was located in Nashau, New Hampshire, where there was an abundance of stout lumber for its tubs. The founders had patented a special gearbox that drove the cream can and dasher in opposite directions. The dasher blades scraped ice crystals off the sides of the turning can and blended them with the slowly solidifying mixture. Ice-cream freezers still work off the same principle today.

Nowadays, White Mountain Freezers are made by Rival, an appliance manufacturer in Kansas City, Missouri, but the product retains its old-fashioned quality. That is to say, it churns up the same wonderful ice cream that White Mountain Freezers have been making for almost 150 years.

White Mountain Freezers are not cheap, but they last forever. Electric motor-driven models are also available, but why mess up a good thing with all that newfangled technology? Hand-cranked is best.

Every family has, or should have, its own recipe for ice cream. Of course, vanilla is always a favorite, but home freezers excel at making fruit varieties. Usually, it's best to use fruit that is a little past ripe; that way it is softer and juicier. Peach may be the best flavor for home freezers (see "Georgia Peaches" on page 132), but don't tell that to folks who favor strawberry.

White Mountain Freezers can be found in many hardware and appliance stores. For more information, write to Rival Company, Marketing Department, 800 East 101st Terrace, Kansas City, MO 64131, or call (800) 343-0065. If you would like to order your old-fashioned ice-cream freezer from an equally old-fashioned supplier, write to Farmers Delight Country Store, Route 2, Box 416, Grafton, WV 26354, or call (800) 273-1945. (Farmers Delight also sells Aladdin Lamps.)

On the next page is a basic recipe to start with. If you are not in the mood for fruit flavors but would like to add a little razzle-dazzle to plain vanilla, add a couple of heaping handfuls of plain M&M's to the mix.

PEACH VANILLA ICE CREAM

6 medium eggs
2 cups sugar
1 can condensed milk
3 teaspoons vanilla flavoring
4 large ripe peaches, peeled and cut into small pieces
1 8-ounce package dairy whipping cream

In a bowl beat the eggs. Add the sugar, condensed milk, and vanilla. Pour into a saucepan and gradually cook. Pour the egg mixture into the freezer tub. Add the peaches and whipped cream and enough milk to fill the freezer. Will make up to one gallon. For strawberry, substitute 1 to 2 pints of halved ripe strawberries for the peaches.

GO TO:

PAGE 52 FOR BLUEBERRIES
PAGE 132 FOR GEORGIA PEACHES
PAGE 191 FOR M&M'S
PAGE 218 FOR PAPER-SHELL PECANS

HANK WILLIAMS

Long Gone Lonesome Blues Singer

THE WORD *legend* is hardly sufficient to describe Hank Williams. He burst into the music world as if from nowhere in 1949, and by 1953 he was gone. During those four brief years, his down-home musical style and plaintive vocals raised him to the top of the country and western charts. Others have accomplished that, and in just as short a time, but they never became a Hank Williams. Today, almost half a century after he died, Williams is recognized as a mountain in the

American cultural landscape. It is difficult to understand why—until you hear his music.

Hank Williams was born in 1923 into a dirt-poor Alabama family. His father was a tree trimmer, his mother a church organist. When he was only seven his father disappeared, never to be heard from again. Young Hank had to sell peanuts and shine shoes to help his family through the lean years of the Great Depression. While he worked he listened constantly to music, especially that of a black street singer named Rufus Payne, who would have an important influence on the bluesy Williams style.

By age fourteen, Williams was playing and singing with his own band, the Drifting Cowboys. For years he worked the Alabama honky-tonks, barely making gas and food money for himself and his band. During World War II, he was forced to quit the band all together and take a job as a welder in a shipyard. Soon after the war, however, he took the gamble that was to be the making of his career. As many other young, ambitious country singers did at that time and still do today, he moved to Nashville, home of the Grand Ole Opry.

In Nashville, Williams's talents were soon recognized by Fred Rose, a well-known music publisher, who got him a recording contract with MGM and a job on a wildly popular Shreveport radio program called the *Louisiana Hayride*. One of the songs Williams sang on the *Hayride* was "Move It on Over," which soared straight to the top of the country charts. Even so, it was not until 1949 that Williams appeared at the Opry, the cathedral of country music. His first Opry performance on June 11 of that year would prove a defining moment in the history of popular entertainment. Mainstream America was about to discover country music.

Before long, Williams was the best-known country musician in America. In fact, during the early 1950s, he ranked among the nation's most popular entertainers of any type. Williams hits such as "Long Gone Lonesome Blues," "Why Don't You Love Me," and "Hey, Good Lookin'" poured from radios and jukeboxes in every city and small town in America. It seemed that every week brought the release of a new Hank Williams chart buster—"Cold Cold Heart," "Jambalaya," "Take These Chains from My Heart," and "Your Cheatin' Heart," to name just a few. In less than four years, Williams placed more than thirty tunes on Billboard's Country Top Ten. Eleven of his songs reached the number one slot. Meanwhile, Williams and his reconstituted Drifting Cowboys band played to packed houses almost every night. But it could not go on forever.

Like so many country music stars, Williams was hard drinking, hard loving, and hard a lot of things. He knew what it was like to perform live at 5:00 a.m. in a backwoods radio studio, drink himself to sleep during the day, drive all night to a gig, and then drive all the next night to another. His was a lifestyle not many could endure, and it took a heavy toll on him. He died of a heart attack in 1953 while on his way to a New Year's Eve concert in Canton, Ohio. Even those who did not care for country and western music mourned him. Hank Williams is still missed by those who love American culture and American music. Who knows what songs he might have sung for us had he lived another fifty years?

If you have never driven down the road humming "Long Gone Lonesome Blues," "Your Cheatin' Heart," or "Take These Chains," maybe you have never been lonely or hopelessly in love. If you know the emotions but for some extraordinary reason are unfamiliar with the work of Hank Williams, visit the country section of your local music store as soon as possible. Collections of his best songs are available on a variety of labels. Keep in mind that Hank Williams Jr., born in 1949, is a big country star in his own right. Hank Jr. is definitely worth a listen, but try his father's music first. You may be surprised at how fresh and up-to-date those old Hank Williams classics sound even today, more than six decades after they first appeared. And even the ones that sound a little old-fashioned are sure hard to forget. For instance, "Hey, Good Lookin'." Sure, you know the words.

GO TO:

PAGE 53 FOR BLUEGRASS
PAGE 91 FOR PATSY CLINE
PAGE 117 FOR ELVIS PRESLEY

GRAY WOLF

My, What Big Ears You Have

WOLVES HAVE found their way into the mythology of nearly every people in the Northern Hemisphere. They usually are portrayed as snarling aggressors or devilish schemers laying clever traps for unwary children, especially boys named Peter or little girls dressed in red capes. Ironically, wolf attacks on humans are so rare that only a few have been documented throughout all of history.

At the same time, a wolf is certainly nobody's puppy dog. *Canis lupus*, also known as the gray wolf or timber wolf, is the largest member of the dog family, but it would be very hard to mistake one for a Border collie. Adult males may stand nearly three feet tall at the shoulder and weigh up to 150 pounds. They are ferocious hunters capable of bringing down a full-grown elk or caribou.

Jack London's Buck would have been an extraordinary and noble animal indeed to take up with a wolf pack and survive, for wolves are themselves extraordinary and noble. London saw in the wolves the embodiment of an utterly wild spirit that lies at the heart of all creatures—our neighbor's mutt and ourselves as well. And he was right.

Wolves once ranged freely across much of the country. After the bear, they ranked as the top predator in the dark forests and on the unfenced plains of pre-colonial America. But like the buffalo and many other species, the wolf retreated quickly from the advance of European-style civilization. Wolves require a lot of open space—about ten square miles per adult. They are poorly suited to settled places and don't make very good neighbors. Shot on sight by farmers, ranchers, and hunters, the gray wolf was driven to near-extinction throughout most of America by the turn of the twentieth century.

Today, only about ninety-two hundred wolves remain in the entire country. As many as seven thousand of these stalk the caribou herds of Alaska. Another two thousand live in the forests of northern Minnesota, the primary bastion of the wolf in the Lower Forty-eight. A few others are known by wildlife experts to exist in Montana, Wyoming, Idaho, Michigan, and Wisconsin, but elsewhere, the wolf is extinct. Efforts are being made to reintroduce the wolf to areas where their predation on domestic livestock can be monitored and controlled.

Wolves are best experienced from a considerable distance. In other words, they should be left alone. However, excellent books and videos on the gray wolf are widely available. For more information on the gray wolf and wolf conservation, write the Defenders of Wildlife at 1130 Seventeenth Street NW, Washington, DC 20036, or call (202) 682-9400. Incidentally, this nonprofit conservation organization has a baying wolf as its logo.

GO TO:

PAGE 64 FOR AMERICAN BUFFALO
PAGE 143 FOR GRIZZLY BEAR
PAGE 183 FOR JACK LONDON
PAGE 200 FOR JOHN MUIR
PAGE 238 FOR RAINBOW TROUT

NERO WOLFE

World's Greatest—and Fattest—Detective

SHOVE IT on over, Sherlock—way over. The greatest private detective of all time is not a thin, nervous, cocaine-addicted Londoner, but rather a fat, lazy New Yorker obsessed with orchids, food, and beer.

Nero Wolfe is a name that should be familiar to anyone who has read more than five or six mystery novels—and who in America hasn't? But just in case you've missed him, here is the *skinny* on Wolfe: Weighing in at a "seventh-of-a-ton," or approximately 286 pounds, Wolfe lives in a brownstone on West Thirty-fifth Street in Manhattan. Here, in the company of his younger and much thinner operative, Archie Goodwin, Wolfe indulges in lavish, gourmet meals prepared by master chef Fritz Brenner.

Every day from 9:00 to 11:00 and 4:00 to 6:00, Wolfe holes up in his beloved rooftop greenhouse where, with the help of his troll-like assistant, Theodore Horstmann, he husbands ten thousand or so rare orchids. For Wolfe, who has no interest whatever in women—he leaves that field entirely to the abundantly amorous Archie—the orchids are his "concubines: insipid, expensive, parasitic, and temperamental." Wolfe's schedule is so inflexible that, if the clock strikes four while he is in the middle of an important crime-solving conference, he will lever himself out of his specially built and reinforced chair and head for the plant rooms, leaving Archie to deal with the consequences.

Wolfe meets his astronomical household expenses by charging his wealthy clients exorbitant fees for the service of unmasking criminals whose dark deeds have so far baffled homicide detective Cramer and the twenty thousand or so other members of the New York City police force. Actually, it is Archie who does most of the investigating, since the reclusive Wolfe almost never leaves the brownstone. Only when all the pertinent facts have been gathered by Archie does Wolfe settle down to work it all out. In fact, *work* is something of a dirty word for Wolfe, and he accepts a case only when economic necessity or Archie's constant hectoring render his malingering untenable. For Wolfe, the only prospect more irksome than work is the thought of shaking hands with a murderer.

If you think this an unlikely setup for a successful mystery series, consider: Author Rex Stout published *Fer-de-Lance*, his first Nero Wolfe mystery, in 1934. A few months after Stout died in 1975 at the age of eighty-eight, Viking Press published *A Family Affair*, his seventy-second Wolfe mystery. During the more than forty years between, Stout's brownstone yarns sold countless millions of hardcovers and paperbacks, and to this day he still has millions of faithful readers.

The broad and continuing appeal of Stout's Nero Wolfe mysteries must be due in part to his strong and consistent handling of the major characters. After reading just a few of the stories, Nero, Archie, Fritz, Theodore, and Cramer are like next-door neighbors. When they do something out of the ordinary, our surprise is real because we feel we know them.

We also know that during the course of every story, we'll be sitting down with Nero and Archie to one or more sumptuous meals. For instance, one of his extremely rare excursions outside the brownstone took the rotund detective all the way to Montana to a ranch owned by Lilly Rowan, Archie's wealthy lady friend. There, in addition to solving a baffling murder mystery and seeing justice done to the culprit, Wolfe treats everyone to a fabulous trout dinner. The following recipe appears in *The Nero Wolfe Cookbook* and is reprinted here with the kind permission of Cumberland House, Viking Press, and Bantam Books:

NEW YORK CITY REAL NERO WOLFE TROUT DEAL

10 brook trout, 6 to 7 inches long
¼ pound mushrooms
2 tablespoons brandy
4 large tomatoes
1 medium onion, minced
½ teaspoon paprika
1 tablespoon minced parsley
2 large eggs
1 tablespoon minced chives
½ cup bread crumbs
1 tablespoon minced chervil
¼ cup grated Parmesan cheese (or ½ teaspoon dried leaves)
1 tablespoon minced tarragon (or ½ teaspoon dried leaves)

Clean the trout and rub them inside and out with the brandy. Add half the onion to the parsley, chives, chervil, and tarragon. Clean the mushrooms, and chop; squeeze their juice into the herbs. Stir this mixture well, and stuff the trout with it.

Peel, chop, and seed the tomatoes. In a saucepan, cook the tomato pulp and the rest of the onion over low heat until it becomes mushy; add the mushrooms, and cook another 5 minutes. Season with paprika, and, if you want a very smooth sauce, put through the fine blade of a meat grinder or puree in a blender. Set aside and keep warm.

Beat the eggs in a shallow bowl, and combine the bread crumbs and cheese in another shallow dish. Dip each trout first into the egg and then into the bread crumbs, until they are thoroughly coated. Place the breaded trout in a generously buttered baking dish, and bake in a 350° oven for 10 to 12 minutes until they are tender and golden brown. Remove to a warm serving dish, and cover with the tomato sauce. (Serves one per trout.)

Mass-market paperback editions of Rex Stout's Nero Wolfe novels are still being published by Bantam Books, and they can be found in almost any bookstore. Since Stout's death, several new and highly entertaining Nero Wolfe novels by author Robert Golds-borough—a longtime fan of Stout—have been released, and you should not miss them. After all, what better way to spend a lazy Sunday afternoon than curled up with a Nero Wolfe mystery?

Nero Wolfe has his own fan club, The Wolfe Pack, with membership open to all who would not willingly shake hands with a murderer. Membership costs $25 for two years. To join, or for additional information, write to Wolfe Pack, P.O. Box 230822, Ansonia Station, New York City, NY 10022.

Can't find your favorite Nero Wolfe mystery? Write to the Black Orchid Bookstore at 303 East Eighty-first Street, New York, NY 10028, or call (212) 734-5980. Tell them Archie recommended the place.

For the benefit of those who would like to sample more of Wolfe's gourmet table, try *The Nero Wolfe Cookbook* republished by Cumberland House Publishing. It features one hundred or more unique recipes along with dozens of classic black-and-white photographs taken in New York City during the 1930s through 1950s, the heyday of Nero and Archie. Look for it in the cooking or mystery sections of your local bookstore.

GO TO:

Page 76 for Carnegie Deli
Page 219 for Dorothy Parker
Page 183 for Jack London
Page 215 for Oz

FRANK LLOYD WRIGHT

Bridging the Hills with Grace

IT IS an astounding house by any standard: beautiful, imminently livable, and charged throughout with ideas. But perhaps its most remarkable feature is a bridge that leads to nowhere. Extending from the living areas of the home, the bridge reaches out over the brow of a wooded Wisconsin hill. It affords a sweeping view of a lake and the lovely surrounding countryside but serves no other apparent purpose. For most of its length, the bridge appears to be unsupported, and you would think twice about walking out onto it if you didn't know the name of the architect who designed it. He was Frank Lloyd Wright, and the house is Taliesin, his home for nearly half a century.

Widely believed to have been America's greatest architect, Wright used concrete, steel, and stone the way poets use words and rhythm, and central to his genius was the metaphor of the bridge. You see that metaphor expressed in the cantilevered balconies at Fallingwater—thought by many to be the most beautiful house in the world—and in dozens of other Frank Lloyd Wright structures. As at Taliesin, his bridges almost never lead any place. Instead, they draw us into nature, into the air, into the open spaces that are, after all, the essence of America.

Born in 1867, Wright was raised in the rich farming country of south-central Wisconsin, a place where the houses and barns were simple but sturdy and the land was held dear. A widowed schoolteacher, his mother had it in mind from the beginning that Frank should become an architect. Apparently, so did he. Teaching salaries being even worse then than they are today, however, there was no money for him to attend a proper school of architecture. Instead, he took a few college courses in Madison and helped support the family by working as a draftsman for a local engineering firm, dreaming all the while of the tall, shining buildings in Chicago.

By age twenty, Wright could no longer contain his dreams and rushed off to the big city, where he landed a job in the firm of noted

Chicago architect Louis Sullivan. Wright proved such a quick study that soon he was serving as Sullivan's chief assistant and accepting design work on the side as well. Inevitably, the freelance assignments got him into trouble with his boss, but rather than knuckle under, he quit and set up his own small company.

Within a few years, the young architect had become the chief figure in an entirely new and uniquely American design movement called the Prairie School. Wright and other young Midwestern architects who looked to him for leadership built homes using mass-produced materials and equipment. Their houses had bold, clean lines and wide-open family areas filled with light. Even the most elaborate Prairie School houses were meant primarily to be lived in—not just to impress.

Wright recognized that the main thrust in modern architecture was vertical, toward taller and taller skyscrapers, for instance. He, on the other hand, believed that the natural requirements of everyday human life called for greater emphasis on the horizontal. As a result, whenever you see a Frank Lloyd Wright building or house, the horizontal lines are what catch your attention—and make you want to live there.

Many of Wright's earliest commissions were for houses built in Oak Park near Chicago. He lived and maintained a studio there from 1889 until 1909. During this period, he designed at least fifty houses in the Prairie style, and many of them still can be seen in the town's quiet residential neighborhoods.

Marital discord and scandal eventually drove Wright back to Wisconsin, where he built a Prairie-style home for himself, naming it Taliesin, which means "shining brow." He would redesign Taliesin several times over the years, using it as a model for many of his most revolutionary ideas.

Wright's personal life remained in unhappy turmoil for years. To escape, he lived for a time in Japan, designing the famed Imperial Hotel. He also traveled extensively in the American West, where he studied the ruins of ancient pueblos. He would later introduce details borrowed from Native American cultures into his designs. His travels gave him an even deeper feeling for the expansiveness of the American landscape and added justification for his "horizontal" architectural style. They also gave rise to his single greatest inspiration, that the natural environment, buildings, and people must all live together in harmony. This concept would come to be called "organic architecture," and Wright would be its chief proponent.

"The good building is not one that hurts the landscape," said Wright, "but one that makes the landscape more beautiful than it was before the building was built."

To achieve that ideal, Wright tried to make his structures as much a part of the land as possible. "No house should ever be on a hill or on anything," he said. "It should be of the hill, belonging to it, so hill and house could live together each the happier for the other."

This approach would lead Wright to create what many believe is the most beautiful building in the world, the Edgar J. Kaufmann House in Pennsylvania, also known as Fallingwater. A natural waterfall is actually incorporated into the design of the house. Or rather, the house is made part of the fall.

Luckily for those of us who love beautiful architecture, Wright's career was a long one. He worked almost up until the day he died, on April 8, 1959, at the age of ninety-two. During his more than seven-decade career, he designed 380 homes and other buildings, of which 280 still stand.

Looking out at the rolling country around his home in Wisconsin, Wright once remarked, "I'll bridge these hills with graceful arches." His homes especially are like bridges linking the earth to the human spirit, the soul-nurturing land to the universe of ideas.

The best place to see Frank Lloyd Wright architecture is Oak Park, Illinois, where the master worked for more than a decade furthering Prairie School design concepts. In all, there are twenty-five Wright-designed homes in Oak Park, including the architect's home and studio, which is open to the public. Write to the Frank Lloyd Wright Home and Studio, 951 Chicago Avenue, Oak Park, IL 60302, or call (708) 848-1976.

Taliesin, Wright's home in Spring Green, Wisconsin, near Madison, is now part of a complex of buildings dedicated to the architect's work and memory. Most were designed by Wright himself. For information or advance reservations, call the Frank Lloyd Wright Visitor Center at (608) 588-7900.

For information on other Frank Lloyd Wright structures and how you can help preserve them, contact the Frank Lloyd Wright Building Conservancy at 5132 South Woodlawn Avenue, Chicago, IL 60615, or call (773) 324-5600. If you would like to build a house influenced by Frank Lloyd Wright, several firms around the country occasionally work in the Prairie Style. A good choice would be Marcus and Willers Architects, 415 First Street West, Suite 3, Sonoma, CA 95476; call (707) 996-2396. Wright designed not just homes, but furniture that made his houses even more beautiful and livable. Several makers specialize in furniture inspired by his designs, including Prairie Woodworking at 343 Harrison Street, Oak Park, IL 60304; call (708) 386-0603.

GO TO:

PAGE 88 FOR CHICAGO, CHICAGO
PAGE 115 FOR THOMAS EDISON
PAGE 124 FOR FALLINGWATER
PAGE 215 FOR OZ

WURLITZER JUKEBOXES

Put Another Nickel In

WHEN YOU met at the diner for a soda that afternoon, Patsy Cline was singing "I Fall to Pieces" on the jukebox. Practically every loving American couple share an important memory something like that. Of course, it didn't have to be Patsy Cline. It could have been Elvis Presley, Nat "King" Cole, or just about anybody. But the essential detail, the one most likely to bring the emotions of the moment rushing back, is the song playing on the jukebox.

Music goes with romance—or heartbreak—like sugar and cream go with coffee. That is why jukeboxes, especially Wurlitzer jukeboxes, have made such an indelible mark on American culture. Some would say the jukebox owed its success to the rise of swing and other forms of recorded popular music. But the real reason we Americans fell in love with the jukebox was not because our musical tastes changed. It was because we changed the way we met and fell in love with one another. Increasingly, as the century progressed and we became more mobile, our special times together came at diners, restaurants, and corner ice-cream shops. And where there was love or the prospect of love, we wanted music.

A man named Rudolph Wurlitzer saw all this coming. Born in Germany in 1829, he was descended from a long line of gifted artisans famed for their finely crafted musical instruments. As a young man, Wurlitzer sailed to America, where in 1856 he founded his own piano manufacturing company. His pianos gained popularity among both professional and amateur musicians, but Wurlitzer believed the market for music extended far beyond the concert hall or even the family parlor. Searching endlessly for ways to bring music into the everyday lives of ordinary people, he pioneered the production of electric pianos and other automated instruments. In 1896, Wurlitzer introduced the Tonophon, the world's first coin-operated piano.

The company Wurlitzer founded already had a solid foundation in the nickelodeon trade when in 1933 it purchased a patented mechanism, improved on it, and gave America its first true jukebox. Called the Debutante, this wonder would slap a record onto a turntable and play it for anyone with a nickel and a yen to dance. More than forty-five thousand Debutantes and similar models were sold annually, and people everywhere were soon listening to their favorite tunes while they ate, drank, and danced—even in places far from the nearest bandstand.

Nobody knows who first applied the name jukebox to these coin-operated record players. Apparently, the "juke" was borrowed from a West Africa word meaning "wicked," but a better translation might be "good times."

Wurlitzer's "good-times boxes" serenaded the country through the Great Depression and the great war that followed. The Victory model that appeared in 1942 featured a keyboard for making selections and could play twenty-four different tunes. No doubt, Glenn Miller's big band numbers were frequently among them.

After World War II, the nation celebrated victory with music and dance, and the jukebox jitterbugged off into its golden age. Many of the jukeboxes of this era were in fact golden or red, or decorated in a rainbow of brightly illuminated colors. Designer Paul Fuller's Wurlitzers were, perhaps, the ultimate celebration of the streamlined styling of the 1940s and 1950s that also gave us the chrome diner and fins on automobiles.

While people may have been drawn to Wurlitzers by their flashy looks, it was the music they wanted. And that was exactly what jukeboxes gave them: musical selections by the dozen—that is, if they had some change to spare. During the 1950s, Americans grew excited about music as never before, and as country and western, blue grass, and rock 'n' roll surged in popularity, so did Wurlitzers. With a few nickels in your hand, you could dance to your favorites anytime you wanted; you could literally "rock around the clock."

According to the Wurlitzer archives, here are the all-time top ten jukebox hits: (1) "Hound Dog," Elvis Presley, 1956; (2) "Crazy," Patsy Cline, 1961; (3) "Old Time Rock & Roll," Bob Seger, 1979; (4) "I Heard It Through the Grapevine," Marvin Gaye, 1968; (5) "Don't Be Cruel," Elvis Presley, 1956; (6) "Rock Around the Clock," Bill Haley and His Comets, 1955; (7) "Hey Jude," The Beatles, 1968; (8) "The Dock of the Bay," Otis Redding (1968); (9) "Lady," Kenny Rogers, 1980; (10) "Cherry Pink and Apple Blossom White," Perez Prado, 1955.

You may have noticed that the most recent song on the above list came out in 1980, and most of the top ten selections appeared as far back as the 1950s and 1960s. This is not because music has been declining in popularity. Rather, it shows how over the years jukeboxes themselves have lost ground to television and other forms of entertainment. Recently, however, jukeboxes, and especially Wurlitzers, have been making a comeback among collectors who see them as an investment in a valuable piece of Americana, and among the rest of us who don't want to forget all those happy times.

Anybody got some change?

Jukeboxes still can be found in eating and drinking establishments everywhere. Beautiful antique Wurlitzers often take center stage in restaurants that emphasize nostalgia and a happy-time feeling. You can buy your own Wurlitzer, but be prepared to part with a lot of change. For information, contact the Wurlitzer Jukebox Company, 235 Moonachie Road, Moonachie, NJ 07074, or call (800) 987-5480. Wurlitzer recently introduced an Elvis Presley model, complete with sparkly 1950s styling and a likeness of the King.

GO TO:

PAGE 53 FOR BLUEGRASS
PAGE 91 FOR PATSY CLINE
PAGE 117 FOR ELVIS PRESLEY
PAGE 179 FOR LINDY HOP
PAGE 285 FOR VICTROLA
PAGE 291 FOR HANK WILLIAMS

X

XEROX

The Billions That Nobody Wanted

IT HAS been called "the world-changing invention that nobody wanted," and the mountains of money it has earned over the years have been described as "the billions that nobody wanted." Okay, maybe a lot of people wanted those billions, but no one imagined they could be earned with a photocopying machine—no one, that is, except Chester Carlson, the man who made the first one.

Like more than a few inventors, Carlson grew up hoping that he could use his wits to get out of poverty. Born in Seattle in 1906, by the age of fourteen, he was already the primary family breadwinner. Somehow Carlson, while shouldering this responsibility, managed to earn a degree in physics from the California Institute of Technology. Unfortunately, it was the height of the Great Depression, and his degree really didn't count for much in terms of earning potential. He managed to land a job at the Bell Labs in New York City for $35 a week but was soon laid off. Eventually, he got a mundane position working with patents. While laboriously copying page after page of patent material, it occurred to him that his and countless other jobs could be made much easier if he could find a fast, mechanical method for reproducing documents.

Carlson set up a shop in his own kitchen and began to work out a way to use a photoconductive plate to re-create an image on paper. Carlson had patented some of the necessary components by 1937, but progress on a functional copier moved ahead at a snail's pace. Eventually, Carlson's exasperated wife drove him out of the kitchen, and he set up shop in the back of a beauty salon owned by his mother-in-law. In time, he was able to assemble a very primitive working model.

Between 1939 and 1944, Carlson trotted his invention around to dozens of companies, more than a few of them corporate giants the likes of IBM, Kodak, and RCA. Nobody was interested. Here was the problem. Carlson's potential partners could easily see one of his machines sitting in, say, a library, but they couldn't imagine anyone would go to the trouble and expense of photocopying a page from a book when they could simply go to the desk and check out that same book for free. It seemed to them that photocopying machines would be of use to only a few people with highly specialized copying needs—patent clerks, for instance. They were to be proven wrong, billions, if not trillions of times over.

Eventually, Carlson's project found a home with Battelle, a non-profit research organization. In turn, Battelle managed to interest Halloid, a small photographic products firm in Rochester, New York. It took Halloid nearly fifteen years to bring a practical copier to the market, but when the first one became available in 1960, people were amazed. Suddenly it was possible to make copies that you could read without squinting. And as it turned out, there were plenty of things people wanted to copy—tax returns, for instance, recipes, manuals, magazine articles, even love letters. The Xerox era had arrived.

Halloid called its copier a Xerox, a named derived from the term "xerography," which in turn was taken from a pair of Greek words: *xeros*, meaning "dry," and *graphos*, meaning "writing." The new Xerox machine proved so successful that Halloid soon changed its name to the Xerox Corporation. Anyone who invested in Xerox stock at that time and held on to it would now be obscenely wealthy.

The photocopier he had invented eventually earned Carlson nearly $150 million, enough to make him one of the richest men in the world—not bad for a $35-a-week lab technician. Although many other successful men of humble origins have allowed their wealth to transform them into greedy tycoons, not so Carlson. In fact, by the time he died in 1968, he had given $100 million—more than two-thirds of his fortune—to charity. Now there's a page worth copying.

If you want to learn more about Xerox products or the Xerox Corporation, call (800) ASK-XEROX ([800] 275-9376).

GO TO:
PAGE 115 FOR THOMAS EDISON
PAGE 193 FOR MODEL T FORD
PAGE 166 FOR IVORY SOAP
PAGE 285 FOR VICTROLA

THE MAN WITH X-RAY EYES

Great Caesar's Ghost, It's Superman

HE WAS and is a "Man of Steel," but perhaps it is worth remember-
ing that Joseph Stalin and Genghis Khan were also described in this
way. Fortunately for us all, however, Superman is one of the good
guys, and has been since his first appearance in a 1938 issue of Action
Comics. Writer Jerry Siegel and artist Joe Shuster had created the
superhero in 1933, but there was a depression on, and it took them
five years to find him a home. Even so, as soon as the first thirteen-
page Superman story—complete with Clark Kent, Lois Lane, and the
Daily Star (not *Planet*)—hit the streets, Siegel, Shuster, and Action
knew they had a winner.

So, too, did comic book readers everywhere. Soon they were clambering for more news about this man who could fly at supersonic
speeds—airplanes of that era could not—could turn away bullets and
locomotives, and could see through solid walls with his x-ray vision.
So Action gave them more: Lex Luthor, Perry White, Kryptonite, the
whole Superman, Superboy, Supergirl, Superdog thing.

Superman became a sort of action-hero Santa Claus. Little kids
believed in him, while older children and adults didn't necessary
believe, but still loved him. This author once heard a little boy say
the following: "I know Superman can't really fly. What they do is
drop him out of an airplane onto a foam-rubber city."

In time, the Superman legend would outgrow Action and outlive its creators, and today, the Man of Steel remains as strong as

ever. People never seem to tire of him, despite his appearance in countless comic books, two popular television series, and a string of big-budget movies. Nowadays, Americans often know more about the personal history of Superman than they do, say, the president of the United States. We all know, for instance, that Superman hails from the planet Krypton, the source of his unearthly powers. What none of us understand very well is why we care. Where's the drama in a story featuring an invulnerable character who will never lose a fight—he can't. Still, for some reason, he's an awful lot of fun.

From the first, the Superman stories and legend contained what appeared to be an important logical inconsistency. If Superman was invincible, then why didn't he vanquish all the bad guys once and for all? Over the years, the writers of Superman stories have tried to deal with this problem by suggesting that, being sent here from another planet, Superman was somehow morally bound not to interfere in human history. This makes about as much sense as the foam-rubber city theory.

Actually, there is a perfectly reasonable explanation for Superman's unwillingness to use his powers for purposes other than to rescue small children, catch people who have fallen out of buildings, lasso a few bank robbers, and vanquish the occasional cosmic villain. Superman's x-ray vision allows him to see through walls but not into the human heart. This means that like the rest of us, he has a hard time distinguishing the good guys from the bad and cannot afford to set himself up as judge and jury. He understands that superpowers must never be used unless one is sure of the facts.

Ironically, the actor who portrayed Superman in a string of blockbuster movies understands better than anyone the important distinction between physical and moral strength. A few years after completing his last Superman movie in 1987, Christopher Reeve broke his neck in a tragic riding accident. Although paralyzed from the neck down, Reeve has inspired the world with his effort to continue his career while raising money for research on and treatment of spinal injuries. Only after losing nearly all his physical strength did he get his chance to become a true superhero.

Don't miss the super movies *Superman* and *Superman II, III,* and *IV.* If you should happen to find an old Action Comics *Superman* issue dated before, say, 1950, hang on to it. You may be able to sell it to a collector for thousands, or you could just relax and enjoy it yourself.

GO TO:
PAGE 45 FOR BATMAN AND ROBIN
PAGE 211 FOR OLD HOLLYWOOD

Y

YELLOWSTONE PARK

Where Nature Picks Up Steam

As is the case with movie stars and sports personalities, some of America's natural attractions are better known and more popular than others, but it is probably safe to say that Yellowstone National Park is *hot*—in more ways than one. The world's first national park, Yellowstone was founded in 1872, just a few years after the Civil War and four years before Custer made his famous last stand on the Little Bighorn. At that time, it might have taken a year or more to reach the park from Washington, D.C., or New York City. Nowadays, you can make the same trip in a day or so, if you have the right airline connections and a confirmed rental car reservation at the airport in Jackson, Wyoming, or Bozeman, Montana. Even so, Yellowstone remains well off the beaten path and a very long way from any place a reasonable person might describe as civilization. So why is it that during the height of the summer travel season, the park population swells to that of a fair-sized city? To put it simply, Yellowstone is awesome.

In case you haven't been there and don't know it yet, there is a lot more to Yellowstone than Old Faithful and a few beggarly bears. In addition to the geysers, there are mighty falls and cataracts, crystalline streams filled with brightly colored rocks and equally colorful fish, pots of steaming mud, hot-spring ledges sculpted into fantastic shapes by mineral-laden waters, not to mention elk, buffalo, wolves, grizzlies, and other denizens of the wild, wild West. Although perhaps not so immense as the one in Arizona, there is even a Grand Canyon with enormous yellow rocks forming its walls. Apparently, these rocks explain how the Yellowstone country got its name. Native Americans called this place Mi-tsi-a-da-zi, meaning "Yellow Rock River."

You cannot properly grasp the phenomenon that is Yellow-stone—if it can be grasped at all—until you drive along one of its hundreds of miles of road and notice that the ditch beside you is fizzing and fuming. It may strike you that the ditch is not one of the park's key attractions, it's just a ditch. There are no signs, no parking areas, no rangers to "interpret" its activities for wide-eyed tourists. Even so, the ditch puts on its spewing and sputtering show to remind you that nature here is not playing around. It's deadly serious.

At Yellowstone, you get the feeling the molten rock that is sup-posed to stay far beneath the earth's crust is about to break through and pay us all a very unwelcome visit. That is, in fact, more or less the case. The wonders of Yellowstone are largely the work of a so-called "hot spot" not unlike the one that created the Hawaiian volca-noes. The planetary crust is unusually thin here, so the earth's internal furnace can reach up and announce its presence. Old Faith-ful, the park's most famous geyser, makes this announcement once about every sixty-five minutes, throwing a column of scalding water and steam as high as a fifteen-story building.

There are hundreds of other geysers and thermal features in Yel-lowstone and so much more to see. Unfortunately, most people never get more than a few yards from their automobiles. Don't you be one of these lazy folks. Plan to take a long walk in the backcountry so you can see this part of America as the nineteenth-century moun-tain men saw it. Just be sure you keep well clear of the bears.

Your adventure in Yellowstone will be a major undertaking and should be carefully planned. Helpful guides can be found in the travel section of any well-stocked bookstore. You can download a free Yellowstone trip planner from the official Yellowstone National Park website (www.nps.gov/yell). Otherwise, write to Yellowstone National Park, P.O. Box 168, Yellowstone National Park, WY 82190-0168, or call (307) 344-7381. For recorded information, call (307) 344-2386.

GO TO:

PAGE 294 FOR GRAY WOLF
PAGE 143 FOR GRIZZLY BEAR
PAGE 169 FOR CHIEF JOSEPH'S LAST STAND

PAGE 200 FOR JOHN MUIR
PAGE 249 FOR CHIEF SEATTLE'S PLEA

YOGI

It Ain't Over Till It's Over

To MILLIONS who have long admired his baseball skills and talent for turning misfired diction into sheer poetry, he has always been known as "Yogi," so perhaps we can be forgiven for listing Lawrence Peter "Yogi" Berra under the Ys. Born in 1925, the man and baseball legend we might otherwise have known as Larry Berra picked up the nickname Yogi from a childhood friend, who thought he resembled an Indian swami he had seen at the movies.

A rare natural talent, Yogi was only seventeen and already playing in the minor leagues in 1942 when he was signed by the St. Louis Cardinals for a whopping bonus of $500—he had turned down an earlier offer of $250. Obviously, the Cards had got themselves a good one, as later that year Yogi drove in twenty-three runs in a single day for their Norfolk, Virginia, minor-league franchise.

World War II put Yogi's career on hold for a while, and when he emerged from the U.S. Navy in 1946, he entered the majors as a Yankee instead of a Cardinal. Yogi remained a Yank for the better part of two decades, playing in fourteen World Series and fifteen All Star matchups, while earning his reputation as one of the best catchers ever to play the game. Equipped with a cannon for a throwing arm, he gunned down armies of hapless base runners. Anyone who stole a base on Yogi had to have wings on their heels and a lot of luck. As a hitter Yogi had few equals, and he almost never struck out. In 1950, Yogi had 597 trips to the plate and struck out only twelve times, a performance that may be unmatched in baseball history. After retiring from active play, Yogi went on to manage the Yankees, Mets, and Astros, leading teams to pennants in both the American and National Leagues.

Of course, Yogi is famous not just for baseball but for his contributions to the English language. He was the one who first said, "It was déjà vu all over again." Nowadays, sportscasters and politicians toss this line into monologues without a second's thought, and it is tempting to think that many of them have no idea they've said something ridiculous. They have, as Yogi might have put it, "made a wrong mistake." Actually, no one has ever delivered a Yogi line as well as Yogi himself. Over the years, he has concocted some beauties; for instance:

- "Baseball is 90 percent mental, and the other half is physical."

- "If you can't imitate him, don't copy him."

- "I knew I was going to take the wrong train, so I left early."

- "You can observe a lot by watching."

- "A nickel isn't worth a dime, today."

And then, there's the author's personal favorite: "You better cut that pizza into four pieces because I'm not hungry enough to eat six."

It's easy to laugh at that sort of stuff, and Yogi has always laughed right along with us, but some of his remarks are more true than funny. One Yogi Berra line in particular is so meaningful and filled with folk/sports wisdom that it will likely live forever. You guessed it: "It ain't over till it's over."

GO TO:

PAGE 21 FOR HANK AARON
PAGE 93 FOR TY COBB
PAGE 272 FOR JOHNNY UNITAS

Z

ZINFANDEL

The Grape That Makes You Blush

SUPPOSEDLY THE great winemaking grapes all come from Europe, but if that is true, the ancestry of this one is—like that of most Americans—a little murky. No one is at all sure where the first Zinfandel vines grew. It may have been Italy, France, Greece, or Germany, but who can say for certain? However, it was definitely a place with lots of sunshine and dense blankets of moist fog that usually burned off about the middle of the day—a place, for instance, like California.

Here's what we know. Sometime in the early 1880s, bottles of California wine turned up with the word ZINFANDEL on their labels. Like Chardonnay, Cabernet, or Sauvignon, Zinfandel is a variety of grape. It flourishes in the rich, well-drained soils of California's coastal valleys. And as far as anyone knows, until those first Zinfandels appeared, the grape had never been widely used for wines.

Those early Zins must have tasted awfully good, because this distinctly American variety soon attracted a large following. Its popularity has kept right on growing, like the vines themselves, some of which may live to a ripe old age—several generations, if not longer. Nowadays, it is the most widely planted grape in California.

One reason for the popularity of Zinfandel grapes is its extraordinary versatility. With a little coaxing from talented hands, it can be used for rich, full-bodied reds, ports, whites, and rose wines. Quality red Zins often offer an aromatic array of berrylike or peppery flavors.

During the last couple of decades, innovative California vineyards have introduced a new concept—the "blush" wine. Usually, white Zinfandels are made by removing the grape skins from the juice before fermentation, but with blush wines, the skins are allowed to lend the wine a touch of their ruby-red color. Some blush wines are

315

so subtle that one must hold up a glass to a light before the liquid—like a girl who has just been told she's pretty—reveals a hint of red.

Except for the color, blush wines are not very sophisticated. They are meant to be served chilled and enjoyed at picnics, barbecues, and other lighthearted affairs, and like most other Zinfandels, they'll go well with just about any meal.

Some worldly wine connoisseurs do not count the Zinfandel among the earth's truly "noble" grapes. Here in America, however, a thing or a person may be considered noble simply because they are good. And Zinfandel? Yeah!

You can find a delicious California Zinfandel in almost any supermarket or wine shop. But to fully appreciate them and other unsurpassed American wines, such as the Cabernet Sauvignon, you should visit the California Wine Country. You'll find many sources of information about the wine country in bookstores, online, and elsewhere. An especially good source is the Napa Valley Visitors Bureau at 1310 Napa Town Center, Napa, CA 94559; call (707) 226-7459. Another is the Sonoma Valley Visitors Bureau at 453 First Street East, Sonoma, CA 95476; call (707) 996-1090.

GO TO:

PAGE 26 FOR SAMUEL ADAMS BEER

PAGE 136 FOR GOLDEN GATE BRIDGE

PAGE 168 FOR JACK DANIEL'S

PAGE 183 FOR JACK LONDON

NATIONAL ZOO

Lions, Tigers, and Bears, Oh Yes!

THE GREAT herds of wild buffalo had only recently disappeared from the western plains, and Teddy Roosevelt would not move into the White House for yet another dozen years when Washington D.C.'s National Zoo was founded in 1889. Its mission then, as now, was to protect the worldwide diversity of animals and their habitats. Along the way, it has also delighted many a five-year-old and, for that matter, eighty-five-year-old.

If you have never enjoyed a trip to the National Zoo or even just your local zoo, perhaps you were born without the capacity to see an elephant, a lemur, or a spadefoot toad through the eyes of a child. Most of have that ability—at any age.

Created by an act of Congress and operated by the Smithsonian since 1890, the National Zoo is one of the world's best. Located off Connecticut Avenue in the northwest corner of the District, it is home to more than 2,750 animals representing 419 distinct species. For instance, here you will find the *Macroclemys temminckii*. No, that's not meant as an insult, it's an alligator snapping turtle. You may also encounter the *Tylototriton shanjing*. No that's not a Chinese science-fiction movie, it's a mandarin newt. And, of course, there are everybody's favorites, the Pandas.

A gift from the citizens of China to the American people, the zoo's first pandas were Hsing Hsing and Ling Ling, who arrived in 1972 during a very distinct thaw in relations between our two nations. Apparently, animals make far better ambassadors than people, a fact the pandas proved by quickly becoming more famous than any State Department functionary. However, Hsing Hsing and Ling Ling did most of their negotiating with children, whom they delighted with their roly-poly antics. Having finally passed into the bamboo forests of legend, their place at the zoo has been taken over by a fresh pair of black-and-white bear-like critters named Mel Xiang and Tian Tian.

In the wild, the panda remain threatened, as is the case with countless species. For years now, the National Zoo has focused on preserving our planet's diverse wildlife and the environment that nourishes it. Since 1975, the zoo has maintained a 3,200-acre Conservation and Research Center in Virginia to further these goals. While the center is closed to the public, you should consider supporting its efforts with your donations.

For more information or to make a donation, write to Smithsonian National Zoological Park, 3001 Connecticut Avenue, Washington, DC 20008. The zoo can be reached by telephone at (202)

673-7800, or for the recorded information, call the twenty-four-hour hot line at (202) 673-4800.

GO TO:

PAGE 64 FOR AMERICAN BUFFALO

PAGE 102 FOR COYOTE

PAGE 294 FOR GRAY WOLF

PAGE 143 FOR GRIZZLY BEAR

PAGE 200 FOR JOHN MUIR

PAGE 287 FOR WASHINGTON MEMORIAL

CONCLUSION

Antique Cannon, Watermelon, and Fireflies

OKAY, DOES Batman have anything to do with New England bean suppers? Sam Adams with Elvis Presley? Daffy Duck with Dorothy Parker? The Statue of Liberty with Harley-Davidson motorcycles? The author hopes you think so. He also hopes you've enjoyed reading *USA to Z* as much as he enjoyed writing it.

As you read *USA to Z*, you may have wondered why it left out one or another of your favorite American things—Cracker Jacks, for instance. After all, Cracker Jacks go so great with a baseball game, and there is always an amazing little surprise inside the box. But America offers so many treats, how could we include them all? *USA to Z* was never intended as a comprehensive guide to American culture. Instead, it is meant as a celebration—like the Fourth of July—of all those special American things and people, the ones we included and the ones that maybe we'll get around to next time.

When you think about it, every day should be the Fourth of July. Why? Because we as Americans have so much to celebrate: our freedom for one thing, all the stuff mentioned in *USA to Z* for another, and so many other wonders not mentioned. The Fourth is a magical occasion, a fine time to be eight years old or eighty. There are flags and parades. Picnics of fried chicken, ham, and barbecue are laid out on blankets in the park grass—as close as possible to the bandstand or to the ancient, green-tinted, bird-spattered cannon. Slices of watermelon are served up, and if there is an orchestra, it plays the

1812 Overture (ironically, a Russian piece). And finally, when night comes, fireworks streak the sky with color.

However, you don't need fireworks or even a day off to celebrate America. Something as simple and delightful as watching an old classic movie on the tube, turning up a Hank Williams tune on the radio, polishing off a bagel and cream cheese, or buying a rag doll for a little girl can be a patriotic statement. It's all a matter of the spirit you bring to the occasion.

You never have to look very far or very hard to detect a spark of the American spirit. It's all around us, lighting every room and every backyard. And, indeed, every day can be Independence Day. For a great American picnic, all we need is a couple of slices of bread and enough leftovers to throw together a towering dagwood sandwich. For music, all we need is an old Benny Goodman record. And for fireworks . . . Well, in the summer, at least, and not just on the Fourth, there are fireflies in the air, and any child—or octogenarian—who is quick and gentle enough can always catch a few in a bottle.

So for now . . .

That's all, folks!